Python 101

Michael Driscoll

D0218984

Published by Michael Driscoll
Ankeny, IA

Cover art by Tyler Sowles

ISBN-13:978-0-9960628-1-7

ISBN 978-0-9960628-1-7

90000

9 780996 062817

Contents

CONTENTS

Introduction

Welcome to Python 101! I wrote this book to help you learn Python 3. It is not meant to be an exhaustive reference book. Instead, the object is to get you acquainted with the building blocks of Python so that you can actually write something useful yourself. A lot of programming textbooks only teach you the language, but do not go much beyond that. I will endeavour to not only get you up to speed on the basics, but also to show you how to create useful programs. Now you may be wondering why just learning the basics isn't enough. In my experience, when I get finished reading an introductory text, I want to then create something, but I don't know how! I've got the learning, but not the glue to get from point A to point B. I think it's important to not only teach you the basics, but also cover intermediate material.

Thus, this book will be split into five parts:

- Part one will cover Python's basics
- Part two will be on a small subset of Python's Standard Library
- Part three will be intermediate material
- Part four will be a series of small tutorials
- Part five will cover Python packaging and distribution

Let me spend a few moments explaining what each part has to offer. In part one, we will cover the following:

- Python types (strings, lists, dicts, etc)
- Conditional statements
- Loops
- List and dictionary comprehensions
- Exception Handling
- File I/O
- Functions and Classes

Part two will talk about some of Python's standard library. The standard library is what comes pre-packaged with Python. It is made up of modules that you can import to get added functionality. For example, you can import the **math** module to gain some high level math functions. I will be cherry picking the modules I use the most as a day-to-day professional and explaining how they work. The reason I think this is a good idea is that they are common, every day modules that I think you will benefit knowing about at the beginning of your Python education. This section will also cover

1

various ways to install 3rd party modules. Finally, I will cover how to create your own modules and packages and why you'd want to do that in the first place. Here are some of the modules we will be covering:

- csv
- ConfigParser
- logging
- os
- smtplib / email
- subprocess
- sys
- thread / queues
- time / datetime

Part three will cover intermediate odds and ends. These are topics that are handy to know, but not necessarily required to be able to program in Python. The topics covered are:

- the Python debugger (pdb)
- decorators
- the lambda function
- code profiling
- a testing introduction

Part four will be made up of small tutorials that will help you to learn how to use Python in a practical way. In this way, you will learn how to create Python programs that can actually do something useful! You can take the knowledge in these tutorials to create your own scripts. Ideas for further enhancements to these mini-applications will be provided at the end of each tutorial so you will have something that you can try out on your own. Here are a few of the 3rd party packages that we'll be covering:

- pip and easy_install
- configobj
- lxml
- requests
- virtualenv
- pylint / pychecker
- SQLAlchemy

Part four is going to cover how to take your code and give it to your friends, family and the world! You will learn the following:

- How to turn your reusable scripts into Python "eggs", "wheels" and more
- How to upload your creation to the Python Package Index (PyPI)
- How to create binary executables so you can run your application without Python
- How to create an installer for your application

The chapters and sections may not all be the same length. While every topic will be covered well, not every topic will require the same page count.

A Brief History of Python

I think it helps to know the background of the Python programming language. Python was created in the late 1980s[1]. Everyone agrees that its creator is Guido van Rossum when he wrote it as a successor to the ABC programming language that he was using. Guido named the language after one of his favorite comedy acts: Monty Python. The language wasn't released until 1991 and it has grown a lot in terms of the number of included modules and packages included. At the time of this writing, there are two major versions of Python: the 2.x series and the 3.x (sometimes known as Python 3000) . The 3.x series is not backwards compatible with 2.x because the idea when creating 3.x was to get rid of some of the idiosyncrasies in the original. The current versions are 2.7.7 and 3.3.0. Most of the features in 3.x have been backported to 2.x; however, 3.x is getting the majority of Python's current development, so it is the version of the future.

Some people think Python is just for writing little scripts to glue together "real" code, like C++ or Haskell. However you will find Python to be useful in almost any situation. Python is used by lots of big name companies such as Google, NASA, LinkedIn, Industrial Light & Magic, and many others. Python is used not only on the backend, but also on the front. In case you're new to the computer science field, backend programming is the stuff that's behind the scenes; things like database processing, document generation, etc. Frontend processing is the pretty stuff most users are familiar with, such as web pages or desktop user interfaces. For example, there are some really nice Python GUI toolkits such as wxPython, PySide, and Kivy. There are also several web frameworks like Django, Pyramid, and Flask. You might find it surprising to know that Django is used for Instagram and Pinterest. If you have used these or many other websites, then you have used something that's powered by Python without even realizing it!

About the Author

You may be wondering about who I am and why I might be knowledgeable enough about Python to write about it, so I thought I'd give you a little information about myself. I started programming in Python in the Spring of 2006 for a job. My first assignment was to port Windows login scripts from

---

[1]http://www.artima.com/intv/pythonP.html

Kixtart to Python. My second project was to port VBA code (basically a GUI on top of Microsoft Office products) to Python, which is how I first got started in wxPython. I've been using Python ever since, doing a variation of backend programming and desktop front end user interfaces.

I realized that one way for me to remember how to do certain things in Python was to write about them and that's how my Python blog came about: http://www.blog.pythonlibrary.org/. As I wrote, I would receive feedback from my readers and I ended up expanding the blog to include tips, tutorials, Python news, and Python book reviews. I work regularly with Packt Publishing as a technical reviewer, which means that I get to try to check for errors in the books before they're published. I also have written for the Developer Zone (DZone) and i-programmer websites as well as the Python Software Foundation. In November 2013, DZone published **The Essential Core Python Cheat Sheet** that I co-authored.

Conventions

As with most technical books, this one includes a few conventions that you need to be aware of. New topics and terminology will be in **bold**. You will also see some examples that look like the following:

```
1    >>> myString = "Welcome to Python!"
```

The >>> is a Python prompt symbol. You will see this in the Python **interpreter** and in **IDLE**. You will learn more about each of these in the first chapter. Other code examples will be shown in a similar manner, but without the >>>.

Requirements

You will need a working Python 3 installation. The examples should work in either Python 2.x or 3.x unless specifically marked otherwise. Most Linux and Mac machines come with Python already installed. However, if you happen to find yourself without Python, you can go download a copy from http://python.org/download/[2]. There are up-to-date installation instructions on their website, so I won't include any installation instructions in this book. Any additional requirements will be explained later on in the book.

Reader Feedback

I welcome feedback about my writings. If you'd like to let me know what you thought of the book, you can send comments to the following address:

comments@pythonlibrary.org

---

[2]http://python.org/download/

Errata

I try my best not to publish errors in my writings, but it happens from time to time. If you happen to see an error in this book, feel free to let me know by emailing me at the following:

errata@pythonlibrary.org

Part I - Learning the Basics

In Part I, we will learn the basics of the Python programming language. This section of the book should get you ready to use all the building blocks of Python so that you will be ready to tackle the following sections confidently.

Let's go over what we'll be covering:

- IDLE
- Strings
- Lists, Dictionaries and Tuples
- Conditional statements
- Loops
- Comprehensions
- Exception Handling
- File I/O
- Importing modules and packages
- Functions
- Classes

The first chapter in this section will familiarize you with Python's built-in development environment that is known as IDLE. The next couple of chapters will go over some of Python's types, such as strings, lists, and dictionaries. After that we'll look at conditional statements in Python and looping using Python's **for** and **while** loops.

In the second half of this section, we will go into comprehensions, such as list and dictionary comprehensions. Then we'll look at Python's exception handling capabilities and how Python's file operations work. Next up is learning how to import pre-made modules and packages. The last two chapters cover Python functions and classes.

Let's get started!

image

Chapter 1 - IDLE Programming

Using IDLE

Python comes with its own code editor: **IDLE**. There is some unconfirmed lore that the name for IDLE comes from Eric Idle, an actor in *Monty Python*. I have no idea if that's true or not, but it would make sense in this context as it appears to be a pun on the acronym IDE or Integrated Development Environment. An IDE is an editor for programmers that provides color highlighting of key words in the language, auto-complete, a debugger and lots of other fun things. You can find an IDE for most popular languages and a number of IDEs will work with multiple languages. IDLE is kind of a lite IDE, but it does have all those items mentioned. It allows the programmer to write Python and debug their code quite easily. The reason I call it "lite" is the debugger is very basic and it's missing other features that programmers who have a background using products like *Visual Studio* will miss. You might also like to know that IDLE was created using Tkinter, a Python GUI toolkit that comes with Python.

To open up IDLE, you will need to find it and you'll see something like this:

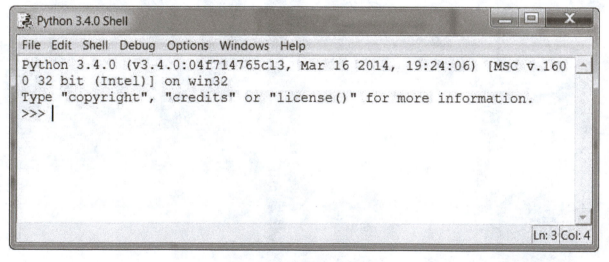

image

Yes, it's a Python shell where you can type short scripts and see their output immediately and even interact with code in real time. There is no compiling of the code as Python is an interpretive language and runs in the Python interpreter. Let's write your first program now. Type the following after the command prompt (>>>) in IDLE:

8

```
1   print("Hello from Python!")
```

You have just written your first program! All your program does is write a string to the screen, but you'll find that very helpful later on. Please note that the **print** statement has changed in Python 3.x. In Python 2.x, you would have written the above like this:

```
1   print "Hello from Python!"
```

In Python 3, the **print** statement was turned into a **print function**, which is why parentheses are required. You will learn what functions are in chapter 10.

If you want to save your code into a file, go to the File menu and choose New Window (or press CTRL+N). Now you can type in your program and save it here. The primary benefit of using the Python shell is that you can experiment with small snippets to see how your code will behave before you put the code into a real program. The code editor screen looks a little different than the IDLE screenshot above:

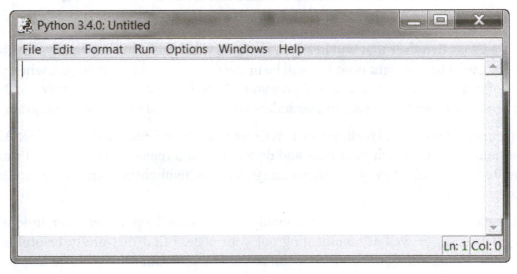

image

Now we'll spend a little time looking at IDLE's other useful features.

Python comes with lots of modules and packages that you can import to add new features. For example, you can import the **math** module for all kinds of good math functions, like square roots, cosines, etcetera. In the **File** menu, you'll find a **Path Browser** which is useful for figuring out where Python looks for module imports. You see, Python first looks in the same directory as the script that is running to see if the file it needs to import is there. Then it checks a predefined list of other locations. You can actually add and remove locations as well. The Path Browser will show you where these files are located on your hard drive, if you have imported anything. My Path Browser looks like this:

image

Next there's a **Class Browser** that will help you navigate your code. This is actually something that won't be very useful to you right now, but will be in the future. You'll find it helpful when you have lots of lines of code in a single file as it will give you a "tree-like" interface for your code. Note that you won't be able to load the Class Browser unless you have actually saved your program.

The **Edit** menu has your typical features, such as Copy, Cut, Paste, Undo, Redo and Select All. It also contains various ways to search your code and do a search and replace. Finally, the Edit menu has some menu items that will Show you various things, such as highlighting parentheses or displaying the auto-complete list.

The **Format** menu has lots of useful functionality. It has some helpful items for **indenting** and **dedenting** your code, as well as commenting out your code. I find that pretty helpful when I'm testing my code. Commenting out your code can be very helpful. One way it can be helpful is when you have a lot of code and you need to find out why it's not working correctly. Commenting out portions of it and re-running the script can help you figure out where you went wrong. You just go along slowly uncommenting out stuff until you hit your bug. Which reminds me; you may have noticed that the main IDLE screen has a **Debugger** menu. That is nice for debugging, but only in the **Shell** window. Sadly you cannot use the debugger in your main editing menu. If you need a more versatile debugger, you should either find a different IDE or try Python's debugger found in the **pdb** library.

What are Comments?

A comment is a way to leave un-runnable code that documents what you are doing in your code. Every programming language uses a different symbol to demarcate where a comment starts and ends. What do comments look like in Python though? A comment is anything that begins with an octothorpe (i.e. a hash or pound sign). The following is an example of some comments in action:

```
1   # This is a comment before some code
2   print("Hello from Python!")
3   print("Winter is coming") # this is an in-line comment
```

You can write comments on a line all by themselves or following a statement, like the second **print** statement above. The Python interpreter ignores comments, so you can write anything you want in them. Most programmers I have met don't use comments very much. However, I highly recommend using comments liberally not just for yourself, but for anyone else who might have to maintain or enhance your code in the future. I have found my own comments useful when I come back to a script that I wrote 6 months ago and I have found myself working with code that didn't have comments and wishing that it did so I could figure it out faster.

Examples of good comments would include explanations about complex code statements, or adding an explanation for acronyms in your code. Sometimes you'll need to leave a comment to explain why you did something a certain way because it's just not obvious.

Now we need to get back to going over the menu options of IDLE:

The **Run** menu has a couple of handy options. You can use it to bring up the Python Shell, check your code for errors, or run your code. The Options menu doesn't have very many items. It does have a Configure option that allows you to change the code highlighting colors, fonts and key shortcuts. Other than that, you get a Code Context option that is helpful in that it puts an overlay in the editing window which will show you which class or function you're currently in. We will be explaining functions and classes near the end of Part I. You will find this feature is useful whenever you have a lot of code in a function and the name has scrolled off the top of the screen. With this option enabled, that doesn't happen. Of course, if the function is too large to fit on one screen, then it may be getting too long and it could be time to break that function down into multiple functions.

The **Windows** menu shows you a list of currently open Windows and allows you to switch between them.

Last but not least is the **Help** menu where you can learn about IDLE, get help with IDLE itself or load up a local copy of the Python documentation. The documentation will explain how each piece of Python works and is pretty exhaustive in its coverage. The Help menu is probably the most helpful in that you can get access to the docs even when you're not connected to the internet. You can search the documentation, find HOWTOs, read about any of the builtin libraries, and learn so much your head will probably start spinning.

Other Tips

When you see code examples in the following chapters, you can write and run them in IDLE. I wrote all my programs in IDLE for the first couple of years of my Python programming life and I was pretty happy with it. There are lots of free Python IDEs out there though and several IDEs that you have to pay for. If you want to go cheap, you might want to take a look at Eclipse+PyDev, Editra or even Notepad++. For a paid IDE, I would recommend WingWare's IDE or possibly PyCharm. They have many more features such as integration with code repositories, better debuggers, refactoring help, etc.

In this book, we will be using IDLE in our examples because it comes with Python and will provide a common test bed. I still think IDLE has the best, most consistent code highlighting of any IDE I have used. Code highlighting is important in my mind in that it helps prevent me from using one of Python's keywords (or built-ins) for a variable name. In case you're wondering, here is a list of those key words:

1	and	del	from	**not**	**while**
2	as	elif	global	or	with
3	assert	else	if	pass	yield
4	break	except	import	**print**	
5	class	**exec**	in	raise	
6	continue	finally	is	return	
7	def	for	lambda	try	

Let's see what happens as we type out a few things in Python:

```
Python 3.4.0 Shell
File  Edit  Shell  Debug  Options  Windows  Help
Python 3.4.0 (v3.4.0:04f714765c13, Mar 16 2014, 19:24:06) [MSC v.160
0 32 bit (Intel)] on win32
Type "copyright", "credits" or "license()" for more information.
>>> print("I'm a string") # I'm a comment
I'm a string
>>>
                                                                Ln: 5 Col: 4
```

image

As you can see, IDLE color coded everything. A key word is orange, a string of text is in green, a comment is in red and the output from the print function is in blue.

Wrapping Up

In this chapter we learned how to use Python's integrated development environment, IDLE. We also learned what **comments** are and how to use them. At this point, you should be familiar enough with IDLE to use it in the rest of this book. There are many other integrated development environments (IDEs) for Python. There are free ones like PyDev and Editra, and there are some others that you have to pay for, such as WingWare and PyCharm. There are also plug-ins for regular text editors that allow you to code in Python too. I think IDLE is a good place to start, but if you already have a favorite editor, feel free to continue using that.

At this point, we are ready to move on and start learning about Python's various data types. We will start with Strings in the following chapter.

Chapter 2 - All About Strings

There are several data types in Python. The main data types that you'll probably see the most are string, integer, float, list, dict and tuple. In this chapter, we'll cover the string data type. You'll be surprised how many things you can do with strings in Python right out of the box. There's also a string module that you can import to access even more functionality, but we won't be looking at that in this chapter. Instead, we will be covering the following topics:

- How to create strings
- String concatenation
- String methods
- String slicing
- String substitution

How to Create a String

Strings are usually created in one of three ways. You can use single, double or triple quotes. Let's take a look!

```
1  >>> my_string = "Welcome to Python!"
2  >>> another_string = 'The bright red fox jumped the fence.'
3  >>> a_long_string = '''This is a
4  multi-line string. It covers more than
5  one line'''
```

The triple quoted line can be done with three single quotes or three double quotes. Either way, they allow the programmer to write strings over multiple lines. If you print it out, you will notice that the output retains the line breaks. If you need to use single quotes in your string, then wrap it in double quotes. See the following example.

```
1  >>> my_string = "I'm a Python programmer!"
2  >>> otherString = 'The word "python" usually refers to a snake'
3  >>> tripleString = """Here's another way to embed "quotes" in a string"""
```

The code above demonstrates how you could put single quotes or double quotes into a string. There's actually one other way to create a string and that is by using the **str** method. Here's how it works:

```
1  >>> my_number = 123
2  >>> my_string = str(my_number)
```

If you type the code above into your interpreter, you'll find that you have transformed the integer value into a string and assigned the string to the variable *my_string*. This is known as **casting**. You can cast some data types into other data types, like numbers into strings. But you'll also find that you can't always do the reverse, such as casting a string like 'ABC' into an integer. If you do that, you'll end up with an error like the one in the following example:

```
1  >>> int('ABC')
2  Traceback (most recent call last):
3    File "<string>", line 1, in <fragment>
4  ValueError: invalid literal for int() with base 10: 'ABC'
```

We will look at exception handling in a later chapter, but as you may have guessed from the message, this means that you cannot convert a literal into an integer. However, if you had done

```
1  >>> x = int("123")
```

then that would have worked fine.

It should be noted that a string is one of Python immutable types. What this means is that you cannot change a string's content after creation. Let's try to change one to see what happens:

```
1  >>> my_string = "abc"
2  >>> my_string[0] = "d"
3  Traceback (most recent call last):
4    File "<string>", line 1, in <fragment>
5  TypeError: 'str' object does not support item assignment
```

Here we try to change the first character from an "a" to a "d"; however this raises a TypeError that stops us from doing so. Now you may think that by assigning a new string to the same variable that you've changed the string. Let's see if that's true:

```
1   >>> my_string = "abc"
2   >>> id(my_string)
3   19397208
4   >>> my_string = "def"
5   >>> id(my_string)
6   25558288
7   >>> my_string = my_string + "ghi"
8   >>> id(my_string)
9   31345312
```

By checking the id of the object, we can determine that any time we assign a new value to the variable, its identity changes.

Note that in Python 2.x, strings can only contain **ASCII** characters. If you require **unicode** in Python 2.x, then you will need to precede your string with a **u**. Here's an example:

```
1   my_unicode_string = u"This is unicode!"
```

The example above doesn't actually contain any unicode, but it should give you the general idea. In Python 3.x, all strings are unicode.

String Concatenation

Concatenation is a big word that means to combine or add two things together. In this case, we want to know how to add two strings together. As you might suspect, this operation is very easy in Python:

```
1   >>> string_one = "My dog ate "
2   >>> string_two = "my homework!"
3   >>> string_three = string_one + string_two
```

The '+' operator concatenates the two strings into one.

String Methods

A string is an object in Python. In fact, everything in Python is an object. However, you're not really ready for that. If you want to know more about how Python is an object oriented programming language, then you'll need to skip to that chapter. In the meantime, it's enough to know that strings have their very own methods built into them. For example, let's say you have the following string:

```
1  >>> my_string = "This is a string!"
```

Now you want to cause this string to be entirely in uppercase. To do that, all you need to do is call its **upper()** method, like this:

```
1  >>> my_string.upper()
```

If you have your interpreter open, you can also do the same thing like this:

```
1  >>> "This is a string!".upper()
```

There are many other string methods. For example, if you wanted everything to be lowercase, you would use the **lower()** method. If you wanted to remove all the leading and trailing white space, you would use **strip()**. To get a list of all the string methods, type the following command into your interpreter:

```
1  >>> dir(my_string)
```

You should end up seeing something like the following:

['__add__', '__class__', '__contains__', '__delattr__', '__doc__', '__eq__', '__format__', '__ge__', '__getattribute__', '__getitem__', '__getnewargs__', '__getslice__', '__gt__', '__hash__', '__init__', '__le__', '__len__', '__lt__', '__mod__', '__mul__', '__ne__', '__new__', '__reduce__', '__reduce_ex__', '__repr__', '__rmod__', '__rmul__', '__setattr__', '__sizeof__', '__str__', '__subclasshook__', '_formatter_field_name_split', '_formatter_parser', 'capitalize', 'center', 'count', 'decode', 'encode', 'endswith', 'expandtabs', 'find', 'format', 'index', 'isalnum', 'isalpha', 'isdigit', 'islower', 'isspace', 'istitle', 'isupper', 'join', 'ljust', 'lower', 'lstrip', 'partition', 'replace', 'rfind', 'rindex', 'rjust', 'rpartition', 'rsplit', 'rstrip', 'split', 'splitlines', 'startswith', 'strip', 'swapcase', 'title', 'translate', 'upper', 'zfill']

You can safely ignore the methods that begin and end with double-underscores, such as __add__. They are not used in every day Python coding. Focus on the other ones instead. If you'd like to know what one of them does, just ask for **help**. For example, say you want to learn what **capitalize** is for. To find out, you would type

```
1  >>> help(my_string.capitalize)
```

This would return the following information:

Help on built-in function capitalize:

capitalize(...)
    S.capitalize() -> string

Return a copy of the string S with only its first character capitalized.

You have just learned a little bit about a topic called **introspection**. Python allows easy introspection of all its objects, which makes it very easy to use. Basically, introspection allows you to ask Python about itself. In an earlier section, you learned about casting. You may have wondered how to tell what type the variable was (i.e. an int or a string). You can ask Python to tell you that!

```
1  >>> type(my_string)
2  <type 'str'>
```

As you can see, the my_string variable is of type str!

String Slicing

One subject that you'll find yourself doing a lot of in the real world is string slicing. I have been surprised how often I have needed to know how to do this in my day-to-day job. Let's take a look at how slicing works with the following string:

```
1  >>> my_string = "I like Python!"
```

Each character in a string can be accessed using slicing. For example, if I want to grab just the first character, I could do this:

```
1  >>> my_string[0:1]
```

This grabs the first character in the string up to, but **not** including, the 2nd character. Yes, Python is zero-based. It's a little easier to understand if we map out each character's position in a table:

0 1 2 3 4 5 6 7 8 9 10 11 12 13 - - - - - - - - - - - - - - I l i k e P y t h o n !

Thus we have a string that is 14 characters long, starting at zero and going through thirteen. Let's do a few more examples to get these concepts into our heads better.

```
1  >>> my_string[:1]
2  'I'
3  >>> my_string[0:12]
4  'I like Pytho'
5  >>> my_string[0:13]
6  'I like Python'
7  >>> my_string[0:14]
8  'I like Python!'
9  >>> my_string[0:-5]
10 'I like Py'
11 >>> my_string[:]
12 'I like Python!'
13 >>> my_string[2:]
14 'like Python!'
```

As you can see from these examples, we can do a slice by just specifying the beginning of the slice (i.e. my_string[2:]), the ending of the slice (i.e. my_string[:1]) or both (i.e. my_string[0:13]). We can even use negative values that start at the end of the string. So the example where we did my_string[0:-5] starts at zero, but ends 5 characters before the end of the string.

You may be wondering where you would use this. I find myself using it for parsing fixed width records in files or occasionally for parsing complicated file names that follow a very specific naming convention. I have also used it in parsing out values from binary-type files. Any job where you need to do text file processing will be made easier if you understand slicing and how to use it effectively.

You can also access individual characters in a string via indexing. Here is an example:

```
1  >>> print(my_string[0])
```

The code above will print out the first character in the string.

String Formatting

String formatting (AKA substitution) is the topic of substituting values into a base string. Most of the time, you will be inserting strings within strings; however you will also find yourself inserting integers and floats into strings quite often as well. There are two different ways to accomplish this task. We'll start with the old way of doing things and then move on to the new.

Ye Olde Way of Substituting Strings

The easiest way to learn how to do this is to see a few examples. So here we go:

```
 1  >>> my_string = "I like %s" % "Python"
 2  >>> my_string
 3  'I like Python'
 4  >>> var = "cookies"
 5  >>> newString = "I like %s" % var
 6  >>> newString
 7  'I like cookies'
 8  >>> another_string = "I like %s and %s" % ("Python", var)
 9  >>> another_string
10  'I like Python and cookies'
```

As you've probably guessed, the **%s** is the important piece in the code above. It tells Python that you may be inserting text soon. If you follow the string with a percent sign and another string or variable, then Python will attempt to insert it into the string. You can insert multiple strings by putting multiple instances of **%s** inside your string. You'll see that in the last example. Just note that when you insert more than one string, you have to enclose the strings that you're going to insert with parentheses.

Now let's see what happens if we don't insert enough strings:

```
 1  >>> another_string = "I like %s and %s" % "Python"
 2  Traceback (most recent call last):
 3    File "<string>", line 1, in <fragment>
 4  TypeError: not enough arguments for format string
```

Oops! We didn't pass enough arguments to format the string! If you look carefully at the example above, you'll notice it has two instances of %s, so to insert strings into it, you have to pass it the same number of strings! Now we're ready to learn about inserting integers and floats. Let's take a look!

```
 1  >>> my_string = "%i + %i = %i" % (1,2,3)
 2  >>> my_string
 3  '1 + 2 = 3'
 4  >>> float_string = "%f" % (1.23)
 5  >>> float_string
 6  '1.230000'
 7  >>> float_string2 = "%.2f" % (1.23)
 8  >>> float_string2
 9  '1.23'
10  >>> float_string3 = "%.2f" % (1.237)
11  >>> float_string3
12  '1.24'
```

The first example above is pretty obvious. We create a string that accept three arguments and we pass them in. Just in case you hadn't figured it out yet, no, Python isn't actually doing any addition in that first example. For the second example, we pass in a float. Note that the output includes a lot of extra zeroes. We don't want that, so we tell Python to limit it to two decimal places in the 3rd example ("%.2f"). The last example shows you that Python will do some rounding for you if you pass it a float that's greater than two decimal places.

Now let's see what happens if we pass it bad data:

```
1  >>> int_float_err = "%i + %f" % ("1", "2.00")
2  Traceback (most recent call last):
3    File "<string>", line 1, in <fragment>
4  TypeError: %d format: a number is required, not str
```

In this example, we pass it two strings instead of an integer and a float. This raises a TypeError and tells us that Python was expecting a number. This refers to not passing an integer, so let's fix that and see if that fixes the issue:

```
1  >>> int_float_err = "%i + %f" % (1, "2.00")
2  Traceback (most recent call last):
3    File "<string>", line 1, in <fragment>
4  TypeError: float argument required, not str
```

Nope. We get the same error, but a different message that tells us we should have passed a float. As you can see, Python gives us pretty good information about what went wrong and how to fix it. If you fix the inputs appropriately, then you should be able to get this example to run.

Let's move on to the new method of string formatting!

Templates and the New String Formatting Methodology

This new method was actually added back in Python 2.4 as string templates, but was added as a regular string method via the **format** method in Python 2.6. So it's not really a new method, just newer. Anyway, let's start with templates!

```
1  >>> print("%(lang)s is fun!" % {"lang":"Python"})
2  Python is fun!
```

This probably looks pretty weird, but basically we just changed our %s into **%(lang)s**, which is basically the %s with a variable inside it. The second part is actually called a Python dictionary that we will be studying in the next section. Basically it's a key:value pair, so when Python sees the key "lang" in the string AND in the key of the dictionary that is passed in, it replaces that key with its value. Let's look at some more samples:

```
1  >>> print("%(value)s %(value)s %(value)s !" % {"value":"SPAM"})
2  SPAM SPAM SPAM !
3  >>> print("%(x)i + %(y)i = %(z)i" % {"x":1, "y":2})
4  Traceback (most recent call last):
5    File "<string>", line 1, in <fragment>
6  KeyError: 'z'
7  >>> print("%(x)i + %(y)i = %(z)i" % {"x":1, "y":2, "z":3})
8  1 + 2 = 3
```

In the first example, you'll notice that we only passed in one value, but it was inserted 3 times! This is one of the advantages of using templates. The second example has an issue in that we forgot to pass in a key, namely the "z" key. The third example rectifies this issue and shows the result. Now let's look at how we can do something similar with the string's format method!

```
1  >>> "Python is as simple as {0}, {1}, {2}".format("a", "b", "c")
2  'Python is as simple as a, b, c'
3  >>> "Python is as simple as {1}, {0}, {2}".format("a", "b", "c")
4  'Python is as simple as b, a, c'
5  >>> xy = {"x":0, "y":10}
6  >>> print("Graph a point at where x={x} and y={y}".format(**xy))
7  Graph a point at where x=0 and y=10
```

In the first two examples, you can see how we can pass items positionally. If we rearrange the order, we get a slightly different output. The last example uses a dictionary like we were using in the templates above. However, we have to extract the dictionary using the double asterisk to get it to work correctly here.

There are lots of other things you can do with strings, such as specifying a width, aligning the text, converting to different bases and much more. Be sure to take a look at some of the references below for more information.

- Python's official documentation on the str type[3]
- String Formatting[4]
- More on String Formatting[5]
- Python 2.x documentation on unicode[6]

---

[3]https://docs.python.org/3/library/functions.html#func-str
[4]https://docs.python.org/3/library/string.html#string-formatting
[5]https://docs.python.org/3/library/string.html#formatexamples
[6]http://docs.python.org/2/library/functions.html#unicode

Wrapping Up

We have covered a lot in this chapter. Let's review:

First we learned how to create strings themselves, then we moved on to the topic of string concatenation. After that we looked at some of the methods that the string object gives us. Next we looked at string slicing and we finished up by learning about string substitution.

In the next chapter, we will look at three more of Python's built-in data types: lists, tuples and dictionaries. Let's get to it!

Chapter 3 - Lists, Tuples and Dictionaries

Python has several other important data types that you'll probably use every day. They are called lists, tuples and dictionaries. This chapter's aim is to get you acquainted with each of these data types. They are not particularly complicated, so I expect that you will find learning how to use them very straight forward. Once you have mastered these three data types plus the string data type from the previous chapter, you will be quite a ways along in your education of Python. You'll be using these four building blocks in 99% of all the applications you will write.

Lists

A Python list is similar to an array in other languages. In Python, an empty list can be created in the following ways.

```
1  >>> my_list = []
2  >>> my_list = list()
```

As you can see, you can create the list using square brackets or by using the Python built-in, **list**. A list contains a list of elements, such as strings, integers, objects or a mixture of types. Let's take a look at some examples:

```
1  >>> my_list = [1, 2, 3]
2  >>> my_list2 = ["a", "b", "c"]
3  >>> my_list3 = ["a", 1, "Python", 5]
```

The first list has 3 integers, the second has 3 strings and the third has a mixture. You can also create lists of lists like this:

```
1  >>> my_nested_list = [my_list, my_list2]
2  >>> my_nested_list
3  [[1, 2, 3], ['a', 'b', 'c']]
```

Occasionally, you'll want to combine two lists together. The first way is to use the extend method:

```
1  >>> combo_list = []
2  >>> one_list = [4, 5]
3  >>> combo_list.extend(one_list)
4  >>> combo_list
5  [4, 5]
```

A slightly easier way is to just add two lists together.

```
1  >>> my_list = [1, 2, 3]
2  >>> my_list2 = ["a", "b", "c"]
3  >>> combo_list = my_list + my_list2
4  >>> combo_list
5  [1, 2, 3, 'a', 'b', 'c']
```

Yes, it really is that easy. You can also sort a list. Let's spend a moment to see how to do that:

```
1  >>> alpha_list = [34, 23, 67, 100, 88, 2]
2  >>> alpha_list.sort()
3  >>> alpha_list
4  [2, 23, 34, 67, 88, 100]
```

Now there is a got-cha above. Can you see it? Let's do one more example to make it obvious:

```
1  >>> alpha_list = [34, 23, 67, 100, 88, 2]
2  >>> sorted_list = alpha_list.sort()
3  >>> sorted_list
4  >>> print(sorted_list)
5  None
```

In this example, we try to assign the sorted list to a variable. However, when you call the **sort()** method on a list, it sorts the list in-place. So if you try to assign the result to another variable, then you'll find out that you'll get a None object, which is like a Null in other languages. Thus when you want to sort something, just remember that you sort them in-place and you cannot assign it to a different variable.

You can slice a list just like you do with a string:

```
1  >>> alpha_list[0:3]
2  [2, 23, 34]
```

This code returns a list of just the first 3 elements.

Tuples

A tuple is similar to a list, but you create them with parentheses instead of square brackets. You can also use the **tuple** built-in. The main difference is that a tuple is immutable while the list is mutable. Let's take a look at a few examples:

```
1   >>> my_tuple = (1, 2, 3, 4, 5)
2   >>> my_tuple[0:3]
3   (1, 2, 3)
4   >>> another_tuple = tuple()
5   >>> abc = tuple([1, 2, 3])
```

The code above demonstrates one way to create a tuple with five elements. It also shows that you can do tuple slicing. However, you cannot sort a tuple! The last two examples shows how to create tuples using the **tuple** keyword. The first one just creates an empty tuple whereas the second example has three elements inside it. Notice that it has a list inside it. This is an example of **casting**. We can change or **cast** an item from one data type to another. In this case, we cast a list into a tuple. If you want to turn the **abc** tuple back into a list, you can do the following:

```
1   >>> abc_list = list(abc)
```

To reiterate, the code above casts the tuple (abc) into a list using the **list** function.

Dictionaries

A Python dictionary is basically a **hash table** or a hash mapping. In some languages, they might be referred to as **associative memories** or **associative arrays**. They are indexed with keys, which can be any immutable type. For example, a string or number can be a key. You need to be aware that a dictionary is an unordered set of key:value pairs and the keys must be unique. You can get a list of keys by calling a dictionary instance's **keys** method. To check if a dictionary has a key, you can use Python's **in** keyword. In some of the older versions of Python (2.3 and older to be specific), you will see the **has_key** keyword used for testing if a key is in a dictionary. This keyword is deprecated in Python 2.x and removed entirely from Python 3.x.

Let's take a moment to see how we create a dictionary.

```
1  >>> my_dict = {}
2  >>> another_dict = dict()
3  >>> my_other_dict = {"one":1, "two":2, "three":3}
4  >>> my_other_dict
5  {'three': 3, 'two': 2, 'one': 1}
```

The first two examples show how to create an empty dictionary. All dictionaries are enclosed with curly braces. The last line is printed out so you can see how unordered a dictionary is. Now it's time to find out how to access a value in a dictionary.

```
1  >>> my_other_dict["one"]
2  1
3  >>> my_dict = {"name":"Mike", "address":"123 Happy Way"}
4  >>> my_dict["name"]
5  'Mike'
```

In the first example, we use the dictionary from the previous example and pull out the value associated with the key called "one". The second example shows how to acquire the value for the "name" key. Now let's see how to tell if a key is in a dictionary or not:

```
1  >>> "name" in my_dict
2  True
3  >>> "state" in my_dict
4  False
```

So, if the key is in the dictionary, Python returns a **Boolean True**. Otherwise it returns a Boolean **False**. If you need to get a listing of all the keys in a dictionary, then you do this:

```
1  >>> my_dict.keys()
2  dict_keys(['name', 'address'])
```

In Python 2, the **keys** method returns a list. But in Python 3, it returns a *view object*. This gives the developer the ability to update the dictionary and the view will automatically update too. Also note that when using the **in** keyword for dictionary membership testing, it is better to do it against the dictionary instead of the list returned from the **keys** method. See below:

```
1  >>> "name" in my_dict          # this is good
2  >>> "name" in my_dict.keys()   # this works too, but is slower
```

While this probably won't matter much to you right now, in a real job situation, seconds matter. When you have thousands of files to process, these little tricks can save you a lot of time in the long run!

Wrapping Up

In this chapter you just learned how to construct a Python list, tuple and dictionary. Make sure you understand everything in this section before moving on. These concepts will assist you in designing your programs. You will be building complex data structures using these building blocks every day if you choose to pursue employment as a Python programmer. Each of these data types can be nested inside the others. For example, you can have a nested dictionary, a dictionary of tuples, a tuple made up of several dictionaries, and on and on.

When you are ready to move on, we will learn about Python's support for conditional statements.

Chapter 4 - Conditional Statements

Every computer language I have ever used has had at least one conditional statement. Most of the time that statement is the **if/elif/else** structure. This is what Python has. Other languages also include the **case/switch** statement which I personally enjoy, however Python does not include it. You can make your own if you really want to, but this book is focused on learning Python fundamentals, so we're going to be only focusing on what's included with Python in this chapter.

The conditional statement checks to see if a statement is True or False. That's really all it does. However we will also be looking at the following Boolean operations: **and**, **or**, and **not**. These operations can change the behaviour of the conditional in simple and complex ways, depending on your project.

The if statement

Python's if statement is pretty easy to use. Let's spend a few minutes looking at some examples to better acquaint ourselves with this construct.

```
1  >>> if 2 > 1:
2          print("This is a True statement!")
3      This is a True Statement!
```

This conditional tests the "truthfulness" of the following statement: 2 > 1. Since this statement evaluates to True, it will cause the last line in the example to print to the screen or **standard out** (stdout).

Python Cares About Space

The Python language cares a lot about space. You will notice that in our conditional statement above, we indented the code inside the **if** statement four spaces. This is very important! If you do not indent your blocks of code properly, the code will not execute properly. It may not even run at all.

Also, do **not** mix tabs and spaces. IDLE will complain that there is an issue with your file and you will have trouble figuring out what the issue is. The recommended number of spaces to indent a block of code is four. You can actually indent your code any number of spaces as long as you are consistent. However, the 4-space rule is one that is recommended by the Python Style Guide and is the rule that is followed by the Python code developers.

29

Let's look at another example:

```
1  >>> var1 = 1
2  >>> var2 = 3
3  >>> if var1 > var2:
4          print("This is also True")
```

In this one, we compare two variables that translate to the question: Is 1 > 3? Obviously one is not greater than three, so it doesn't print anything. But what is we wanted it to print something? That's where the **else** statement comes in. Let's modify the conditional to add that piece:

```
1  if var1 > var2:
2      print("This is also True")
3  else:
4      print("That was False!")
```

If you run this code, it will print the string that follows the **else** statement. Let's change gears here and get some information from the user to make this more interesting. In Python 2.x, you can get information using a built-in called **raw_input**. If you are using Python 3.x, then you'll find that raw_input no longer exists. It was renamed to just **input**. They function in the same way though. To confuse matters, Python 2.x actually has a built-in called **input** as well; however it tries to execute what is entered as a Python expression whereas raw_input returns a string. Anyway, we'll be using Python 2.x's **raw_input** for this example to get the user's age.

```
1  # Python 2.x code
2  value = raw_input("How much is that doggy in the window? ")
3  value = int(value)
4
5  if value < 10:
6      print("That's a great deal!")
7  elif 10 <= value <= 20:
8      print("I'd still pay that...")
9  else:
10     print("Wow! That's too much!")
```

Let's break this down a bit. The first line asks the user for an amount. In the next line, it converts the user's input into an integer. So if you happen to type a floating point number like **1.23**, it will get truncated to just **1**. If you happen to type something other than a number, then you'll receive an exception. We'll be looking at how to handle exceptions in a later chapter, so for now, just enter an integer.

In the next few lines, you can see how we check for 3 different cases: less than 10, greater than or equal to 10 but less than or equal to 20 or something else. For each of these cases, a different string is printed out. Try putting this code into IDLE and save it. Then run it a few times with different inputs to see how it works.

You can add multiple **elif** statements to your entire conditional. The **else** is optional, but makes a good default.

Boolean Operations

Now we're ready to learn about Boolean operations (and, or, not). According to the Python documentation, their order of priority is first **or**, then **and**, then **not**. Here's how they work:

- **or** means that if any conditional that is "ored" together is True, then the following statement runs
- **and** means that all statements must be True for the following statement to run
- **not** means that if the conditional evaluates to False, it is True. This is the most confusing, in my opinion.

Let's take a look at some examples of each of these. We will start with **or**.

```
1  x = 10
2  y = 20
3
4  if x < 10 or y > 15:
5      print("This statement was True!")
```

Here we create a couple of variables and test if one is less than ten or if the other is greater than 15. Because the latter is greater than 15, the print statement executes. As you can see, if one or both of the statements are True, it will execute the statement. Let's take a look at how **and** works:

```
1  x = 10
2  y = 10
3  if x == 10 and y == 15:
4      print("This statement was True")
5  else:
6      print("The statement was False!")
```

If you run the code above, you will see that first statement does not get run. Instead, the statement under the **else** is executed. Why is that? Well, it is because we are testing is both x **and** y are 10 and 15 respectively. In this case, they are not, so we drop to the else. Thus, when you **and** two statements together, **both** statements have to evaluate to True for it to execute the following code. Also note that to test equality in Python, you have to use a double equal sign. A single equals sign is known as the **assignment operator** and is only for assigning a value to a variable. If you had tried to run the code above with one of those statement only having one equals sign, you would have received a message about invalid syntax.

Note that you can also **or** and **and** more than two statements together. However, I do not recommend that as the more statements that you do that too, the harder it can be to understand and debug.

Now we're ready to take a look at the **not** operation.

```
1   my_list = [1, 2, 3, 4]
2   x = 10
3   if x not in my_list:
4       print("'x' is not in the list, so this is True!")
```

In this example, we create a list that contains four integers. Then we write a test that asks if "x" is not in that list. Because "x" equals 10, the statement evaluates to True and the message is printed to the screen. Another way to test for **not** is be using the exclamation point, like this:

```
1   x = 10
2   if x != 11:
3       print("x is not equal to 11!")
```

If you want to, you can combine the **not** operation with the other two to create more complex conditional statements. Here is a simple example:

```
1   my_list = [1, 2, 3, 4]
2   x = 10
3   z = 11
4   if x not in my_list and z != 10:
5       print("This is True!")
```

Checking for Nothing

Because we are talking about statements that evaluate to True, we probably need to cover what evaluates to False. Python has the keyword **False** which I've mentioned a few times. However an empty string, tuple or list also evaluates to False. There is also another keyword that basically evaluates to False which is called **None**. The None value is used to represent the absence of value. It's kind of analogous to Null, which you find in databases. Let's take a look at some code to help us better understand how this all works:

```
 1  empty_list = []
 2  empty_tuple = ()
 3  empty_string = ""
 4  nothing = None
 5
 6  if empty_list == []:
 7      print("It's an empty list!")
 8
 9  if empty_tuple:
10      print("It's not an empty tuple!")
11
12  if not empty_string:
13      print("This is an empty string!")
14
15  if not nothing:
16      print("Then it's nothing!")
```

The first four lines set up four variables. Next we create four conditionals to test them. The first one checks to see if the **empty_list** is really empty. The second conditional checks to see if the **empty_tuple** has something in it. Yes, you read that right, The second conditional only evaluates to True if the tuple is **not** empty! The last two conditionals are doing the opposite of the second. The third is checking if the string **is** empty and the fourth is checking if the **nothing** variable is really None.

The **not** operator means that we are checking for the opposite meaning. In other words, we are checking if the value is NOT True. So in the third example, we check if the empty string is REALLY empty. Here's another way to write the same thing:

```
 1  if empty_string == "":
 2      print("This is an empty string!")
```

To really nail this down, let's set the **empty_string** variable to actually contain something:

```
 1  >>> empty_string = "something"
 2  >>> if empty_string == "":
 3          print("This is an empty string!")
```

If you run this, you will find that nothing is printed as we will only print something if the variable is an empty string.

Please note that none of these variables equals the other. They just evaluate the same way. To prove this, we'll take a look at a couple of quick examples:

```
1  >>> empty_list == empty_string
2  False
3  >>> empty_string == nothing
4  False
```

As you can see, they do not equal each other. You will find yourself checking your data structures for data a lot in the real world. Some programmers actually like to just wrap their structures in an exception handler and if they happen to be empty, they'll catch the exception. Others like to use the strategy mentioned above where you actually test the data structure to see if it has something in it. Both strategies are valid.

Personally, I find the **not** operator a little confusing and don't use it that much. But you will find it useful from time to time.

Special Characters

Strings can contain special characters, like tabs or new lines. We need to be aware of those as they can sometimes crop up and cause problems. For example, the new line character is defined as "n", while the tab character is defined as "t". Let's see a couple of examples so you will better understand what these do:

```
1  >>> print("I have a \n new line in the middle")
2  I have a
3   new line in the middle
4  >>> print("This sentence is \ttabbed!")
5  This sentence is    tabbed!
```

Was the output as you expected? In the first example, we have a "n" in the middle of the sentence, which forces it to print out a new line. Because we have a space after the new line character, the second line is indented by a space. The second example shows what happens when we have a tab character inside of a sentence.

Sometimes you will want to escape characters in a string, such as a backslash. To escape characters, you have to actually use a backslash, so in the case of a backslash, you would actually type two backslashes. Let's take a look:

```
1  >>> print("This is a backslash \")
2  Traceback (most recent call last):
3    File "<string>", line 1, in <fragment>
4  EOL while scanning string literal: <string>, line 1, pos 30
5  >>> print("This is a backslash \\")
6  This is a backslash \
```

You will notice that the first example didn't work so well. Python thought we were escaping the double-quote, so it couldn't tell where the end of the line (EOL) was and it threw an error. The second example has the backslash appropriately escaped.

if __name__ == "__main__"

You will see a very common conditional statement used in many Python examples. This is what it looks like:

```
1  if __name__ == "__main__":
2      # do something!
```

You will see this at the end of a file. This tells Python that you only want to run the following code if this program is executed as a standalone file. I use this construct a lot to test that my code works in the way I expect it to. We will be discussing this later in the book, but whenever you create a Python script, you create a Python module. If you write it well, you might want to import it into another module. When you do import a module, it will **not** run the code that's under the conditional because **__name__** will no longer equal "**__main__**". We will look at this again in **Chapter 11** when we talk about **classes**.

Wrapping Up

We've covered a fair bit of ground in this chapter. You have learned how to use conditional statements in several different ways. We have also spent some time getting acquainted with Boolean operators. As you have probably guessed, each of these chapters will get slightly more complex as we'll be using each building block that we learn to build more complicated pieces of code. In the next chapter, we will continue that tradition by learning about Python's support of loops!

Chapter 5 - Loops

Every programming language I have tried has some kind of looping construct. Most have more than one. The Python world has two types of loops:

- the **for** loop and
- the **while** loop

You will find that the **for** loop is by far the most popular of the two. Loops are used when you want to do something many times. Usually you will find that you need to do some operation or a set of operations on a piece of data over and over. This is where loops come in. They make it really easy to apply this sort of logic to your data.

Let's get started learning how these fun structures work!

The for Loop

As mentioned above, you use a loop when you want to iterate over something n number of times. It's a little easier to understand if we see an example. Let's use Python's builtin **range** function. The range function will create a list that is n in length. In Python 2.x, there is actually another function called **xrange** that is a number generator and isn't as resource intensive as range. They basically changed **xrange** into **range** in Python 3. Here is an example:

```
1  >>> range(5)
2  range(0, 5)
```

As you can see, the range function above took an integer and returned a **range** object. The range function also accepts a beginning value, an end value and a step value. Here are two more examples:

```
1  >>> range(5,10)
2  range(5, 10)
3  >>> list(range(1, 10, 2))
4  [1, 3, 5, 7, 9]
```

The first example demonstrates that you can pass a beginning and end value and the range function will return the numbers from the beginning value up to but not including the end value. So in the case of 5-10, we get 5-9. The second example shows how to use the **list** function to cause the range function to return every second element between 1 and 10. So it starts with one, skips two, etc. Now you're probably wondering what this has to do with loops. Well one easy way to show how a loop works is if we use the range function! Take a look:

```
1   >>> for number in range(5):
2           print(number)
3
4   0
5   1
6   2
7   3
8   4
```

What happened here? Let's read it from left to right to figure it out. For each number in a range of 5, print the number. We know that if we call range with a value of 5, it will return a list of 5 elements. So each time through the loop, it prints out each of the elements. The for loop above would be the equivalent of the following:

```
1   >>> for number in [0, 1, 2, 3, 4]:
2           print(number)
```

The range function just makes it a little bit smaller. The for loop can loop over any kind of Python iterator. We've already seen how it can iterate over a list. Let's see if it can also iterate over a dictionary.

```
1   >>> a_dict = {"one":1, "two":2, "three":3}
2   >>> for key in a_dict:
3           print(key)
4
5   three
6   two
7   one
```

When you use a **for** loop with a dictionary, you'll see that it automatically loops over the keys. We didn't have to say **for key in a_dict.keys()** (although that would have worked too). Python just did the right thing for us. You may be wondering why the keys printed in a different order than they were defined in the dictionary. As you may recall from chapter 3, dictionaries are unordered, so when we iterate over it, the keys could be in any order.

Now if you know that the keys can be sorted, then you can do that before you iterate over them. Let's change the dictionary slightly to see how that works.

```
1  >>> a_dict = {1:"one", 2:"two", 3:"three"}
2  >>> keys = a_dict.keys()
3  >>> keys = sorted(keys)
4  >>> for key in keys:
5          print(key)
6
7  1
8  2
9  3
```

Let's take a moment to figure out what this code does. First off, we create a dictionary that has integers for keys instead of strings. Then we extract the keys from the dictionary. Whenever you call the keys() method, it will return an unordered list of the keys. If you print them out and find them to be in ascending order, then that's just happenstance. Now we have a view of the dictionary's keys that are stored in a variable called **keys**. We sort it and then we use the **for** loop to loop over it.

Now we're ready to make things a little bit more interesting. We are going to loop over a range, but we want to print out only the even numbers. To do this, we want to use a conditional statement instead of using the range's step parameter. Here's one way you could do this:

```
1  >>> for number in range(10):
2          if number % 2 == 0:
3              print(number)
4
5  0
6  2
7  4
8  6
9  8
```

You're probably wondering what's going on here. What's up with the percent sign? In Python, the % is called a modulus operator. When you use the modulus operator, it will return the remainder. There is no remainder when you divide an even number by two, so we print those numbers out. You probably won't use the modulus operator a lot in the wild, but I have found it useful from time to time.

Now we're ready to learn about the **while** loop.

The while Loop

The while loop is also used to repeat sections of code, but instead of looping n number of times, it will only loop until a specific condition is met. Let's look at a very simple example:

```
1    >>> i = 0
2    >>> while i < 10:
3            print(i)
4            i = i + 1
```

The while loop is kind of like a conditional statement. Here's what this code means: while the variable **i** is less than ten, print it out. Then at the end, we increase i's value by one. If you run this code, it should print out 0-9, each on its own line and then stop. If you remove the piece where we increment i's value, then you'll end up with an infinite loop. This is usually a bad thing. Infinite loops are to be avoided and are known as logic errors.

There is another way to break out of a loop. It is by using the **break** builtin. Let's see how that works:

```
1    >>> while i < 10:
2            print(i)
3            if i == 5:
4                break
5            i += 1
6
7    0
8    1
9    2
10   3
11   4
12   5
```

In this piece of code, we add a conditional to check if the variable i ever equals 5. If it does, then we break out of the loop. As you can see from the sample output, as soon as it reaches 5, the code stops even though we told the while loop to keep looping until it reached 10. You will also note that we changed how we increment the value by using +=. This is a handy shortcut that you can also use with other math operations, like subtraction (-=) and multiplication (*=).

The break builtin is known as a **flow control tool**. There is another one called **continue** that is used to basically skip an iteration or continue with the next iteration. Here's one way to use it:

```
1   i = 0
2
3   while i < 10:
4       if i == 3:
5           i += 1
6           continue
7
8       print(i)
9
10      if i == 5:
11          break
12      i += 1
```

This is a little confusing, no? Basically we added a second conditional that checks if **i** equals 3. If it does, we increment the variable and continue with the next loop, which effectively skips printing the value 3 to the screen. As before, when we reach a value of 5, we break out of the loop.

There's one more topic we need to cover regarding loops and that's the **else** statement.

What else is for in loops

The **else** statement in loops only executes if the loop completes successfully. The primary use of the else statement is for searching for items:

```
1   my_list = [1, 2, 3, 4, 5]
2
3   for i in my_list:
4       if i == 3:
5           print("Item found!")
6           break
7       print(i)
8   else:
9       print("Item not found!")
```

In this code, we break out of the loop when **i** equals 3. This causes the else statement to be skipped. If you want to experiment, you can change the conditional to look for a value that's not in the list, which will cause the else statement to execute. To be honest, I have never seen anyone use this structure in all my years as a programmer. Most of the examples I have seen are bloggers trying to explain what it is used for. I have seen several who use it to raise an error if an item is not found in the iterable that you were searching. You can read a fairly in depth article by one of the Python core developers here[7].

---

[7] https://ncoghlan_devs-python-notes.readthedocs.org/en/latest/python_concepts/break_else.html

Wrapping Up

Hopefully at this point you can see the value in Python loops. They make repetition easier and pretty easy to understand. You will likely see the **for** loop much more often than the **while** loop. In fact, we are going to look at another way **for** loops are used in the next chapter when we learn about comprehensions! If you're still not quite sure how all this works, you may want to re-read this chapter before continuing.

Chapter 6 - Python Comprehensions

The Python language has a couple of methods for creating lists and dictionaries that are known as comprehensions. There is also a third type of comprehension for creating a Python set. In this chapter we will learn how to use each type of comprehension. You will find that the comprehension constructs build on the knowledge you have acquired from the previous chapters as they contain loops and conditionals themselves.

List Comprehensions

List comprehensions in Python are very handy. They can also be a little hard to understand when and why you would use them. List comprehensions tend to be harder to read than just using a simple **for** loop as well. You may want to review the looping chapter before you continue.

If you are ready, then we'll spend some time looking at how to construct list comprehensions and learn how they can be used. A list comprehension is basically a one line **for** loop that produces a Python **list** data structure. Here's a simple example:

```
1  >>> x = [i for i in range(5)]
```

Let's break this down a bit. Python comes with a range function that can return a list of numbers. By default, it returns integers starting at 0 and going up to but not including the number you pass it. So in this case, it returns a list containing the integers 0-4. This can be useful if you need to create a list very quickly. For example, say you're parsing a file and looking for something in particular. You could use a list comprehension as a kind of filter:

```
1  if [i for i in line if "SOME TERM" in i]:
2      # do something
```

I have used code similar to this to look through a file quickly to parse out specific lines or sections of the file. When you throw functions into the mix, you can start doing some really cool stuff. Say you want to apply a function to every element in a list, such as when you need to cast a bunch of strings into integers:

```
1  >>> x = ['1', '2', '3', '4', '5']
2  >>> y = [int(i) for i in x]
3  >>> y
4  [1, 2, 3, 4, 5]
```

This sort of thing comes up more often than you'd think. I have also had to loop over a list of strings and call a string method, such as strip on them because they had all kinds of leading or ending white space:

```
1  >>> myStrings = [s.strip() for s in myStringList]
```

There are also occasions where one needs to create a nested list comprehension. One reason to do that is to flatten multiple lists into one. This example comes from the Python documentation:

```
1  >>> vec = [[1,2,3], [4,5,6], [7,8,9]]
2  >>> [num for elem in vec for num in elem]
3  [1, 2, 3, 4, 5, 6, 7, 8, 9]
```

The documentation shows several other interesting examples for nested list comprehensions as well. I highly recommend taking a look at it! At this point, you should now be capable of using list comprehensions in your own code and use them well. Just use your imagination and you'll start seeing lots of good places where you too can use them.

Now we're ready to move on to Python's dictionary comprehensions!

Dictionary Comprehensions

Dictionary comprehensions started life in Python 3.0, but were backported to Python 2.7. They were originally proposed in the Python Enhancement Proposal 274 (PEP 274)[8] back in 2001. They are pretty similar to a list comprehension in the way that they are organized.

The best way to understand is to just do one!

```
1  >>> print( {i: str(i) for i in range(5)} )
2  {0: '0', 1: '1', 2: '2', 3: '3', 4: '4'}
```

This is a pretty straightforward comprehension. Basically it is creating an integer key and string value for each item in the range. Now you may be wondering how you could use a dictionary comprehension in real life. Mark Pilgrim[9] mentioned that you could use a dictionary comprehension for swapping the dictionary's keys and values. Here's how you would do that:

---

[8]http://www.python.org/dev/peps/pep-0274/
[9]http://www.diveintopython3.net/comprehensions.html

```
1  >>> my_dict = {1:"dog", 2:"cat", 3:"hamster"}
2  >>> print( {value:key for key, value in my_dict.items()} )
3  {'hamster': 3, 'dog': 1, 'cat': 2}
```

This will only work if the dictionary values are of a non-mutable type, such as a string. Otherwise you will end up causing an exception to be raised.

I could also see a dictionary comprehension being useful for creating a table out of class variables and their values. However, we haven't covered classes at this point, so I won't confuse you with that here.

Set Comprehensions

Set comprehensions are created in much the same way as dictionary comprehensions. Now a Python set is much like a mathematical set in that it doesn't have any repeated elements. You can create a normal set like this:

```
1  >>> my_list = [1, 2, 2, 3, 4, 5, 5, 7, 8]
2  >>> my_set = set(my_list)
3  >>> my_set
4  set([1, 2, 3, 4, 5, 7, 8])
```

As you can see from the example above, the call to set has removed the duplicates from the list. Now let's rewrite this code to use a set comprehension:

```
1  >>> my_list = [1, 2, 2, 3, 4, 5, 5, 7, 8]
2  >>> my_set = {x for x in my_list}
3  >>> my_set
4  set([1, 2, 3, 4, 5, 7, 8])
```

You will notice that to create a set comprehension, we basically changed the square brackets that a list comprehension uses to the curly braces that the dictionary comprehension has.

Wrapping Up

Now you know how to use the various Python comprehensions. You will probably find the list comprehension the most useful at first and also the most popular. If you start using your imagination, I am sure you will be able to find uses for all three types of comprehensions. Now we're ready to move on and learn about exception handling!

Chapter 7 - Exception Handling

What do you do when something bad happens in your program? Let's say you try to open a file, but you typed in the wrong path or you ask the user for information and they type in some garbage. You don't want your program to crash, so you implement exception handling. In Python, the construct is usually wrapped in what is know as a **try/except**. We will be looking at the following topics in this chapter:

- Common exception types
- Handling exceptions with **try/except**
- Learn how **try/except/finally** works
- Discover how the **else** statement works in conjunction with the **try/except**

Let's start out by learning about some of the most common exceptions that you'll see in Python. Note: an error and an exception are just different words that describe the same thing when we are talking about exception handling.

Common Exceptions

You have seen a few exceptions already. Here is a list of the most common built-in exceptions (definitions from the Python documentation[10]):

- **Exception** (this is what almost all the others are built off of)
- **AttributeError** - Raised when an attribute reference or assignment fails.
- **IOError** - Raised when an I/O operation (such as a print statement, the built-in open() function or a method of a file object) fails for an I/O-related reason, e.g., "file not found" or "disk full".
- **ImportError** - Raised when an import statement fails to find the module definition or when a **from ... import** fails to find a name that is to be imported.
- **IndexError** - Raised when a sequence subscript is out of range.
- **KeyError** - Raised when a mapping (dictionary) key is not found in the set of existing keys.
- **KeyboardInterrupt** - Raised when the user hits the interrupt key (normally Control-C or Delete).
- **NameError** - Raised when a local or global name is not found.
- **OSError** - Raised when a function returns a system-related error.
- **SyntaxError** - Raised when the parser encounters a syntax error.

---

[10]http://docs.python.org/2/library/exceptions.html

- **TypeError** - Raised when an operation or function is applied to an object of inappropriate type. The associated value is a string giving details about the type mismatch.
- **ValueError** - Raised when a built-in operation or function receives an argument that has the right type but an inappropriate value, and the situation is not described by a more precise exception such as IndexError.
- **ZeroDivisionError** - Raised when the second argument of a division or modulo operation is zero.

There are a lot of other exceptions as well, but you probably won't see them all that often. However, if you are interested, you can go and read all about them in the Python documentation[11].

How to Handle Exceptions

Handling exceptions in Python is really easy. Let's spend some time writing some examples that will cause exceptions. We will start with one of the most common computer science problems: division by zero.

```
1   >>> 1 / 0
2   Traceback (most recent call last):
3       File "<string>", line 1, in <fragment>
4   ZeroDivisionError: integer division or modulo by zero
5
6   >>> try:
7           1 / 0
8       except ZeroDivisionError:
9           print("You cannot divide by zero!")
10
11  You cannot divide by zero!
```

If you think back to elementary math class, you will recall that you cannot divide by zero. In Python, this operation will cause an error, as you can see in the first half of the example. To catch the error, we wrap the operation with a **try/except** statement.

Bare Excepts

Here's another way to catch the error:

---

[11]http://docs.python.org/2/library/exceptions.html

```
1  >>> try:
2          1 / 0
3      except:
4          print("You cannot divide by zero!")
```

This is **not** recommended! In Python, this is known as a **bare except**, which means it will catch any and all exceptions. The reason this is not recommended is that you don't know which exception you are catching. When you have something like **except ZeroDivisionError**, you are obviously trying to catch a division by zero error. In the code above, you cannot tell what you are trying to catch.

Let's take a look at a couple of other examples.

```
1  >>> my_dict = {"a":1, "b":2, "c":3}
2  >>> try:
3          value = my_dict["d"]
4      except KeyError:
5          print("That key does not exist!")
6
7  That key does not exist!
8  >>> my_list = [1, 2, 3, 4, 5]
9  >>> try:
10         my_list[6]
11     except IndexError:
12         print("That index is not in the list!")
13
14 That index is not in the list!
```

In the first example, we create a 3-element dictionary. Then we try to access a key that is not in the dictionary. Because the key is not in the dictionary, it raises a **KeyError**, which we catch. The second example shows a list that is 5 items in length. We try to grab the 7th item from the index. Remember, Python lists are zero-based, so when you say [6], you're asking for the 7th item. Anyway, because there are only 5 items, it raises an **IndexError**, which we also catch.

You can also catch multiple exceptions with a single statement. There are a couple of different ways to do this. Let's take a look:

```
1  my_dict = {"a":1, "b":2, "c":3}
2  try:
3      value = my_dict["d"]
4  except IndexError:
5      print("This index does not exist!")
6  except KeyError:
7      print("This key is not in the dictionary!")
8  except:
9      print("Some other error occurred!")
```

This is a fairly standard way to catch multiple exceptions. First we try to access a key that doesn't exist in the dictionary. The try/except checks to see if you are catching a KeyError, which you are in the second **except** statement. You will also note that we have a bare except at the end. This is usually not recommended, but you'll probably see it from time to time, so it's good to know about it. Also note that most of the time, you won't need to wrap a block of code in multiple **except** handlers. You normally just need to wrap it in one.

Here's another way to catch multiple exceptions:

```
1  try:
2      value = my_dict["d"]
3  except (IndexError, KeyError):
4      print("An IndexError or KeyError occurred!")
```

Notice that in this example, we are putting the errors that we want to catch inside of parentheses. The problem with this method is that it's hard to tell which error has actually occurred, so the previous example is recommended.

Most of the time when an exception occurs, you will need to alert the user by printing to the screen or logging the message. Depending on the severity of the error, you may need to exit your program. Sometimes you will need to clean up before you exit the program. For example, if you have opened a database connection, you will want to close it before you exit your program or you may end up leaving connections open. Another example is closing a file handle that you have been writing to. You will learn more about file handling in the next chapter. But first, we need to learn how to clean up after ourselves. This is facilitated with the **finally** statement.

The finally Statement

The **finally** statement is really easy to use. Let's take a look at a silly example:

```
1  my_dict = {"a":1, "b":2, "c":3}
2
3  try:
4      value = my_dict["d"]
5  except KeyError:
6      print("A KeyError occurred!")
7  finally:
8      print("The finally statement has executed!")
```

If you run the code above, it will print the statement in the **except** and the **finally**. This is pretty simple, right? Now you can use the **finally** statement to clean up after yourself. You would also put the exit code at the end of the **finally** statement.

try, except, or else!

The **try/except** statement also has an **else** clause. The **else** will only run if there are no errors raised. We will spend a few moments looking at a couple examples:

```
1  my_dict = {"a":1, "b":2, "c":3}
2
3  try:
4      value = my_dict["a"]
5  except KeyError:
6      print("A KeyError occurred!")
7  else:
8      print("No error occurred!")
```

Here we have a dictionary with 3 elements and in the **try/except** we access a key that exists. This works, so the **KeyError** is **not** raised. Because there is no error, the **else** executes and "No error occurred!" is printed to the screen. Now let's add in the **finally** statement:

```
1   my_dict = {"a":1, "b":2, "c":3}
2
3   try:
4       value = my_dict["a"]
5   except KeyError:
6       print("A KeyError occurred!")
7   else:
8       print("No error occurred!")
9   finally:
10      print("The finally statement ran!")
```

If you run this example, it will execute the **else** and **finally** statements. Most of the time, you won't see the **else** statement used as any code that follows a **try/except** will be executed if no errors were raised. The only good usage of the **else** statement that I've seen mentioned is where you want to execute a **second** piece of code that can **also** raise an error. Of course, if an error is raised in the **else**, then it won't get caught.

Wrapping Up

Now you should be able to handle exceptions in your code. If you find your code raising an exception, you will know how to wrap it in such a way that you can catch the error and exit gracefully or continue without interruption.

Now we're ready to move on and learn about how to work with files in Python.

Chapter 8 - Working with Files

This chapter introduces the topic of reading and writing data to files on your hard drive. You will find that reading and writing files in Python is very easy to do. Let's get started!

How to Read a File

Python has a builtin function called **open** that we can use to open a file for reading. Create a text file name "test.txt" with the following contents:

```
1  This is a test file
2  line 2
3  line 3
4  this line intentionally left blank
```

Here are a couple of examples that show how to use **open** for reading:

```
1  handle = open("test.txt")
2  handle = open(r"C:\Users\mike\py101book\data\test.txt", "r")
```

The first example will open a file named **test.txt** in read-only mode. This is the default mode of the **open** function. Note that we didn't pass a fully qualified path to the file that we wanted to open in the first example. Python will automatically look in the folder that the script is running in for **test.txt**. If it doesn't find it, then you will receive an IOError.

The second example does show a fully qualified path to the file, but you'll notice that it begins with an "r". This means that we want Python to treat the string as a raw string. Let's take a moment to see the difference between specifying a raw string versus a regular string:

```
1  >>> print("C:\Users\mike\py101book\data\test.txt")
2  C:\Users\mike\py101book\data     est.txt
3  >>> print(r"C:\Users\mike\py101book\data\test.txt")
4  C:\Users\mike\py101book\data\test.txt
```

As you can see, when we don't specify it as a raw string, we get an invalid path. Why does this happen? Well, as you might recall from the strings chapter, there are certain special characters that need to be escaped, such as "n" or "t". In this case, we see there's a "t" (i.e. a tab), so the string obediently adds a tab to our path and screws it up for us.

The second argument in the second example is also an "r". This tells **open** that we want to open the file in read-only mode. In other words, it does the same thing as the first example, but it's more explicit. Now let's actually read the file!

Put the following lines into a Python script and save it in the same location as your test.txt file:

```
1  handle = open("test.txt", "r")
2  data = handle.read()
3  print(data)
4  handle.close()
```

If you run this, it will open the file and read the entire file as a string into the **data** variable. Then we print that data and close the file handle. You should always close a file handle as you never know when another program will want to access it. Closing the file will also help save memory and prevent strange bugs in your programs. You can tell Python to just read a line at a time, to read all the lines into a Python list or to read the file in chunks. The last option is very handy when you are dealing with really large files and you don't want to read the whole thing in, which might fill up the PC's memory.

Let's spend some time looking at different ways to read files.

```
1  handle = open("test.txt", "r")
2  data = handle.readline() # read just one line
3  print(data)
4  handle.close()
```

If you run this example, it will only read the first line of your text file and print it out. That's not too useful, so let's try the file handle's readlines() method:

```
1  handle = open("test.txt", "r")
2  data = handle.readlines() # read ALL the lines!
3  print(data)
4  handle.close()
```

After running this code, you will see a Python list printed to the screen because that's what the **readlines** method returns: a list! Let's take a moment to learn how to read a file in smaller chunks.

How To Read Files Piece by Piece

The easiest way to read a file in chunks is to use a loop. First we will learn how to read a file line by line and then we will learn how to read it a kilobyte at a time. We will use a **for** loop for our first example:

```
1  handle = open("test.txt", "r")
2
3  for line in handle:
4      print(line)
5
6  handle.close()
```

Here we open up a read-only file handle and then we use a **for** loop to iterate over it. You will find that you can iterate over all kinds of objects in Python (strings, lists, tuples, keys in a dictionary, etc). That was pretty simple, right? Now let's do it in chunks!

```
1  handle = open("test.txt", "r")
2
3  while True:
4      data = handle.read(1024)
5      print(data)
6      if not data:
7          break
```

In this example, we use Python's **while** loop to read a kilobyte of the file at a time. As you probably know, a kilobyte is 1024 bytes or characters. Now let's pretend that we want to read a binary file, like a PDF.

How to Read a Binary File

Reading a binary file is very easy. All you need to do is change the file mode:

```
1  handle = open("test.pdf", "rb")
```

So this time we changed the file mode to **rb**, which means **read-binary**. You will find that you may need to read binary files when you download PDFs from the internet or transfer files from PC to PC.

Writing Files in Python

If you have been following along, you can probably guess what the file-mode flag is for writing files: "w" and "wb" for write-mode and write-binary-mode. Let's take a look at a simple example, shall we?

CAUTION: When using "w" or "wb" modes, if the file already exists, it will be overwritten with no warning! You can check if a file exists before you open it by using Python's **os** module. See **Chapter 16** in the **os.path.exists** section.

```
1   handle = open("output.txt", "w")
2   handle.write("This is a test!")
3   handle.close()
```

That was easy! All we did here was change the file mode to "w" and we called the file handle's **write** method to write some text to the file. The file handle also has a **writelines** method that will accept a list of strings that the handle will then write to disk in order.

Using the with Operator

Python has a neat little builtin called **with** which you can use to simplify reading and writing files. The **with** operator creates what is known as a **context manager** in Python that will automatically close the file for you when you are done processing it. Let's see how this works:

```
1   with open("test.txt") as file_handler:
2       for line in file_handler:
3           print(line)
```

The syntax for the **with** operator is a little strange, but you'll pick it up pretty quickly. Basically what we're doing is replacing:

```
1   handle = open("test.txt")
```

with this:

```
1   with open("test.txt") as file_handler:
```

You can do all the usual file I/O operations that you would normally do as long as you are within the **with** code block. Once you leave that code block, the file handle will close and you won't be able to use it any more. Yes, you read that correctly. You no longer have to close the file handle explicitly as the **with** operator does it automatically! See if you can change some of the earlier examples from this chapter so that they use the **with** method too.

Catching Errors

Sometimes when you are working with files, bad things happen. The file is locked because some other process is using it or you have some kind of permission error. When this happens, an **IOError** will probably occur. In this section, we will look at how to catch errors the normal way and how to catch them using the **with** operator. Hint: the idea is basically the same in both!

```
1  try:
2      file_handler = open("test.txt")
3      for line in file_handler:
4          print(line)
5  except IOError:
6      print("An IOError has occurred!")
7  finally:
8      file_handler.close()
```

In the example above, we wrap the usual code inside of a **try/except** construct. If an error occurs, we print out a message to the screen. Note that we also make sure we close the file using the **finally** statement. Now we're ready to look at how we would do this same thing using **with**:

```
1  try:
2      with open("test.txt") as file_handler:
3          for line in file_handler:
4              print(line)
5  except IOError:
6      print("An IOError has occurred!")
```

As you might have guessed, we just wrapped the **with** block in the same way as we did in the previous example. The difference here is that we do not need the **finally** statement as the context manager handles that for us.

Wrapping Up

At this point you should be pretty well versed in dealing with files in Python. Now you know how to read and write files using the older style and the newer **with** style. You will most likely see both styles in the wild. In the next chapter, we will learn how to import other modules that come with Python. This will allow us to create programs using pre-built modules. Let's get started!

Chapter 9 - Importing

Python comes with lots of pre-made code baked in. These pieces of code are known as modules and packages. A module is a single importable Python file whereas a package is made up of two or more modules. A package can be imported the same way a module is. Whenever you save a Python script of your own, you have created a module. It may not be a very useful module, but that's what it is. In this chapter, we will learn how to import modules using several different methods. Let's get started!

import this

Python provides the **import** keyword for importing modules. Let's give it a try:

```
1  import this
```

If you run this code in your interpreter, you should see something like the following as your output:

```
1   The Zen of Python, by Tim Peters
2
3   Beautiful is better than ugly.
4   Explicit is better than implicit.
5   Simple is better than complex.
6   Complex is better than complicated.
7   Flat is better than nested.
8   Sparse is better than dense.
9   Readability counts.
10  Special cases aren't special enough to break the rules.
11  Although practicality beats purity.
12  Errors should never pass silently.
13  Unless explicitly silenced.
14  In the face of ambiguity, refuse the temptation to guess.
15  There should be one-- and preferably only one --obvious way to do it.
16  Although that way may not be obvious at first unless you're Dutch.
17  Now is better than never.
18  Although never is often better than *right* now.
19  If the implementation is hard to explain, it's a bad idea.
20  If the implementation is easy to explain, it may be a good idea.
21  Namespaces are one honking great idea -- let's do more of those!
```

You have found an "Easter egg" in Python known as the "Zen of Python". It's actually a sort of an unofficial best practices for Python. The **this** module doesn't actually do anything, but it provided a fun little way to show how to import something. Let's actually import something we can use, like the **math** module:

```
1  >>> import math
2  >>> math.sqrt(4)
3  2.0
```

Here we imported the **math** module and then we did something kind of new. We called one of its functions, **sqrt** (i.e. square root). To call a method of an imported module, we have to use the following syntax: **module_name.method_name(argument)**. In this example, we found the square root of 4. The **math** module has many other functions that we can use, such as **cos** (cosine), **factorial**, **log** (logarithm), etc. You can call these functions in much the same way you did **sqrt**. The only thing you'll need to check is if they accept more arguments or not. Now let's look at another way to import.

Using from to import

Some people don't like having to preface everything they type with the module name. Python has a solution for that! You can actually import just the functions you want from a module. Let's pretend that we want to just import the **sqrt** function:

```
1  >>> from math import sqrt
2  >>> sqrt(16)
3  4.0
```

This works pretty much exactly how it is read: **from the math module, import the sqrt function**. Let me explain it another way. We use Python's **from** keyword to import the **sqrt** function **from** the **math** module. You can also use this method to import multiple functions from the math function:

```
1  >>> from math import pi, sqrt
```

In this example, we import both **pi** and **sqrt**. If you tried to access **pi** you may have noticed that it's actually a value and not a function that you can call. It just returns the value of pi. When you do an import, you may end up importing a value, a function or even another module! There's one more way to import stuff that we need to cover. Let's find out how to import everything!

Importing Everything!

Python provides a way to import **all** the functions and values from a module as well. This is actually a **bad** idea as it can contaminate your **namespace**. A namespace is where all your variables live during the life of the program. So let's say you have your own variable named **sqrt**, like this:

```
1   >>> from math import sqrt
2   >>> sqrt = 5
```

Now you have just changed the **sqrt** function into a variable that holds the value of 5. This is known as **shadowing**. This becomes especially tricky when you import everything from a module. Let's take a look:

> >>> from math import * >>> sqrt = 5 >>> sqrt(16) Traceback (most recent call last): File "<string>", line 1, in <fragment> TypeError: 'int' object is not callable

To import everything, instead of specifying a list of items, we just use the " " *wildcard which means we want to import everything. If we don't know what's in themath** module, we won't realize that we've just clobbered one of the functions we imported. When we try to call the **sqrt** function after reassigning it to an integer, we find out that it no longer works.

Thus it is recommended that in most cases, you should import items from modules using one of the previous methods mentioned in this chapter. There are a few exceptions to this rule. Some modules are made to be imported using the "*" method. One prominent example is Tkinter, a toolkit included with Python that allows you to create desktop user interfaces. The reason that it is supposedly okay to import Tkinter in this way is that the modules are named so that it is unlikely you would reuse one yourself.

Wrapping Up

Now you know all about Python imports. There are dozens of modules included with Python that you can use to give extra functionality to your programs. You can use the builtin modules to query your OS, get information from the Windows Registry, set up logging utilities, parse XML, and much, much more. We will be covering a few of these modules in Part II of this book.

In the next chapter, we will be looking at building our own functions. I think you'll find this next topic to be very helpful.

Chapter 10 - Functions

A function is a structure that you define. You get to decide if they have arguments or not. You can add keyword arguments and default arguments too. A function is a block of code that starts with the **def** keyword, a name for the function and a colon. Here's a simple example:

```
1  >>> def a_function():
2          print("You just created a function!")
```

This function doesn't do anything except print out some text. To call a function, you need to type out the name of the function followed by an open and close parentheses:

```
1  >>> a_function()
2  You just created a function!
```

Simple, eh?

An Empty Function (the stub)

Sometimes when you are writing out some code, you just want to write the function definitions without putting any code in them. I've done this as kind of an outline. It helps you to see how your application is going to be laid out. Here's an example:

```
1  >>> def empty_function():
2          pass
```

Here's something new: the **pass** statement. It is basically a null operation, which means that when **pass** is executed, nothing happens.

Passing Arguments to a Function

Now we're ready to learn about how to create a function that can accept arguments and also learn how to pass said arguments to the function. Let's create a simple function that can add two numbers together:

```
1   >>> def add(a, b):
2           return a + b
3
4   >>> add(1, 2)
5   3
```

All functions return something. If you don't tell it to return something, then it will return None. In this case, we tell it to return **a + b**. As you can see, we can call the function by passing in two values. If you don't pass enough or you pass too many arguments, then you'll get an error:

```
1   >>> add(1)
2   Traceback (most recent call last):
3     File "<string>", line 1, in <fragment>
4   TypeError: add() takes exactly 2 arguments (1 given)
```

You can also call the function by passing the name of the arguments:

```
1   >>> add(a=2, b=3)
2   5
3   >>> total = add(b=4, a=5)
4   >>> print(total)
5   9
```

You'll notice that it doesn't matter what order you pass them to the function as long as they are named correctly. In the second example, you can see that we assign the result of the function to a variable named **total**. This is the usual way of calling a function as you'll want to do something with the result. You are probably wondering what would happen if we passed in arguments with the wrong names attached. Would it work? Let's find out:

```
1   >>> add(c=5, d=2)
2   Traceback (most recent call last):
3     File "<string>", line 1, in <fragment>
4   TypeError: add() got an unexpected keyword argument 'c'
```

Whoops! We received an error. This means that we passed in a keyword argument that the function didn't recognize. Coincidentally, keyword arguments are our next topic!

Keyword Arguments

Functions can also accept keyword arguments! They can actually accept both regular arguments and keyword arguments. What this means is that you can specify which keywords are which and pass them in. You saw this behavior in a previous example.

```
1   >>> def keyword_function(a=1, b=2):
2           return a+b
3
4   >>> keyword_function(b=4, a=5)
5   9
```

You could have also called this function without specifying the keywords. This function also demonstrates the concept of default arguments. How? Well, try calling the function without any arguments at all!

```
1   >>> keyword_function()
2   3
```

The function returned the number 3! Why? The reason is that **a** and **b** have default values of 1 and 2 respectively. Now let's create a function that has both a regular argument and a couple keyword arguments:

```
1    >>> def mixed_function(a, b=2, c=3):
2            return a+b+c
3
4    >>> mixed_function(b=4, c=5)
5    Traceback (most recent call last):
6      File "<string>", line 1, in <fragment>
7    TypeError: mixed_function() takes at least 1 argument (2 given)
8    >>> mixed_function(1, b=4, c=5)
9    10
10   >>> mixed_function(1)
11   6
```

There are 3 example cases in the above code. Let's go over each of them. In the first example, we try calling our function using just the keyword arguments. This will give us a confusing error. The Traceback says that our function accepts at least one argument, but that two were given. What's going on here? The fact is that the first argument is required because it's not set to anything, so if you only call the function with the keyword arguments, that causes an error.

For the second example, we call the mixed function with 3 values, naming two of them. This works and gives us the expected result, which was 1+4+5=10. The third example shows what happens if we only call the function by passing in just one value...the one that didn't have a default. This also works by taking the "1" and adding it to the two default values of "2" and "3" to get a result of "6"! Isn't that cool?

*args and **kwargs

You can also set up functions to accept any number of arguments or keyword arguments by using a special syntax. To get infinite arguments, use *args and for infinite keyword arguments, use *kwargs. The "args" and "kwargs" words are not important. That's just convention. You could have called them *bill and *ted and it would work the same way. The key here is in the number of asterisks.

Note: in addition to the convention of *args and *kwargs, you will also see a andkw from time to time.

Let's take a look at a quick example:

```
1  >>> def many(*args, **kwargs):
2          print(args)
3          print(kwargs)
4
5  >>> many(1, 2, 3, name="Mike", job="programmer")
6  (1, 2, 3)
7  {'job': 'programmer', 'name': 'Mike'}
```

First we create our function using the new syntax and then we call it with three regular arguments and two keyword arguments. The function itself will print out both types of arguments. As you can see, the **args** parameter turns into a tuple and **kwargs** turns into a dictionary. You will see this type of coding used in the Python source and in many 3rd party Python packages.

A Note on Scope and Globals

Python has the concept of **scope** just like most programming languages. Scope will tell us when a variable is available to use and where. If we define the variables inside of a function, those variables can only be used inside that function. Once that function ends, they can no longer be used because they are **out of scope**. Let's take a look at an example:

```
1  def function_a():
2      a = 1
3      b = 2
4      return a+b
5
6  def function_b():
7      c = 3
8      return a+c
9
10 print( function_a() )
11 print( function_b() )
```

If you run this code, you will receive the following error:

```
1   NameError: global name 'a' is not defined
```

This is caused because the variable **a** is only defined in the first function and is not available in the second. You can get around this by telling Python that **a** is a **global** variable. Let's take a look at how that's done:

```
1   def function_a():
2       global a
3       a = 1
4       b = 2
5       return a+b
6
7   def function_b():
8       c = 3
9       return a+c
10
11  print(function_a())
12  print(function_b())
```

This code will work because we told Python to make **a** global, which means that that variable is available everywhere in our program. This is usually a bad idea and not recommended. The reason it is not recommended is that it makes it difficult to tell when the variable is defined. Another problem is that when we define a global in one place, we may accidentally redefine its value in another which may cause logic errors later that are difficult to debug.

Coding Tips

One of the biggest problems that new programmers need to learn is the idea of "Don't Repeat Yourself (DRY)". This concept is that you should avoid writing the same code more than once. When you find yourself doing that, then you know that chunk of code should go into a function. One great reason to do this is that you will almost certainly need to change that piece of code again in the future and if it's in multiple places, then you will need to remember where all those locations are AND change them.

Copying and pasting the same chunk of code all over is an example of **spaghetti code**. Try to avoid this as much as possible. You will regret it at some point either because you'll be the one having to fix it or because you'll find someone else's code that you have to maintain with these sorts of problems.

Wrapping Up

You now have the foundational knowledge necessary to use functions effectively. You should practice creating some simple functions and try calling them in different ways. Once you've played around with functions a bit or you just think you thoroughly understand the concepts involved, you can turn to the next chapter on classes.

Chapter 11 - Classes

Everything in Python is an object. That's a very vague statement unless you've taken a computer programming class or two. What this means is that every *thing* in Python has methods and values. The reason is that everything is based on a class. A class is the blueprint of an object. Let's take a look at what I mean:

```
1  >>> x = "Mike"
2  >>> dir(x)
3  ['__add__', '__class__', '__contains__', '__delattr__', '__doc__', '__eq__',
4  '__format__', '__ge__', '__getattribute__', '__getitem__', '__getnewargs__',
5  '__getslice__', '__gt__', '__hash__', '__init__', '__le__', '__len__', '__lt__',
6  '__mod__', '__mul__', '__ne__', '__new__', '__reduce__', '__reduce_ex__', '__rep\
7  r__',
8  '__rmod__', '__rmul__', '__setattr__', '__sizeof__', '__str__', '__subclasshook_\
9  _',
10 '_formatter_field_name_split', '_formatter_parser', 'capitalize', 'center', 'cou\
11 nt',
12 'decode', 'encode', 'endswith', 'expandtabs', 'find', 'format', 'index', 'isalnu\
13 m',
14 'isalpha', 'isdigit', 'islower', 'isspace', 'istitle', 'isupper', 'join', 'ljust\
15 ',
16 'lower', 'lstrip', 'partition', 'replace', 'rfind', 'rindex', 'rjust', 'rpartiti\
17 on',
18 'rsplit', 'rstrip', 'split', 'splitlines', 'startswith', 'strip', 'swapcase', 't\
19 itle',
20 'translate', 'upper', 'zfill']
```

Here we have a string assigned to the variable **x**. It might not look like much, but that string has a lot of methods. If you use Python's **dir** keyword, you can get a list of all the methods you can call on your string. There are 71 methods here! Technically we're not supposed to call the methods that start with underscores directly, so that reduces the total to 38, but that's still a lot of methods! What does this mean though? It means that a string is based on a class and **x** is an **instance** of that class!

In Python we can create our own classes. Let's get started!

Creating a Class

Creating a class in Python is very easy. Here is a very simple example:

```
1  # Python 2.x syntax
2  class Vehicle(object):
3      """docstring"""
4
5      def __init__(self):
6          """Constructor"""
7          pass
```

This class doesn't do anything in particular, however it is a very good learning tool. For example, to create a class, we need to use Python's **class** keyword, followed by the name of the class. In Python, convention says that the class name should have the first letter capitalized. Next we have an open parentheses followed by the word **object** and a closed parentheses. The **object** is what the class is based on or inheriting from. This is known as the base class or parent class. Most classes in Python are based on **object**. Classes have a special method called __init__ (for initialization). This method is called whenever you create (or instantiate) an object based on this class. The __init__ method is only called once and is not to be called again inside the program. Another term for __init__ is **constructor**, although this term isn't used that much in Python.

You may be wondering why I keep saying **method** instead of **function**. A function changes its name to "method" when it is within a class. You will also notice that every method has to have at least one argument (i.e. self), which is not true with a regular function.

In Python 3, we don't need to explicitly say we're inheriting from **object**. Instead, we could have written the above like this:

```
1  # Python 3.x syntax
2  class Vehicle:
3      """docstring"""
4
5      def __init__(self):
6          """Constructor"""
7          pass
```

You will notice that the only difference is that we no longer need the parentheses if we're basing our class on **object**. Let's expand our class definition a bit and give it some attributes and methods.

```
1   class Vehicle(object):
2       """docstring"""
3
4       def __init__(self, color, doors, tires):
5           """Constructor"""
6           self.color = color
7           self.doors = doors
8           self.tires = tires
9
10      def brake(self):
11          """
12          Stop the car
13          """
14          return "Braking"
15
16      def drive(self):
17          """
18          Drive the car
19          """
20          return "I'm driving!"
```

The code above added three attributes and two methods. The three attributes are:

```
1   self.color = color
2   self.doors = doors
3   self.tires = tires
```

Attributes describe the vehicle. So the vehicle has a color, some number of doors and some number of tires. It also has two methods. A method describes what a class does. So in this case, a vehicle can **brake** and **drive**. You may have noticed that all of the methods, including the first one have a funny argument called **self**. Let's talk about that!

What is self?

Python classes need a way to refer to themselves. This isn't some kind of narcissistic navel-gazing on the part of the class. Instead, it's a way to tell one instance from another. The word **self** is a way to describe itself, literally. Let's take a look at an example as I always find that helpful when I'm learning something new and strange:

Add the following code to the end of that class you wrote above and save it:

```
1  if __name__ == "__main__":
2      car = Vehicle("blue", 5, 4)
3      print(car.color)
4
5      truck = Vehicle("red", 3, 6)
6      print(truck.color)
```

The conditional statement above is a common way of telling Python that you only want to run the following code if this code is executed as a standalone file. If you had imported your module into another script, then the code underneath the conditional would not run. Anyway, if you run this code, you will create two instances of the Vehicle class: a car instance and a truck instance. Each instance will have its own attributes and methods. This is why when we print out the color of each instance, they are different. The reason is that the class is using that **self** argument to tell itself which is which. Let's change the class a bit to make the methods more unique:

```
1  class Vehicle(object):
2      """docstring"""
3
4      def __init__(self, color, doors, tires, vtype):
5          """Constructor"""
6          self.color = color
7          self.doors = doors
8          self.tires = tires
9          self.vtype = vtype
10
11     def brake(self):
12         """
13         Stop the car
14         """
15         return "%s braking" % self.vtype
16
17     def drive(self):
18         """
19         Drive the car
20         """
21         return "I'm driving a %s %s!" % (self.color, self.vtype)
22
23 if __name__ == "__main__":
24     car = Vehicle("blue", 5, 4, "car")
25     print(car.brake())
26     print(car.drive())
27
```

```
28    truck = Vehicle("red", 3, 6, "truck")
29    print(truck.drive())
30    print(truck.brake())
```

In this example, we pass in another parameter to tell the class which vehicle type we're creating. Then we call each method for each instance. If you run this code, you should see the following output:

```
1    car braking
2    I'm driving a blue car!
3    I'm driving a red truck!
4    truck braking
```

This demonstrates how the instance keeps track of its "self". You will also notice that we are able to get the values of the attributes from the __init__ method into the other methods. The reason is because all those attributes are prepended with **self.**. If we hadn't done that, the variables would have gone out of scope at the end of the __init__ method.

Subclasses

The real power of classes becomes apparent when you get into subclasses. You may not have realized it, but we've already created a subclass when we created a class based on **object**. In other words, we subclassed **object**. Now because **object** isn't very interesting, the previous examples don't really demonstrate the power of subclassing. So let's subclass our Vehicle class and find out how all this works.

```
1    class Car(Vehicle):
2        """
3        The Car class
4        """
5
6        #----------------------------------------------------------------
7        def brake(self):
8            """
9            Override brake method
10           """
11           return "The car class is breaking slowly!"
12
13   if __name__ == "__main__":
14       car = Car("yellow", 2, 4, "car")
15       car.brake()
```

```
16      'The car class is breaking slowly!'
17      car.drive()
18      "I'm driving a yellow car!"
```

For this example, we subclassed our **Vehicle** class. You will notice that we didn't include an __init__ method or a **drive** method. The reason is that when you subclass Vehicle, you get all its attributes and methods unless you override them. Thus you will notice that we did override the **brake** method and made it say something different from the default. The other methods we left the same. So when you tell the car to brake, it uses the original method and we learn that we're driving a yellow car. Wasn't that neat?

Using the default values of the parent class is known as **inheriting** or **inheritance**. This is a big topic in Object Oriented Programming (OOP). This is also a simple example of **polymorphism**. Polymorphic classes typically have the same interfaces (i.e. methods, attributes), but they are not aware of each other. In Python land, polymorphism isn't very rigid about making sure the interfaces are exactly the same. Instead, it follows the concept of **duck typing**. The idea of **duck typing** is that if it walks like a duck and talks like a duck, it must be a duck. So in Python, as long as the class has method names that are the same, it doesn't matter if the implementation of the methods are different.

Anyway, you really don't need to know the nitty gritty details of all that to use classes in Python. You just need to be aware of the terminology so if you want to dig deeper, you will be able to. You can find lots of good examples of Python polymorphism that will help you figure out if and how you might use that concept in your own applications.

Now, when you subclass, you can override as much or as little from the parent class as you want. If you completely override it, then you would probably be just as well off just creating a new class.

Wrapping Up

Classes are a little complicated, but they are very powerful. They allow you to use variables across methods which can make code reuse even easier. I would recommend taking a look at Python's source for some excellent examples of how classes are defined and used.

We are now at the end of Part I. Congratulations for making it this far! You now have the tools necessary to build just about anything in Python! In Part II, we will spend time learning about using some of the wonderful modules that Python includes in its distribution. This will help you to better understand the power of Python and familiarize yourself with using the Standard Library. Part II will basically be a set of tutorials to help you on your way to becoming a great Python programmer!

Part II - Learning from the Library

In Part II, you will get an abbreviated tour of some of the Python Standard Library. The reason it's abbreviated is that the Python Standard Library is HUGE! So this section is to get you acquainted with using the modules that come with Python. I will be going over the modules I use the most in my day-to-day job and the modules I've seen used by my co-workers. I think this mini-tour will prepare you for digging in on your own.

Let's take a look at what we'll be covering:

- Introspection
- csv
- ConfigParser
- logging
- os
- smtplib / email
- subprocess
- sys
- thread / queues
- time / datetime

The first chapter in this section will give you a quick tutorial into Python's **introspection** abilities; basically you'll learn how to make Python tell you about itself, which sounds kind of weird but is really quite valuable to know about. Next we'll learn how to use **ConfigParser**, a neat little module that let's you read and write config files. After that we'll take a look at **logging**. The **os** module can do lots of fun things, but we'll try to focus on the ones that I think you'll find most useful. The **subprocess** allows you to open other processes.

You will find the **sys** module allows you to exit a program, get the Python path, acquire version information, redirect stdout and a whole lot more. The thread module allows you to create **threads** in your program. We won't dive too deep into that subject as it can get confusing pretty quickly. The **time** and **datetime** modules allow you to manipulate dates and time in Python, which has many applications when it comes to developing programs.

Let's get started!

image

Chapter 12 - Introspection

Whether you're new to Python, been using it for a few years or you're an expert, knowing how to use Python's introspection capabilities can help your understanding of your code and that new package you just downloaded with the crappy documentation. Introspection is a fancy word that means to observe oneself and ponder one's thoughts, senses, and desires. In Python world, introspection is actually kind of similar. Introspection in this case is to use Python to figure out Python. In this chapter, you can learn how to use Python to give yourself a clue about the code you're working on or trying to learn. Some might even call it a form of debugging.

Here's what we're going to cover:

- type
- dir
- help

The Python Type

You may not know this, but Python may just be your type. Yes, Python can tell you what type of variable you have or what type is returned from a function. It's a very handy little tool. Let's look at a few examples to make it all clear:

```
1  >>> x = "test"
2  >>> y = 7
3  >>> z = None
4  >>> type(x)
5  <class 'str'>
6  >>> type(y)
7  <class 'int'>
8  >>> type(z)
9  <class 'NoneType'>
```

As you can see, Python has a keyword called **type** that can tell you what is what. In my real-life experiences, I've used **type** to help me figure out what is going on when my database data is corrupt or not what I expect. I just add a couple lines and print out each row's data along with its type. This has helped me a lot when I've been dumbfounded by some stupid code I wrote.

The Python Dir

What is dir? Is it something you say when someone says or does something stupid? Not in this context! No, here on Planet Python, the dir keyword is used to tell the programmer what attributes and methods there are in the passed in object. If you forget to pass in an object, dir will return a list of names in the current scope. As usual, this is easier to understand with a few examples.

```
1  >>> dir("test")
2  ['__add__', '__class__', '__contains__', '__delattr__',
3   '__doc__', '__eq__', '__ge__', '__getattribute__',
4   '__getitem__', '__getnewargs__', '__getslice__', '__gt__',
5   '__hash__', '__init__', '__le__', '__len__', '__lt__',
6   '__mod__', '__mul__', '__ne__', '__new__', '__reduce__',
7   '__reduce_ex__', '__repr__', '__rmod__', '__rmul__',
8   '__setattr__', '__str__', 'capitalize', 'center',
9   'count', 'decode', 'encode', 'endswith', 'expandtabs',
10  'find', 'index', 'isalnum', 'isalpha', 'isdigit', 'islower',
11  'isspace', 'istitle', 'isupper', 'join', 'ljust', 'lower',
12  'lstrip', 'replace', 'rfind', 'rindex', 'rjust', 'rsplit',
13  'rstrip', 'split', 'splitlines', 'startswith', 'strip',
14  'swapcase', 'title', 'translate', 'upper', 'zfill']
```

Since everything in Python is an object, we can pass a string to dir and find out what methods it has. Pretty neat, huh? Now let's try it with an imported module:

```
1  >>> import sys
2  >>> dir(sys)
3  ['__displayhook__', '__doc__', '__egginsert', '__excepthook__',
4   '__name__', '__plen', '__stderr__', '__stdin__', '__stdout__',
5   '_getframe', 'api_version', 'argv', 'builtin_module_names',
6   'byteorder', 'call_tracing', 'callstats', 'copyright',
7   'displayhook', 'dllhandle', 'exc_clear', 'exc_info',
8   'exc_traceback', 'exc_type', 'exc_value', 'excepthook',
9   'exec_prefix', 'executable', 'exit', 'exitfunc',
10  'getcheckinterval', 'getdefaultencoding', 'getfilesystemencoding',
11  'getrecursionlimit', 'getrefcount', 'getwindowsversion', 'hexversion',
12  'maxint', 'maxunicode', 'meta_path', 'modules', 'path', 'path_hooks',
13  'path_importer_cache', 'platform', 'prefix', 'setcheckinterval',
14  'setprofile', 'setrecursionlimit', 'settrace', 'stderr', 'stdin',
15  'stdout', 'version', 'version_info', 'warnoptions', 'winver']
```

Now, that's handy! If you haven't figured it out yet, the **dir** function is extremely handy for those 3rd party packages that you have downloaded (or will soon download) that have little to no documentation. How do you find out about what methods are available in these cases? Well, **dir** will help you figure it out. Of course, sometimes the documentation is in the code itself, which brings us to the builtin help utility.

Python Help!

Python comes with a handy help utility. Just type "help()" (minus the quotes) into a Python shell and you'll see the following directions (Python version may vary)

```
1   >>> help()
2
3   Welcome to Python 2.6!  This is the online help utility.
4
5   If this is your first time using Python, you should definitely check out
6   the tutorial on the Internet at http://www.python.org/doc/tut/.
7
8   Enter the name of any module, keyword, or topic to get help on writing
9   Python programs and using Python modules.  To quit this help utility and
10  return to the interpreter, just type "quit".
11
12  To get a list of available modules, keywords, or topics, type "modules",
13  "keywords", or "topics".  Each module also comes with a one-line summary
14  of what it does; to list the modules whose summaries contain a given word
15  such as "spam", type "modules spam".
16
17  help>
```

Note that you now have a "help>" prompt instead of the ">>>". When you are in help mode, you can explore the various modules, keywords and topics found in Python. Also note that when typing the word "modules", you will see a delay as Python searches its library folder to acquire a list. If you have installed a lot of 3rd party modules, this can take quite a while, so be prepared to go fix yourself a mocha while you wait. Once it's done, just follow the directions and play around with it and I think you'll get the gist.

Wrapping Up

Now you know how to take an unknown module and learn a lot about it by just using some of Python's built-in functionality. You will find yourself using these commands over and over again to help you learn Python. As I mentioned earlier, you will find these tools especially helpful for the 3rd Party modules that don't believe in documentation.

Chapter 13 - The csv Module

The csv module gives the Python programmer the ability to parse CSV (Comma Separated Values) files. A CSV file is a human readable text file where each line has a number of fields, separated by commas or some other delimiter. You can think of each line as a row and each field as a column. The CSV format has no standard, but they are similar enough that the csv module will be able to read the vast majority of CSV files. You can also write CSV files using the csv module.

Reading a CSV File

There are two ways to read a CSV file. You can use the csv module's **reader** function or you can use the **DictReader** class. We will look at both methods. But first, we need to get a CSV file so we have something to parse. There are many websites that provide interesting information in CSV format. We will be using the World Health Organization's (WHO) website to download some information on Tuberculosis. You can go here to get it: http://www.who.int/tb/country/data/download/en/. Once you have the file, we'll be ready to start. Ready? Then let's look at some code!

```python
import csv

def csv_reader(file_obj):
    """
    Read a csv file
    """
    reader = csv.reader(file_obj)
    for row in reader:
        print(" ".join(row))

if __name__ == "__main__":
    csv_path = "TB_data_dictionary_2014-02-26.csv"
    with open(csv_path, "r") as f_obj:
        csv_reader(f_obj)
```

Let's take a moment to break this down a bit. First off, we have to actually import the **csv** module. Then we create a very simple function called **csv_reader** that accepts a file object. Inside the function, we pass the file object into the **csv.reader** function, which returns a reader object. The reader object allows iteration, much like a regular file object does. This lets us iterate over each row in the reader object and print out the line of data, minus the commas. This works because each row is a list and we can join each element in the list together, forming one long string.

Now let's create our own CSV file and feed it into the **DictReader** class. Here's a really simple one:

```
1  first_name,last_name,address,city,state,zip_code
2  Tyrese,Hirthe,1404 Turner Ville,Strackeport,NY,19106-8813
3  Jules,Dicki,2410 Estella Cape Suite 061,Lake Nickolasville,ME,00621-7435
4  Dedric,Medhurst,6912 Dayna Shoal,Stiedemannberg,SC,43259-2273
```

Let's save this in a file named **data.csv**. Now we're ready to parse the file using the DictReader class. Let's try it out:

```python
1  import csv
2
3  def csv_dict_reader(file_obj):
4      """
5      Read a CSV file using csv.DictReader
6      """
7      reader = csv.DictReader(file_obj, delimiter=',')
8      for line in reader:
9          print(line["first_name"]),
10         print(line["last_name"])
11
12 if __name__ == "__main__":
13     with open("data.csv") as f_obj:
14         csv_dict_reader(f_obj)
```

In the example above, we open a file and pass the file object to our function as we did before. The function passes the file object to our DictReader class. We tell the DictReader that the delimiter is a comma. This isn't actually required as the code will still work without that keyword argument. However, it's a good idea to be explicit so you know what's going on here. Next we loop over the reader object and discover that each line in the reader object is a dictionary. This makes printing out specific pieces of the line very easy.

Now we're ready to learn how to write a csv file to disk.

Writing a CSV File

The csv module also has two methods that you can use to write a CSV file. You can use the **writer** function or the DictWriter class. We'll look at both of these as well. We will be with the writer function. Let's look at a simple example:

```
1    import csv
2
3    def csv_writer(data, path):
4        """
5        Write data to a CSV file path
6        """
7        with open(path, "w", newline='') as csv_file:
8            writer = csv.writer(csv_file, delimiter=',')
9            for line in data:
10               writer.writerow(line)
11
12   if __name__ == "__main__":
13       data = ["first_name,last_name,city".split(","),
14               "Tyrese,Hirthe,Strackeport".split(","),
15               "Jules,Dicki,Lake Nickolasville".split(","),
16               "Dedric,Medhurst,Stiedemannberg".split(",")
17               ]
18       path = "output.csv"
19       csv_writer(data, path)
```

In the code above, we create a **csv_writer** function that accepts two arguments: data and path. The data is a list of lists that we create at the bottom of the script. We use a shortened version of the data from the previous example and split the strings on the comma. This returns a list. So we end up with a nested list that looks like this:

```
1    [['first_name', 'last_name', 'city'],
2     ['Tyrese', 'Hirthe', 'Strackeport'],
3     ['Jules', 'Dicki', 'Lake Nickolasville'],
4     ['Dedric', 'Medhurst', 'Stiedemannberg']]
```

The **csv_writer** function opens the path that we pass in and creates a csv writer object. Then we loop over the nested list structure and write each line out to disk. Note that we specified what the delimiter should be when we created the writer object. If you want the delimiter to be something besides a comma, this is where you would set it.

Now we're ready to learn how to write a CSV file using the **DictWriter** class! We're going to use the data from the previous version and transform it into a list of dictionaries that we can feed to our hungry DictWriter. Let's take a look:

```python
import csv

def csv_dict_writer(path, fieldnames, data):
    """
    Writes a CSV file using DictWriter
    """
    with open(path, "w", newline='') as out_file:
        writer = csv.DictWriter(out_file, delimiter=',', fieldnames=fieldnames)
        writer.writeheader()
        for row in data:
            writer.writerow(row)

if __name__ == "__main__":
    data = ["first_name,last_name,city".split(","),
            "Tyrese,Hirthe,Strackeport".split(","),
            "Jules,Dicki,Lake Nickolasville".split(","),
            "Dedric,Medhurst,Stiedemannberg".split(",")
            ]
    my_list = []
    fieldnames = data[0]
    for values in data[1:]:
        inner_dict = dict(zip(fieldnames, values))
        my_list.append(inner_dict)

    path = "dict_output.csv"
    csv_dict_writer(path, fieldnames, my_list)
```

We will start in the second section first. As you can see, we start out with the nested list structure that we had before. Next we create an empty list and a list that contains the field names, which happens to be the first list inside the nested list. Remember, lists are zero-based, so the first element in a list starts at zero! Next we loop over the nested list construct, starting with the second element:

```python
for values in data[1:]:
    inner_dict = dict(zip(fieldnames, values))
    my_list.append(inner_dict)
```

Inside the **for** loop, we use Python builtins to create dictionary. The **zip** method will take two iterators (lists in this case) and turn them into a list of tuples. Here's an example:

```
1  zip(fieldnames, values)
2  [('first_name', 'Dedric'), ('last_name', 'Medhurst'), ('city', 'Stiedemannberg')]
```

Now when your wrap that call in **dict**, it turns that list of tuples into a dictionary. Finally we append the dictionary to the list. When the **for** finishes, you'll end up with a data structure that looks like this:

[{'city': 'Strackeport', 'first_name': 'Tyrese', 'last_name': 'Hirthe'},
      {'city': 'Lake Nickolasville', 'first_name': 'Jules', 'last_name': 'Dicki'}, {'city': 'Stiede-
      mannberg', 'first_name': 'Dedric', 'last_name': 'Medhurst'}]

At the end of the second session, we call our **csv_dict_writer** function and pass in all the required arguments. Inside the function, we create a DictWriter instance and pass it a file object, a delimiter value and our list of field names. Next we write the field names out to disk and loop over the data one row at a time, writing the data to disk. The DictWriter class also supports the **writerows** method, which we could have used instead of the loop. The **csv.writer** function also supports this functionality.

You may be interested to know that you can also create **Dialects** with the csv module. This allows you to tell the csv module how to read or write a file in a very explicit manner. If you need this sort of thing because of an oddly formatted file from a client, then you'll find this functionality invaluable.

Wrapping Up

Now you know how to use the csv module to read and write CSV files. There are many websites that put out their data in this format and it is used a lot in the business world. In our next chapter, we will begin learning about the ConfigParser module.

Chapter 14 - configparser

Configuration files are used by both users and programmers. They are usually used for storing your application's settings or even your operating system's settings. Python's core library includes a module called configparser that you can use for creating and interacting with configuration files. We'll spend a few minutes learning how it works in this chapter.

Creating a Config File

Creating a config file with configparser is extremely simple. Let's create some code to demonstrate:

```python
import configparser

def createConfig(path):
    """
    Create a config file
    """
    config = configparser.ConfigParser()
    config.add_section("Settings")
    config.set("Settings", "font", "Courier")
    config.set("Settings", "font_size", "10")
    config.set("Settings", "font_style", "Normal")
    config.set("Settings", "font_info",
               "You are using %(font)s at %(font_size)s pt")

    with open(path, "w") as config_file:
        config.write(config_file)


if __name__ == "__main__":
    path = "settings.ini"
    createConfig(path)
```

The code above will create a config file with one section labelled Settings that will contain four options: font, font_size, font_style and font_info. Also note that in Python 3 we only need to specify that we're writing the file in write-only mode, i.e. "w". Back in Python 2, we had to use "wb" to write in binary mode.

How to Read, Update and Delete Options

Now we're ready to learn how to read the config file, update its options and even how to delete options. In this case, it's easier to learn by actually writing some code! Just add the following function to the code that you wrote above.

```python
import configparser
import os

def crudConfig(path):
    """
    Create, read, update, delete config
    """
    if not os.path.exists(path):
        createConfig(path)

    config = configparser.ConfigParser()
    config.read(path)

    # read some values from the config
    font = config.get("Settings", "font")
    font_size = config.get("Settings", "font_size")

    # change a value in the config
    config.set("Settings", "font_size", "12")

    # delete a value from the config
    config.remove_option("Settings", "font_style")

    # write changes back to the config file
    with open(path, "w") as config_file:
        config.write(config_file)


if __name__ == "__main__":
    path = "settings.ini"
    crudConfig(path)
```

This code first checks to see if the path for the config file exists. If it does not, then it uses the createConfig function we created earlier to create it. Next we create a ConfigParser object and pass it the config file path to read. To read an option in your config file, we call our ConfigParser object's **get** method, passing it the section name and the option name. This will return the option's value. If you want to change an option's value, then you use the **set** method, where you pass the section name, the option name and the new value. Finally, you can use the **remove_option** method to remove an option.

In our example code, we change the value of font_size to **12** and we remove the font_style option completely. Then we write the changes back out to disk.

This isn't really a good example though as you should never have a function that does everything like this one does. So let's split it up into a series of functions instead:

```python
import configparser
import os

def create_config(path):
    """
    Create a config file
    """
    config = configparser.ConfigParser()
    config.add_section("Settings")
    config.set("Settings", "font", "Courier")
    config.set("Settings", "font_size", "10")
    config.set("Settings", "font_style", "Normal")
    config.set("Settings", "font_info",
               "You are using %(font)s at %(font_size)s pt")

    with open(path, "w") as config_file:
        config.write(config_file)


def get_config(path):
    """
    Returns the config object
    """
    if not os.path.exists(path):
        create_config(path)

    config = configparser.ConfigParser()
    config.read(path)
    return config


def get_setting(path, section, setting):
    """
    Print out a setting
```

```
35         """
36         config = get_config(path)
37         value = config.get(section, setting)
38         msg = "{section} {setting} is {value}".format(
39             section=section, setting=setting, value=value)
40         print(msg)
41         return value
42
43
44   def update_setting(path, section, setting, value):
45         """
46         Update a setting
47         """
48         config = get_config(path)
49         config.set(section, setting, value)
50         with open(path, "w") as config_file:
51             config.write(config_file)
52
53
54   def delete_setting(path, section, setting):
55         """
56         Delete a setting
57         """
58         config = get_config(path)
59         config.remove_option(section, setting)
60         with open(path, "w") as config_file:
61             config.write(config_file)
62
63   if __name__ == "__main__":
64       path = "settings.ini"
65       font = get_setting(path, 'Settings', 'font')
66       font_size = get_setting(path, 'Settings', 'font_size')
67
68       update_setting(path, "Settings", "font_size", "12")
69
70       delete_setting(path, "Settings", "font_style")
```

This example is heavily refactored compared to the first one. I even went so far as to name the functions following PEP8. Each function should be self-explanatory and self-contained. Instead of putting all the logic into one function, we separate it out into multiple functions and then demonstrate their functionality within the bottom if statement. Now you can import the module and use it yourself.

Please note that this example has the section hard-coded, so you will want to update this example further to make it completely generic.

How to Use Interpolation

The configparser module also allows **interpolation**, which means you can use some options to build another option. We actually do this with the font_info option in that its value is based on the font and font_size options. We can change an interpolated value using a Python dictionary. Let's take a moment to demonstrate both of these facts.

```python
import configparser
import os

def interpolationDemo(path):
    if not os.path.exists(path):
        createConfig(path)

    config = configparser.ConfigParser()
    config.read(path)

    print(config.get("Settings", "font_info"))

    print(config.get("Settings", "font_info",
                     vars={"font": "Arial", "font_size": "100"}))


if __name__ == "__main__":
    path = "settings.ini"
    interpolationDemo(path)
```

If you run this code, you should see output similar to the following:

```
You are using Courier at 12 pt
You are using Arial at 100 pt
```

Wrapping Up

At this point, you should know enough about the **configparser's** capabilities that you can use it for your own projects. There's another project called **ConfigObj** that isn't a part of Python that you might also want to check out. **ConfigObj** is more flexible and has more features than **configparser**. But if you're in a pinch or your organization doesn't allow 3rd party packages, then **configparser** will probably fit the bill.

Chapter 15 - Logging

Python provides a very powerful logging library in its standard library. A lot of programmers use print statements for debugging (myself included), but you can also use logging to do this. It's actually cleaner to use logging as you won't have to go through all your code to remove the print statements. In this chapter we'll cover the following topics:

- Creating a simple logger
- How to log from multiple modules
- Log formatting
- Log configuration

By the end of this chapter, you should be able to confidently create your own logs for your applications. Let's get started!

Creating a Simple Logger

Creating a log with the logging module is easy and straight-forward. It's easiest to just look at a piece of code and then explain it, so here's some code for you to read:

```
1  import logging
2
3  # add filemode="w" to overwrite
4  logging.basicConfig(filename="sample.log", level=logging.INFO)
5
6  logging.debug("This is a debug message")
7  logging.info("Informational message")
8  logging.error("An error has happened!")
```

As you might expect, to access the logging module you have to first import it. The easiest way to create a log is to use the logging module's basicConfig function and pass it some keyword arguments. It accepts the following: filename, filemode, format, datefmt, level and stream. In our example, we pass it a file name and the logging level, which we set to INFO. There are five levels of logging (in ascending order): DEBUG, INFO, WARNING, ERROR and CRITICAL. By default, if you run this code multiple times, it will append to the log if it already exists. If you would rather have your logger overwrite the log, then pass in a **filemode="w"** as mentioned in the comment in the code. Speaking of running the code, this is what you should get if you ran it once:

```
1  INFO:root:Informational message
2  ERROR:root:An error has happened!
```

Note that the debugging message isn't in the output. That is because we set the level at INFO, so our logger will only log if it's a INFO, WARNING, ERROR or CRITICAL message. The root part just means that this logging message is coming from the root logger or the main logger. We'll look at how to change that so it's more descriptive in the next section. If you don't use **basicConfig**, then the logging module will output to the console / stdout.

The logging module can also log some exceptions to file or wherever you have it configured to log to. Here's an example:

```python
1  import logging
2
3  logging.basicConfig(filename="sample.log", level=logging.INFO)
4  log = logging.getLogger("ex")
5
6  try:
7      raise RuntimeError
8  except RuntimeError:
9      log.exception("Error!")
```

Let's break this down a bit. Here we use the **logging** module's **getLogger** method to return a logger object that has been named **ex**. This is handy when you have multiple loggers in one application as it allows you to identify which messages came from each logger. This example will force a **RuntimeError** to be raised, catch the error and log the entire traceback to file, which can be very handy when debugging.

How to log From Multiple Modules (and Formatting too!)

The more you code, the more often you end up creating a set of custom modules that work together. If you want them all to log to the same place, then you've come to the right place. We'll look at the simple way and then show a more complex method that's also more customizable. Here's one easy way to do it:

```
1   import logging
2   import otherMod
3
4   def main():
5       """
6       The main entry point of the application
7       """
8       logging.basicConfig(filename="mySnake.log", level=logging.INFO)
9       logging.info("Program started")
10      result = otherMod.add(7, 8)
11      logging.info("Done!")
12
13  if __name__ == "__main__":
14      main()
```

Here we import logging and a module of our own creation ("otherMod"). Then we create our log file as before. The other module looks like this:

```
1   # otherMod.py
2   import logging
3
4   def add(x, y):
5       """"""
6       logging.info("added %s and %s to get %s" % (x, y, x+y))
7       return x+y
```

If you run the main code, you should end up with a log that has the following contents:

```
1   INFO:root:Program started
2   INFO:root:added 7 and 8 to get 15
3   INFO:root:Done!
```

Do you see the problem with doing it this way? You can't really tell very easily where the log messages are coming from. This will only get more confusing the more modules there are that write to this log. So we need to fix that. That brings us to the complex way of creating a logger. Let's take a look at a different implementation:

```
1   import logging
2   import otherMod2
3
4   def main():
5       """
6       The main entry point of the application
7       """
8       logger = logging.getLogger("exampleApp")
9       logger.setLevel(logging.INFO)
10
11      # create the logging file handler
12      fh = logging.FileHandler("new_snake.log")
13
14      formatter = logging.Formatter('%(asctime)s - %(name)s - %(levelname)s - %(me\
15   ssage)s')
16      fh.setFormatter(formatter)
17
18      # add handler to logger object
19      logger.addHandler(fh)
20
21      logger.info("Program started")
22      result = otherMod2.add(7, 8)
23      logger.info("Done!")
24
25   if __name__ == "__main__":
26       main()
```

Here we create a logger instance named "exampleApp". We set its logging level, create a logging file handler object and a logging Formatter object. The file handler has to set the formatter object as its formatter and then the file handler has to be added to the logger instance. The rest of the code in main is mostly the same. Just note that instead of "logging.info", it's "logger.info" or whatever you call your logger variable. Here's the updated **otherMod2** code:

```
1   # otherMod2.py
2   import logging
3
4   module_logger = logging.getLogger("exampleApp.otherMod2")
5
6   def add(x, y):
7       """"""
8       logger = logging.getLogger("exampleApp.otherMod2.add")
9       logger.info("added %s and %s to get %s" % (x, y, x+y))
10      return x+y
```

Note that here we have two loggers defined. We don't do anything with the module_logger in this case, but we do use the other one. If you run the main script, you should see the following output in your file:

```
1  2012-08-02 15:37:40,592 - exampleApp - INFO - Program started
2  2012-08-02 15:37:40,592 - exampleApp.otherMod2.add - INFO - added 7 and 8 to get\
3   15
4  2012-08-02 15:37:40,592 - exampleApp - INFO - Done!
```

You will notice that all references to root have been removed. Instead it uses our **Formatter** object which says that we should get a human readable time, the logger name, the logging level and then the message. These are actually known as **LogRecord** attributes. For a full list of **LogRecord** attributes, see the documentation[12] as there are too many to list here.

Configuring Logs for Work and Pleasure

The logging module can be configured 3 different ways. You can configure it using methods (loggers, formatters, handlers) like we did earlier in this article; you can use a configuration file and pass it to fileConfig(); or you can create a dictionary of configuration information and pass it to the dictConfig() function. Let's create a configuration file first and then we'll look at how to execute it with Python. Here's an example config file:

```
1  [loggers]
2  keys=root,exampleApp
3
4  [handlers]
5  keys=fileHandler, consoleHandler
6
7  [formatters]
8  keys=myFormatter
9
10 [logger_root]
11 level=CRITICAL
12 handlers=consoleHandler
13
14 [logger_exampleApp]
15 level=INFO
16 handlers=fileHandler
17 qualname=exampleApp
```

---

[12]https://docs.python.org/3/library/logging.html#logrecord-attributes

```
18
19  [handler_consoleHandler]
20  class=StreamHandler
21  level=DEBUG
22  formatter=myFormatter
23  args=(sys.stdout,)
24
25  [handler_fileHandler]
26  class=FileHandler
27  formatter=myFormatter
28  args=("config.log",)
29
30  [formatter_myFormatter]
31  format=%(asctime)s - %(name)s - %(levelname)s - %(message)s
32  datefmt=
```

You'll notice that we have two loggers specified: root and exampleApp. For whatever reason, "root" is required. If you don't include it, Python will raise a **ValueError** from config.py's **_install_loggers** function, which is a part of the logging module. If you set the root's handler to **fileHandler**, then you'll end up doubling the log output, so to keep that from happening, we send it to the console instead. Study this example closely. You'll need a section for every key in the first three sections. Now let's see how we load it in the code:

```
1   # log_with_config.py
2   import logging
3   import logging.config
4   import otherMod2
5
6   def main():
7       """
8       Based on http://docs.python.org/howto/logging.html#configuring-logging
9       """
10      logging.config.fileConfig('logging.conf')
11      logger = logging.getLogger("exampleApp")
12
13      logger.info("Program started")
14      result = otherMod2.add(7, 8)
15      logger.info("Done!")
16
17  if __name__ == "__main__":
18      main()
```

As you can see, all you need to do is pass the config file path to **logging.config.fileConfig**. You'll also notice that we don't need all that setup code any more as that's all in the config file. Also we can just import the **otherMod2** module with no changes. Anyway, if you run the above, you should end up with the following in your log file:

```
1   2012-08-02 18:23:33,338 - exampleApp - INFO - Program started
2   2012-08-02 18:23:33,338 - exampleApp.otherMod2.add - INFO - added 7 and 8 to get\
3    15
4   2012-08-02 18:23:33,338 - exampleApp - INFO - Done!
```

As you might have guessed, it's very similar to the other example. Now we'll move on to the other config method. The dictionary configuration method (dictConfig) wasn't added until Python 2.7, so make sure you have that or a later version, otherwise you won't be able to follow along. It's not well documented how this works. In fact, the examples in the documentation show **YAML** for some reason. Anyway, here's some working code for you to look over:

```python
1   # log_with_config.py
2   import logging
3   import logging.config
4   import otherMod2
5
6   def main():
7       """
8       Based on http://docs.python.org/howto/logging.html#configuring-logging
9       """
10      dictLogConfig = {
11          "version":1,
12          "handlers":{
13                  "fileHandler":{
14                      "class":"logging.FileHandler",
15                      "formatter":"myFormatter",
16                      "filename":"config2.log"
17                      }
18                  },
19          "loggers":{
20              "exampleApp":{
21                  "handlers":["fileHandler"],
22                  "level":"INFO",
23                  }
24              },
25
26          "formatters":{
```

```
27                "myFormatter":{
28                    "format":"%(asctime)s - %(name)s - %(levelname)s - %(message)s"
29                    }
30                }
31            }
32
33     logging.config.dictConfig(dictLogConfig)
34
35     logger = logging.getLogger("exampleApp")
36
37     logger.info("Program started")
38     result = otherMod2.add(7, 8)
39     logger.info("Done!")
40
41 if __name__ == "__main__":
42     main()
```

If you run this code, you'll end up with the same output as the previous method. Note that you don't need the "root" logger when you use a dictionary configuration.

Wrapping Up

At this point you should know how to get started using loggers and how to configure them in several different ways. You should also have gained the knowledge of how to modify the output using the Formatter object. The logging module is very handy for troubleshooting what went wrong in your application. Be sure to spend some time practicing with this module before writing a large application.

In the next chapter we will be looking at how to use the **os** module.

Chapter 16 - The os Module

The **os** module has many uses. We won't be covering everything that it can do. Instead, we will get an overview of its uses and we'll also take a look at one of its sub-modules, known as **os.path**. Specifically, we will be covering the following:

- os.name
- os.environ
- os.chdir()
- os.getcwd()
- os.getenv()
- os.putenv()
- os.mkdir()
- os.makedirs()
- os.remove()
- os.rename()
- os.rmdir()
- os.startfile()
- os.walk()
- os.path

That looks like a lot to cover, but there is at least ten times as many other actions that the os module can do. This chapter is just going to give you a little taste of what's available. To use any of the methods mentioned in this section, you will need to import the **os** module, like this:

```
1   import os
```

Let's start learning how to use this module!

os.name

The os module has both callable functions and normal values. In the case of **os.name**, it is just a value. When you access os.name, you will get information about what platform you are running on. You will receive one of the following values: 'posix', 'nt', 'os2', 'ce', 'java', 'riscos'. Let's see what we get when we run it on Windows 7:

```
1  >>> import os
2  >>> os.name
3  'nt'
```

This tells us that our Python instance is running on a Windows box. How do we know this? Because Microsoft started calling its operating system NT many years ago. For example, Windows 7 is also known as Windows NT 6.1.

os.environ, os.getenv() and os.putenv()

The **os.environ** value is known as a **mapping** object that returns a dictionary of the user's environmental variables. You may not know this, but every time you use your computer, some environment variables are set. These can give you valuable information, such as number of processors, type of CPU, the computer name, etc. Let's see what we can find out about our machine:

```
1   >>> import os
2   >>> os.environ
3   {'ALLUSERSPROFILE': 'C:\\ProgramData',
4    'APPDATA': 'C:\\Users\\mike\\AppData\\Roaming',
5    'CLASSPATH': '.;C:\\Program Files\\QuickTime\\QTSystem\\QTJava.zip',
6    'COMMONPROGRAMFILES': 'C:\\Program Files\\Common Files',
7    'COMPUTERNAME': 'MIKE-PC',
8    'COMSPEC': 'C:\\Windows\\system32\\cmd.exe',
9    'FP_NO_HOST_CHECK': 'NO',
10   'HOMEDRIVE': 'C:',
11   'HOMEPATH': '\\Users\\mike',
12   'LOCALAPPDATA': 'C:\\Users\\mike\\AppData\\Local',
13   'LOGONSERVER': '\\\\MIKE-PC',
14   'NUMBER_OF_PROCESSORS': '2',
15   'OS': 'Windows_NT',
16   'PATHEXT': '.COM;.EXE;.BAT;.CMD;.VBS;.VBE;.JS;.JSE;.WSF;.WSH;.MSC',
17   'PROCESSOR_ARCHITECTURE': 'x86',
18   'PROCESSOR_IDENTIFIER': 'x86 Family 6 Model 15 Stepping 13, GenuineIntel',
19   'PROCESSOR_LEVEL': '6',
20   'PROGRAMDATA': 'C:\\ProgramData',
21   'PROGRAMFILES': 'C:\\Program Files',
22   'PSMODULEPATH': 'C:\\Windows\\system32\\WindowsPowerShell\\v1.0\\Modules\\',
23   'PUBLIC': 'C:\\Users\\Public',
24   'PYTHONIOENCODING': 'cp437',
25   'QTJAVA': 'C:\\Program Files\\QuickTime\\QTSystem\\QTJava.zip',
26   'SESSIONNAME': 'Console',
```

```
27    'SYSTEMDRIVE': 'C:',
28    'SYSTEMROOT': 'C:\\Windows',
29    'TEMP': 'C:\\Users\\mike\\AppData\\Local\\Temp',
30    'TMP': 'C:\\Users\\mike\\AppData\\Local\\Temp',
31    'USERDOMAIN': 'mike-PC',
32    'USERNAME': 'mike',
33    'USERPROFILE': 'C:\\Users\\mike',
34    'VBOX_INSTALL_PATH': 'C:\\Program Files\\Oracle\\VirtualBox\\',
35    'VS90COMNTOOLS': 'C:\\Program Files\\Microsoft Visual Studio 9.0\\Common7\\Tool\
36    s\\',
37    'WINDIR': 'C:\\Windows',
38    'WINDOWS_TRACING_FLAGS': '3',
39    'WINDOWS_TRACING_LOGFILE': 'C:\\BVTBin\\Tests\\installpackage\\csilogfile.log',
40    'WINGDB_ACTIVE': '1',
41    'WINGDB_PYTHON': 'c:\\python27\\python.exe',
42    'WINGDB_SPAWNCOOKIE': 'rvlxwsGdD7SHYIJm'}
```

Your output won't be the same as mine as everyone's PC configuration is a little different, but you'll see something similar. As you may have noticed, this returned a dictionary. That means you can access the environmental variables using your normal dictionary methods. Here's an example:

```
1    >>> print(os.environ["TMP"])
2    'C:\\Users\\mike\\AppData\\Local\\Temp'
```

You could also use the **os.getenv** function to access this environmental variable:

```
1    >>> os.getenv("TMP")
2    'C:\\Users\\mike\\AppData\\Local\\Temp'
```

The benefit of using os.getenv() instead of the os.environ dictionary is that if you happen to try to access an environmental variable that doesn't exist, the getenv function will just return None. If you did the same thing with os.environ, you would receive an error. Let's give it a try so you can see what happens:

```
1  >>> os.environ["TMP2"]
2  Traceback (most recent call last):
3    File "<pyshell#1>", line 1, in <module>
4      os.environ["TMP2"]
5    File "C:\Python27\lib\os.py", line 423, in __getitem__
6      return self.data[key.upper()]
7  KeyError: 'TMP2'
8
9  >>> print(os.getenv("TMP2"))
10 None
```

os.chdir() and os.getcwd()

The **os.chdir** function allows us to change the directory that we're currently running our Python session in. If you want to actually know what path you are currently in, then you would call **os.getcwd()**. Let's try them both out:

```
1  >>> os.getcwd()
2  'C:\\Python27'
3  >>> os.chdir(r"c:\Users\mike\Documents")
4  >>> os.getcwd()
5  'c:\\Users\\mike\\Documents'
```

The code above shows us that we started out in the Python directory by default when we run this code in IDLE. Then we change folders using **os.chdir()**. Finally we call os.getcwd() a second time to make sure that we changed to the folder successfully.

os.mkdir() and os.makedirs()

You might have guessed this already, but the two methods covered in this section are used for creating directories. The first one is **os.mkdir()**, which allows us to create a single folder. Let's try it out:

```
1  >>> os.mkdir("test")
2  >>> path = r'C:\Users\mike\Documents\pytest'
3  >>> os.mkdir(path)
```

The first line of code will create a folder named **test** in the current directory. You can use the methods in the previous section to figure out where you just ran your code if you've forgotten. The second example assigns a path to a variable and then we pass the path to os.mkdir(). This allows you to create a folder anywhere on your system that you have permission to.

The **os.makedirs()** function will create all the intermediate folders in a path if they don't already exist. Basically this means that you can created a path that has nested folders in it. I find myself doing this a lot when I create a log file that is in a dated folder structure, like Year/Month/Day. Let's look at an example:

```
1  >>> path = r'C:\Users\mike\Documents\pytest\2014\02\19'
2  >>> os.makedirs(path)
```

What happened here? This code just created a bunch of folders! If you still had the **pytest** folder in your system, then it just added a **2014** folder with another folder inside of it which also contained a folder. Try it out for yourself using a valid path on your system.

os.remove() and os.rmdir()

The **os.remove()** and **os.rmdir()** functions are used for deleting files and directories respectively. Let's look at an example of **os.remove()**:

```
1  >>> os.remove("test.txt")
```

This code snippet will attempt to remove a file named **test.txt** from your current working directory. If it cannot find the file, you will likely receive some sort of error. You will also receive an error if the file is in use (i.e. locked) or you don't have permission to delete the file. You might also want to check out **os.unlink**, which does the same thing. The term **unlink** is the traditional Unix name for this procedure.

Now let's look at an example of **os.rmdir()**:

```
1  >>> os.rmdir("pytest")
```

The code above will attempt to remove a directory named **pytest** from your current working directory. If it's successful, you will see that the directory no longer exists. An error will be raised if the directory does not exist, you do not have permission to remove it or if the directory is not empty. You might also want to take a look at **os.removedirs()** which can remove nested empty directories recursively.

os.rename(src, dst)

The **os.rename()** function will rename a file or folder. Let's take a look at an example where we rename a file:

```
1  >>> os.rename("test.txt", "pytest.txt")
```

In this example, we tell **os.rename** to rename a file named **test.txt** to **pytest.txt**. This occurs in our current working directory. You will see an error occur if you try to rename a file that doesn't exist or that you don't have the proper permission to rename the file.

There is also an **os.renames** function that recursively renames a directory or file.

os.startfile()

The **os.startfile()** method allows us to "start" a file with its associated program. In other words, we can open a file with it's associated program, just like when you double-click a PDF and it opens in Adobe Reader. Let's give it a try!

```
1  >>> os.startfile(r'C:\Users\mike\Documents\labels.pdf')
```

In the example above, I pass a fully qualified path to **os.startfile** that tells it to open a file called **labels.pdf**. On my machine, this will open the PDF in Adobe Reader. You should try opening your own PDFs, MP3s, and photos using this method to see how it works.

os.walk()

The **os.walk()** method gives us a way to iterate over a root level path. What this means is that we can pass a path to this function and get access to all its sub-directories and files. Let's use one of the Python folders that we have handy to test this function with. We'll use: C:\Python27\Tools

```
 1  >>> path = r'C:\Python27\Tools'
 2  >>> for root, dirs, files in os.walk(path):
 3          print(root)
 4
 5  C:\Python27\Tools
 6  C:\Python27\Tools\i18n
 7  C:\Python27\Tools\pynche
 8  C:\Python27\Tools\pynche\X
 9  C:\Python27\Tools\Scripts
10  C:\Python27\Tools\versioncheck
11  C:\Python27\Tools\webchecker
```

If you want, you can also loop over **dirs** and **files** too. Here's one way to do it:

```
1  >>> for root, dirs, files in os.walk(path):
2          print(root)
3          for _dir in dirs:
4              print(_dir)
5          for _file in files:
6              print(_file)
```

This piece of code will print a lot of stuff out, so I won't be showing its output here, but feel free to give it a try. Now we're ready to learn about working with paths!

os.path

The **os.path** sub-module of the **os** module has lots of great functionality built into it. We'll be looking at the following functions:

- basename
- dirname
- exists
- isdir and isfile
- join
- split

There are lots of other functions in this sub-module. You are welcome to go read about them in the Python documentation, section 10.1.

os.path.basename

The **basename** function will return just the filename of a path. Here is an example:

```
1  >>> os.path.basename(r'C:\Python27\Tools\pynche\ChipViewer.py')
2  'ChipViewer.py'
```

I have found this useful whenever I need to use a filename for naming some related file, such as a log file. This happens a lot when I'm processing a data file.

os.path.dirname

The **dirname** function will return just the directory portion of the path. It's easier to understand if we take a look at some code:

```
1  >>> os.path.dirname(r'C:\Python27\Tools\pynche\ChipViewer.py')
2  'C:\\Python27\\Tools\\pynche'
```

In this example, we just get the directory path back. This is also useful when you want to store other files next to the file you're processing, like the aforementioned log file.

os.path.exists

The **exists** function will tell you if a path exists or not. All you have to do is pass it a path. Let's take a look:

```
1  >>> os.path.exists(r'C:\Python27\Tools\pynche\ChipViewer.py')
2  True
3  >>> os.path.exists(r'C:\Python27\Tools\pynche\fake.py')
4  False
```

In the first example, we pass the **exists** function a real path and it returns **True**, which means that the path exists. In the second example, we passed it a bad path and it told us that the path did not exist by returning **False**.

os.path.isdir / os.path.isfile

The **isdir** and **isfile** methods are closely related to the **exists** method in that they also test for existence. However, **isdir** only checks if the path is a directory and **isfile** only checks if the path is a file. If you want to check if a path exists regardless of whether it is a file or a directory, then you'll want to use the **exists** method. Anyway, let's study some examples:

```
1  >>> os.path.isfile(r'C:\Python27\Tools\pynche\ChipViewer.py')
2  True
3  >>> os.path.isdir(r'C:\Python27\Tools\pynche\ChipViewer.py')
4  False
5  >>> os.path.isdir(r'C:\Python27\Tools\pynche')
6  True
7  >>> os.path.isfile(r'C:\Python27\Tools\pynche')
8  False
```

Take a moment to study this set of examples. In the first one we pass a path to a file and check if the path is really a file. Then the second example checks the same path to see if it's a directory. You can see for yourself how that turned out. Then in the last two examples, we switched things up a bit by passing a path to a directory to the same two functions. These examples demonstrate how these two functions work.

os.path.join

The **join** method give you the ability to join one or more path components together using the appropriate separator. For example, on Windows, the separator is the backslash, but on Linux, the separator is the forward slash. Here's how it works:

```
1  >>> os.path.join(r'C:\Python27\Tools\pynche', 'ChipViewer.py')
2  'C:\\Python27\\Tools\\pynche\\ChipViewer.py'
```

In this example, we joined a directory path and a file path together to get a fully qualified path. Note however that the **join** method does **not** check if the result actually exists!

os.path.split

The **split** method will split a path into a tuple that contains the directory and the file. Let's take a look:

```
1  >>> os.path.split(r'C:\Python27\Tools\pynche\ChipViewer.py')
2  ('C:\\Python27\\Tools\\pynche', 'ChipViewer.py')
```

This example shows what happens when we path in a path with a file. Let's see what happens if the path doesn't have a filename on the end:

```
1  >>> os.path.split(r'C:\Python27\Tools\pynche')
```

('C:\Python27\Tools', 'pynche')

As you can see, it took the path and split it in such a way that the last sub-folder became the second element of the tuple with the rest of the path in the first element.

For our final example, I thought you might like to see a commmon use case of the **split**:

```
1  >>> dirname, fname = os.path.split(r'C:\Python27\Tools\pynche\ChipViewer.py')
2  >>> dirname
3  'C:\\Python27\\Tools\\pynche'
4  >>> fname
5  'ChipViewer.py'
```

This shows how to do multiple assignment. When you split the path, it returns a two-element tuple. Since we have two variables on the left, the first element of the tuple is assigned to the first variable and the second element to the second variable.

Wrapping Up

At this point you should be pretty familiar with the **os** module. In this chapter you learned the following:

- how to work with environment variables
- change directories and discover your current working directory
- create and remove folders and files
- rename files / folders
- start a file with its associated application
- walk a directory
- work with paths

There are a lot of other functions in the **os** module that are not covered here. Be sure to read the documentation to see what else you can do. In the next chapter, we will be learning about the **email** and **smtplib** modules.

Chapter 17 - The email / smtplib Module

Python provides a couple of really nice modules that we can use to craft emails with. They are the **email** and **smtplib** modules. Instead of going over various methods in these two modules, we'll spend some time learning how to actually use these modules. Specifically, we'll be covering the following:

- The basics of emailing
- How to send to multiple addresses at once
- How to send email using the TO, CC and BCC lines
- How to add an attachment and a body using the email module

Let's get started!

Email Basics - How to Send an Email with smtplib

The **smtplib** module is very intuitive to use. Let's write a quick example that shows how to send an email. Save the following code to a file on your hard drive:

```
1   import smtplib
2
3   HOST = "mySMTP.server.com"
4   SUBJECT = "Test email from Python"
5   TO = "mike@someAddress.org"
6   FROM = "python@mydomain.com"
7   text = "Python 3.4 rules them all!"
8
9   BODY = "\r\n".join((
10      "From: %s" % FROM,
11      "To: %s" % TO,
12      "Subject: %s" % SUBJECT ,
13      "",
14      text
15      ))
```

```
16
17   server = smtplib.SMTP(HOST)
18   server.sendmail(FROM, [TO], BODY)
19   server.quit()
```

We imported two modules, **smtplib** and the **string** module. Two thirds of this code is used for setting up the email. Most of the variables are pretty self-explanatory, so we'll focus on the odd one only, which is **BODY**. Here we use the **string** module to combine all the previous variables into a single string where each lines ends with a carriage return ("/r") plus new line ("/n"). If you print BODY out, it would look like this:

```
1   'From: python@mydomain.com\r\nTo: mike@mydomain.com\r\nSubject: Test email from \
2   Python\r\n\r\nblah blah blah'
```

After that, we set up a server connection to our host and then we call the smtplib module's **sendmail** method to send the email. Then we disconnect from the server. You will note that this code doesn't have a username or password in it. If your server requires authentication, then you'll need to add the following code:

```
1   server.login(username, password)
```

This should be added right after you create the server object. Normally, you would want to put this code into a function and call it with some of these parameters. You might even want to put some of this information into a config file. Let's put this code into a function.

```
1    import smtplib
2
3    def send_email(host, subject, to_addr, from_addr, body_text):
4        """
5        Send an email
6        """
7        BODY = "\r\n".join((
8                "From: %s" % from_addr,
9                "To: %s" % to_addr,
10               "Subject: %s" % subject ,
11               "",
12               body_text
13               ))
14       server = smtplib.SMTP(host)
15       server.sendmail(from_addr, [to_addr], BODY)
16       server.quit()
```

```
17
18  if __name__ == "__main__":
19      host = "mySMTP.server.com"
20      subject = "Test email from Python"
21      to_addr = "mike@someAddress.org"
22      from_addr = "python@mydomain.com"
23      body_text = "Python rules them all!"
24      send_email(host, subject, to_addr, from_addr, body_text)
```

Now you can see how small the actual code is by just looking at the function itself. That's 13 lines! And we could make it shorter if we didn't put every item in the BODY on its own line, but it wouldn't be as readable. Now we'll add a config file to hold the server information and the **from** address. Why? Well in the work I do, we might use different email servers to send email or if the email server gets upgraded and the name changes, then we only need to change the config file rather than the code. The same thing could apply to the **from** address if our company was bought and merged into another.

Let's take a look at the config file (save it as **email.ini**):

```
1  [smtp]
2  server = some.server.com
3  from_addr = python@mydomain.com
```

That is a very simple config file. In it we have a section labelled **smtp** in which we have two items: server and from_addr. We'll use configObj to read this file and turn it into a Python dictionary. Here's the updated version of the code (save it as **smtp_config.py**):

```
1   import os
2   import smtplib
3   import sys
4
5   from configparser import ConfigParser
6
7   def send_email(subject, to_addr, body_text):
8       """
9       Send an email
10      """
11      base_path = os.path.dirname(os.path.abspath(__file__))
12      config_path = os.path.join(base_path, "email.ini")
13
14      if os.path.exists(config_path):
15          cfg = ConfigParser()
```

```
16          cfg.read(config_path)
17      else:
18          print("Config not found! Exiting!")
19          sys.exit(1)
20
21      host = cfg.get("smtp", "server")
22      from_addr = cfg.get("smtp", "from_addr")
23
24      BODY = "\r\n".join((
25          "From: %s" % from_addr,
26          "To: %s" % to_addr,
27          "Subject: %s" % subject ,
28          "",
29          body_text
30      ))
31      server = smtplib.SMTP(host)
32      server.sendmail(from_addr, [to_addr], BODY)
33      server.quit()
34
35  if __name__ == "__main__":
36      subject = "Test email from Python"
37      to_addr = "mike@someAddress.org"
38      body_text = "Python rules them all!"
39      send_email(subject, to_addr, body_text)
```

We've added a little check to this code. We want to first grab the path that the script itself is in, which is what base_path represents. Next we combine that path with the file name to get a fully qualified path to the config file. We then check for the existence of that file. If it's there, we create a **ConfigParser** and if it's not, we print a message and exit the script. We should add an exception handler around the **ConfigParser.read()** call just to be on the safe side though as the file could exist, but be corrupt or we might not have permission to open it and that will throw an exception. That will be a little project that you can attempt on your own. Anyway, let's say that everything goes well and the ConfigParser object is created successfully. Now we can extract the host and from_addr information using the usual ConfigParser syntax.

Now we're ready to learn how to send multiple emails at the same time!

Sending Multiple Emails at Once

Let's modify our last example a little so we send multiple emails!

```python
1   import os
2   import smtplib
3   import sys
4
5   from configparser import ConfigParser
6
7   def send_email(subject, body_text, emails):
8       """
9       Send an email
10      """
11      base_path = os.path.dirname(os.path.abspath(__file__))
12      config_path = os.path.join(base_path, "email.ini")
13
14      if os.path.exists(config_path):
15          cfg = ConfigParser()
16          cfg.read(config_path)
17      else:
18          print("Config not found! Exiting!")
19          sys.exit(1)
20
21      host = cfg.get("smtp", "server")
22      from_addr = cfg.get("smtp", "from_addr")
23
24      BODY = "\r\n".join((
25              "From: %s" % from_addr,
26              "To: %s" % ', '.join(emails),
27              "Subject: %s" % subject ,
28              "",
29              body_text
30              ))
31      server = smtplib.SMTP(host)
32      server.sendmail(from_addr, emails, BODY)
33      server.quit()
34
35  if __name__ == "__main__":
36      emails = ["mike@someAddress.org", "someone@gmail.com"]
37      subject = "Test email from Python"
38      body_text = "Python rules them all!"
39      send_email(subject, body_text, emails)
```

You'll notice that in this example, we removed the to_addr parameter and added an emails parameter, which is a list of email addresses. To make this work, we need to create a comma-separated string in the **To:** portion of the BODY and also pass the email **list** to the **sendmail** method. Thus we do the following to create a simple comma separated string: **', '.join(emails)**. Simple, huh?

Send email using the TO, CC and BCC lines

Now we just need to figure out how to send using the CC and BCC fields. Let's create a new version of this code that supports that functionality!

```python
1   import os
2   import smtplib
3   import sys
4
5   from configparser import ConfigParser
6
7   def send_email(subject, body_text, to_emails, cc_emails, bcc_emails):
8       """
9       Send an email
10      """
11      base_path = os.path.dirname(os.path.abspath(__file__))
12      config_path = os.path.join(base_path, "email.ini")
13
14      if os.path.exists(config_path):
15          cfg = ConfigParser()
16          cfg.read(config_path)
17      else:
18          print("Config not found! Exiting!")
19          sys.exit(1)
20
21      host = cfg.get("smtp", "server")
22      from_addr = cfg.get("smtp", "from_addr")
23
24      BODY = "\r\n".join((
25              "From: %s" % from_addr,
26              "To: %s" % ', '.join(to_emails),
27              "CC: %s" % ', '.join(cc_emails),
28              "BCC: %s" % ', '.join(bcc_emails),
29              "Subject: %s" % subject ,
30              "",
31              body_text
32              ))
33      emails = to_emails + cc_emails + bcc_emails
```

```
34
35      server = smtplib.SMTP(host)
36      server.sendmail(from_addr, emails, BODY)
37      server.quit()
38
39  if __name__ == "__main__":
40      emails = ["mike@somewhere.org"]
41      cc_emails = ["someone@gmail.com"]
42      bcc_emails = ["schmuck@newtel.net"]
43
44      subject = "Test email from Python"
45      body_text = "Python rules them all!"
46      send_email(subject, body_text, emails, cc_emails, bcc_emails)
```

In this code, we pass in 3 lists, each with one email address a piece. We create the CC and BCC fields exactly the same as before, but we also need to combine the 3 lists into one so we can pass the combined list to the sendmail() method. There is some talk on forums like StackOverflow that some email clients may handle the BCC field in odd ways that allow the recipient to see the BCC list via the email headers. I am unable to confirm this behavior, but I do know that Gmail successfully strips the BCC information from the email header.

Now we're ready to move on to using Python's email module!

Add an attachment / body using the email module

Now we'll take what we learned from the previous section and mix it together with the Python email module so that we can send attachments. The email module makes adding attachments extremely easy. Here's the code:

```
1   import os
2   import smtplib
3   import sys
4
5   from configparser import ConfigParser
6   from email import encoders
7   from email.mime.text import MIMEText
8   from email.mime.base import MIMEBase
9   from email.mime.multipart import MIMEMultipart
10  from email.utils import formatdate
11
12  #-------------------------------------------------------------------
13  def send_email_with_attachment(subject, body_text, to_emails,
```

```
14                                 cc_emails, bcc_emails, file_to_attach):
15         """
16         Send an email with an attachment
17         """
18         base_path = os.path.dirname(os.path.abspath(__file__))
19         config_path = os.path.join(base_path, "email.ini")
20         header = 'Content-Disposition', 'attachment; filename="%s"' % file_to_attach
21
22         # get the config
23         if os.path.exists(config_path):
24             cfg = ConfigParser()
25             cfg.read(config_path)
26         else:
27             print("Config not found! Exiting!")
28             sys.exit(1)
29
30         # extract server and from_addr from config
31         host = cfg.get("smtp", "server")
32         from_addr = cfg.get("smtp", "from_addr")
33
34         # create the message
35         msg = MIMEMultipart()
36         msg["From"] = from_addr
37         msg["Subject"] = subject
38         msg["Date"] = formatdate(localtime=True)
39         if body_text:
40             msg.attach( MIMEText(body_text) )
41
42         msg["To"] = ', '.join(to_emails)
43         msg["cc"] = ', '.join(cc_emails)
44
45         attachment = MIMEBase('application', "octet-stream")
46         try:
47             with open(file_to_attach, "rb") as fh:
48                 data = fh.read()
49             attachment.set_payload( data )
50             encoders.encode_base64(attachment)
51             attachment.add_header(*header)
52             msg.attach(attachment)
53         except IOError:
54             msg = "Error opening attachment file %s" % file_to_attach
55             print(msg)
```

```
56            sys.exit(1)
57
58        emails = to_emails + cc_emails
59
60        server = smtplib.SMTP(host)
61        server.sendmail(from_addr, emails, msg.as_string())
62        server.quit()
63
64    if __name__ == "__main__":
65        emails = ["mike@someAddress.org", "nedry@jp.net"]
66        cc_emails = ["someone@gmail.com"]
67        bcc_emails = ["anonymous@circe.org"]
68
69        subject = "Test email with attachment from Python"
70        body_text = "This email contains an attachment!"
71        path = "/path/to/some/file"
72        send_email_with_attachment(subject, body_text, emails,
73                               cc_emails, bcc_emails, path)
```

Here we have renamed our function and added a new argument, **file_to_attach**. We also need to add a header and create a **MIMEMultipart** object. The header could be created any time before we add the attachment. We add elements to the **MIMEMultipart** object (msg) like we would keys to a dictionary. You'll note that we have to use the email module's **formatdate** method to insert the properly formatted date. To add the body of the message, we need to create an instance of **MIMEText**. If you're paying attention, you'll see that we didn't add the BCC information, but you could easily do so by following the conventions in the code above. Next we add the attachment. We wrap it in an exception handler and use the **with** statement to extract the file and place it in our **MIMEBase** object. Finally we add it to the **msg** variable and we send it out. Notice that we have to convert the **msg** to a string in the **sendmail** method.

Wrapping Up

Now you know how to send out emails with Python. For those of you that like mini projects, you should go back and add additional error handling around the **server.sendmail** portion of the code in case something odd happens during the process, such as an **SMTPAuthenticationError** or **SMTPConnectError**. We could also beef up the error handling during the attachment of the file to catch other errors. Finally, we may want to take those various lists of emails and create one normalized list that has removed duplicates. This is especially important if we are reading a list of email addresses from a file.

Also note that our from address is fake. We can spoof emails using Python and other programming languages, but that is very bad etiquette and possibly illegal depending on where you live. You have been warned! Use your knowledge wisely and enjoy Python for fun and profit!

Chapter 18 - The sqlite Module

SQLite is a self-contained, server-less, config-free transactional SQL database engine. Python gained the **sqlite3** module all the way back in version 2.5 which means that you can create SQLite database with any current Python without downloading any additional dependencies. Mozilla uses SQLite databases for its popular Firefox browser to store bookmarks and other various pieces of information. In this chapter you will learn the following:

- How to create a SQLite database
- How to insert data into a table
- How to edit the data
- How to delete the data
- Basic SQL queries

In other words, rather than covering bits and pieces of the **sqlite3** module, we'll go through how to actually use it.

If you want to inspect your database visually, you can use the SQLite Manager plugin for Firefox (just Google for it) or if you like the command line, you can use SQLite's command line shell.

How to Create a Database and INSERT Some Data

Creating a database in SQLite is really easy, but the process requires that you know a little SQL to do it. Here's some code that will create a database to hold music albums:

```
 1   import sqlite3
 2
 3   conn = sqlite3.connect("mydatabase.db") # or use :memory: to put it in RAM
 4
 5   cursor = conn.cursor()
 6
 7   # create a table
 8   cursor.execute("""CREATE TABLE albums
 9                     (title text, artist text, release_date text,
10                      publisher text, media_type text)
11                  """)
```

First we have to import the **sqlite3** module and create a connection to the database. You can pass it a file path, file name or just use use the special string ":memory:" to create the database in memory. In our case, we created it on disk in a file called **mydatabase.db**. Next we create a cursor object, which allows you to interact with the database and add records, among other things. Here we use SQL syntax to create a table named **albums** with 5 text fields: title, artist, release_date, publisher and media_type. SQLite only supports five **data types**: null, integer, real, text and blob. Let's build on this code and insert some data into our new table!

Note: If you run the CREATE TABLE command and the database already exists, you will receive an error message.

```
1   # insert some data
2   cursor.execute("""INSERT INTO albums
3                     VALUES ('Glow', 'Andy Hunter', '7/24/2012',
4                             'Xplore Records', 'MP3')"""
5                  )
6
7   # save data to database
8   conn.commit()
9
10  # insert multiple records using the more secure "?" method
11  albums = [('Exodus', 'Andy Hunter', '7/9/2002', 'Sparrow Records', 'CD'),
12           ('Until We Have Faces', 'Red', '2/1/2011', 'Essential Records', 'CD'),
13           ('The End is Where We Begin', 'Thousand Foot Krutch', '4/17/2012', 'TF\
14  Kmusic', 'CD'),
15           ('The Good Life', 'Trip Lee', '4/10/2012', 'Reach Records', 'CD')]
16  cursor.executemany("INSERT INTO albums VALUES (?,?,?,?,?)", albums)
17  conn.commit()
```

Here we use the INSERT INTO SQL command to insert a record into our database. Note that each item had to have single quotes around it. This can get complicated when you need to insert strings that include single quotes in them. Anyway, to save the record to the database, we have to **commit** it. The next piece of code shows how to add multiple records at once by using the cursor's **executemany** method. Note that we're using question marks (?) instead of string substitution (%s) to insert the values. Using string substitution is NOT safe and should not be used as it can allow SQL injection attacks to occur. The question mark method is much better and using SQLAlchemy is even better because it does all the escaping for you so you won't have to mess with the annoyances of converting embedded single quotes into something that SQLite will accept.

Updating and Deleting Records

Being able to update your database records is key to keeping your data accurate. If you can't update, then your data will become out of date and pretty useless very quickly. Sometimes you will need to delete rows from your data too. We'll be covering both of those topics in this section. First, let's do an update!

```
1   import sqlite3
2
3   conn = sqlite3.connect("mydatabase.db")
4   cursor = conn.cursor()
5
6   sql = """
7   UPDATE albums
8   SET artist = 'John Doe'
9   WHERE artist = 'Andy Hunter'
10  """
11  cursor.execute(sql)
12  conn.commit()
```

Here we use SQL's **UPDATE** command to update out albums table. You can use **SET** to change a field, so in this case we change the artist field to be *John Doe* in any record **WHERE** the artist field is set to *Andy Hunter*. Wasn't that easy? Note that if you don't commit the changes, then your changes won't be written out to the database. The **DELETE** command is almost as easy. Let's check that out!

```
1   import sqlite3
2
3   conn = sqlite3.connect("mydatabase.db")
4   cursor = conn.cursor()
5
6   sql = """
7   DELETE FROM albums
8   WHERE artist = 'John Doe'
9   """
10  cursor.execute(sql)
11  conn.commit()
```

Deleting is even easier than updating. The SQL is only 2 lines! In this case, all we had to do was tell SQLite which table to delete from (albums) and which records to delete using the WHERE clause. Thus it looked for any records that had "John Doe" in its artist field and deleted it.

Basic SQLite Queries

Queries in SQLite are pretty much the same as what you'd use for other databases, such as MySQL or Postgres. You just use normal SQL syntax to run the queries and then have the cursor object execute the SQL. Here are a few examples:

```
1  import sqlite3
2
3  conn = sqlite3.connect("mydatabase.db")
4  #conn.row_factory = sqlite3.Row
5  cursor = conn.cursor()
6
7  sql = "SELECT * FROM albums WHERE artist=?"
8  cursor.execute(sql, [("Red")])
9  print(cursor.fetchall())  # or use fetchone()
10
11 print("\nHere's a listing of all the records in the table:\n")
12 for row in cursor.execute("SELECT rowid, * FROM albums ORDER BY artist"):
13     print(row)
14
15 print("\nResults from a LIKE query:\n")
16 sql = """
17 SELECT * FROM albums
18 WHERE title LIKE 'The%'"""
19 cursor.execute(sql)
20 print(cursor.fetchall())
```

The first query we execute is a **SELECT** * which means that we want to select all the records that match the artist name we pass in, which in this case is "Red". Next we execute the SQL and use **fetchall()** to return all the results. You can also use **fetchone()** to grab the first result. You'll also notice that there's a commented out section related to a mysterious **row_factory**. If you un-comment that line, the results will be returned as Row objects that are kind of like Python dictionaries and give you access to the row's fields just like a dictionary. However, you cannot do item assignment with a Row object.

The second query is much like the first, but it returns every record in the database and orders the results by the artist name in ascending order. This also demonstrates how we can loop over the results. The last query shows how to use SQL's LIKE command to search for partial phrases. In this case, we do a search of the entire table for titles that start with "The". The percent sign (%) is a wildcard operator.

Wrapping Up

Now you know how to use Python to create a SQLite database. You can also create, update and delete records as well as run queries against your database.

Chapter 19 - The subprocess Module

The **subprocess** module gives the developer the ability to start processes or programs from Python. In other words, you can start applications and pass arguments to them using the subprocess module. The subprocess module was added way back in Python 2.4 to replace the **os** modules set of os.popen, os.spawn and os.system calls as well as replace popen2 and the old **commands** module. We will be looking at the following aspects of the subprocess module:

- the call function
- the Popen class
- how to communicate with a spawned process

Let's get started!

The call function

The subprocess module provides a function named **call**. This function allows you to call another program, wait for the command to complete and then return the return code. It accepts one or more arguments as well as the following keyword arguments (with their defaults): stdin=None, stdout=None, stderr=None, shell=False.

Let's look at a simple example:

```
1  >>> import subprocess
2  >>> subprocess.call("notepad.exe")
3  0
```

If you run this on a Windows machine, you should see Notepad open up. You will notice that IDLE waits for you to close Notepad and then it returns a code zero (0). This means that it completed successfully. If you receive anything except for a zero, then it usually means you have had some kind of error.

Normally when you call this function, you would want to assign the resulting return code to a variable so you can check to see if it was the result you expected. Let's do that:

117

```
1  >>> code = subprocess.call("notepad.exe")
2  >>> if code == 0:
3          print("Success!")
4      else:
5          print("Error!")
6  Success!
```

If you run this code, you will see that it prints out **Success!** to the screen. The **call** method also accepts arguments to be passed to the program that you're executing. Let's see how that works:

```
1  >>> code = subprocess.call(["ping", "www.yahoo.com"])
2
3  Pinging ds-any-fp3-real.wa1.b.yahoo.com [98.139.180.149] with 32 bytes of data:
4  Reply from 98.139.180.149: bytes=32 time=66ms TTL=45
5  Reply from 98.139.180.149: bytes=32 time=81ms TTL=45
6  Reply from 98.139.180.149: bytes=32 time=81ms TTL=45
7  Reply from 98.139.180.149: bytes=32 time=69ms TTL=45
8
9  Ping statistics for 98.139.180.149:
10     Packets: Sent = 4, Received = 4, Lost = 0 (0% loss),
11 Approximate round trip times in milli-seconds:
12     Minimum = 66ms, Maximum = 81ms, Average = 74ms
13 >>> code
14 0
```

You will notice that in this example we are passing a list of arguments. The first item in the list is the program we want to call. Anything else in the list are arguments that we want to pass to that program. So in this example, we are executing a ping against Yahoo's website. You will notice that the return code was zero, so everything completed successfully.

You can also execute the program using the operating system's **shell**. This does add a level of abstraction to the process and it raises the possibility of security issues. Here is the Python documentation's official warning on the matter:

Executing shell commands that incorporate unsanitized input from an untrusted source makes a program vulnerable to shell injection, a serious security flaw which can result in arbitrary command execution. For this reason, the use of shell=True is strongly discouraged in cases where the command string is constructed from external input.

The usual recommendation is not to use it if an outside process or person can modify the call's arguments. If you're hard-coding something yourself, then it doesn't matter as much.

The Popen Class

The **Popen** class executes a child program in a new process. Unlike the **call** method, it does not wait for the called process to end unless you tell it to using by using the **wait** method. Let's try running Notepad through Popen and see if we can detect a difference:

```
1  >>> program = "notepad.exe"
2  >>> subprocess.Popen(program)
3  <subprocess.Popen object at 0x01EE0430>
```

Here we create a variable called **program** and assign it the value of "notepad.exe". Then we pass it to the Popen class. When you run this, you will see that it immediately returns the **subprocess.Popen object** and the application that was called executes. Let's make Popen wait for the program to finish:

```
1  >>> program = "notepad.exe"
2  >>> process = subprocess.Popen(program)
3  >>> code = process.wait()
4  >>> print(code)
5  0
```

When you do this in IDLE, Notepad will pop up and may be in front of your IDLE session. Just move Notepad out of the way, but do not close it! You need to tell your process to **wait** for you won't be able to get the return code. Once you've typed that line, close Notepad and print the code out. Or you could just put all this code into a saved Python file and run that.

Note that using the **wait** method can cause the child process to deadlock when using the stdout/stderr=PIPE commands when the process generates enough output to block the pipe. You can use the **communicate** method to alleviate this situation. We'll be looking at that method in the next section.

Now let's try running Popen using multiple arguments:

```
1  >>> subprocess.Popen(["ls", "-l"])
2  <subprocess.Popen object at 0xb7451001>
```

If you run this code in Linux, you'll see it print out the Popen object message and then a listing of the permissions and contents of whatever folder you ran this in. You can use the shell argument with Popen too, but the same caveats apply to Popen as they did to the call method.

Learning to Communicate

There are several ways to communicate with the process you have invoked. We're just going to focus on how to use the subprocess module's **communicate** method. Let's take a look:

```
1  args = ["ping", "www.yahoo.com"]
2  process = subprocess.Popen(args,
3                              stdout=subprocess.PIPE)
4
5  data = process.communicate()
6  print(data)
```

In this code example, we create an **args** variable to hold our list of arguments. Then we redirect standard out (stdout) to our subprocess so we can communicate with it. The **communicate** method itself allows us to communicate with the process we just spawned. We can actually pass input to the process using this method. But in this example, we just use communicate to read from standard out. You will notice when you run this code that communicate will wait for the process to finish and then returns a two-element tuple that contains what was in stdout and stderr. Here is the result from my run:

```
1  ('Pinging ds-any-fp3-real.wa1.b.yahoo.com [98.139.180.149] with 32 bytes of data:
2  Reply from 98.139.180.149: bytes=32 time=139ms TTL=45
3  Reply from 98.139.180.149: bytes=32 time=162ms TTL=45
4  Reply from 98.139.180.149: bytes=32 time=164ms TTL=45
5  Reply from 98.139.180.149: bytes=32 time=110ms TTL=45
6  Ping statistics for 98.139.180.149:
7  Packets: Sent = 4, Received = 4, Lost = 0 (0% loss),
8  Approximate round trip times in milli-seconds:
9  Minimum = 110ms, Maximum = 164ms, Average = 143ms
10 ', None)
```

That's kind of ugly. Let's make it print out the result in a more readable format, shall we?

```
1  import subprocess
2
3  args = ["ping", "www.yahoo.com"]
4  process = subprocess.Popen(args, stdout=subprocess.PIPE)
5
6  data = process.communicate()
7  for line in data:
8      print(line)
```

If you run this code, you should see something like the following printed to your screen:

```
1   Pinging ds-any-fp3-real.wa1.b.yahoo.com [98.139.180.149] with 32 bytes of data:
2   Reply from 98.139.180.149: bytes=32 time=67ms TTL=45
3   Reply from 98.139.180.149: bytes=32 time=68ms TTL=45
4   Reply from 98.139.180.149: bytes=32 time=70ms TTL=45
5   Reply from 98.139.180.149: bytes=32 time=69ms TTL=45
6
7   Ping statistics for 98.139.180.149:
8       Packets: Sent = 4, Received = 4, Lost = 0 (0% loss),
9   Approximate round trip times in milli-seconds:
10      Minimum = 67ms, Maximum = 70ms, Average = 68ms
11
12  None
```

That last line that says "None" is the result of stderr, which means that there were no errors.

Wrapping Up

At this point, you have the knowledge to use the subprocess module effectively. You can open a process in two different ways, you know how to wait for a return code, and you know how to communicate with the child process that you created.

In the next chapter, we will be looking at the **sys** module.

Chapter 20 - The sys Module

The **sys** module provides system specific parameters and functions. We will be narrowing our study down to the following:

- sys.argv
- sys.executable
- sys.exit
- sys.modules
- sys.path
- sys.platform
- sys.stdin/stdout/stderr

sys.argv

The value of **sys.argv** is a Python list of command line arguments that were passed to the Python script. The first argument, **argv[0]** is the name of the Python script itself. Depending on the platform that you are running on, the first argument may contain the full path to the script or just the file name. You should study the documentation for additional details.

Let's try out a few examples to familiarize ourselves with this little tool:

```
1  >>> import sys
2  >>> sys.argv
3  ['']
```

If you run this in the interpreter, you will receive a list with an empty string. Let's create a file named "sysargv.py" with the following contents:

```
1  # sysargv.py
2  import sys
3
4  print(sys.argv)
```

Now run the code in IDLE. You should see it print out a list with a single element that contains the path to your script in it. Let's try passing the script some arguments. Open up a terminal / console screen and change directories (use the "cd" command) to where your script is. Then run something like this:

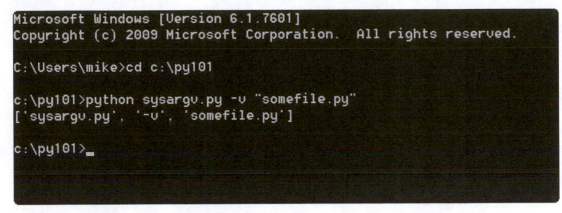

image

You will notice that it outputs the following to the screen:

```
1  ['sysargv.py', '-v', 'somefile.py']
```

The first argument is the name of the script we wrote. The next two arguments in the list are the ones we passed to our script on the command line.

sys.executable

The value of **sys.executable** is the absolute path to the Python interpreter. This is useful when you are using someone else's machine and need to know where Python is installed. On some systems, this command will fail and it will return an empty string or None. Here's how to use it:

```
1  >>> import sys
2  >>> sys.executable
3  'C:\\Python27\\pythonw.exe'
```

sys.exit

The **sys.exit()** function allows the developer to exit from Python. The **exit** function takes an optional argument, typically an integer, that gives an exit status. Zero is considered a "successful termination". Be sure to check if your operating system has any special meanings for its exit statuses so that you can follow them in your own application. Note that when you call **exit**, it will raise the **SystemExit** exception, which allows cleanup functions to work in the **finally** clauses of **try / except** blocks.

Let's take a look at how to call this:

```
1  >>> import sys
2  >>> sys.exit(0)
3
4  Traceback (most recent call last):
5    File "<pyshell#5>", line 1, in <module>
6      sys.exit(0)
7  SystemExit: 0
```

When you run this code in IDLE, you will see the SystemExit error raised. Let's create a couple of scripts to test this out. First you'll want to create a master script, a program that will call another Python script. Let's name it "call_exit.py". Put the following code into it:

```
1  # call_exit.py
2  import subprocess
3
4  code = subprocess.call(["python.exe", "exit.py"])
5  print(code)
```

Now create another Python script called "exit.py" and save it in the same folder. Put the following code into it:

```
1  import sys
2
3  sys.exit(0)
```

Now let's try running this code:

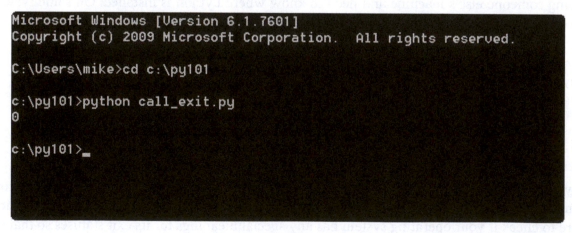

image

In the screenshot above, you can see that the exit script we wrote returned a zero, so it ran successfully. You have also learned how to call another Python script from within Python!

sys.path

The sys module's **path** value is a list of strings that specifies the search path for modules. Basically this tells Python what locations to look in when it tries to import a module. According to the Python documentation, **sys.path** is initialized from an environment variable called PYTHONPATH, plus an installation-dependent default. Let's give it a try:

```
1  >>> import sys
2  >>> print(sys.path)
3  ['',
4  'C:\\Python27\\Lib\\idlelib',
5  'C:\\Python27\\lib\\site-packages\\setuptools-0.9.5-py2.7.egg',
6  'C:\\Python27\\lib\\site-packages\\pip-1.3.1-py2.7.egg',
7  'C:\\Python27\\lib\\site-packages\\sphinx-1.2b3-py2.7.egg',
8  'C:\\Python27\\lib\\site-packages\\docutils-0.11-py2.7.egg',
9  'C:\\Python27\\lib\\site-packages\\pygments-1.6-py2.7.egg',
10 'C:\\Windows\\system32\\python27.zip', '
11 C:\\Python27\\DLLs',
12 'C:\\Python27\\lib',
13 'C:\\Python27\\lib\\plat-win',
14 'C:\\Python27\\lib\\lib-tk',
15 'C:\\Python27',
16 'C:\\Python27\\lib\\site-packages',
17 'C:\\Python27\\lib\\site-packages\\PIL',
18 'C:\\Python27\\lib\\site-packages\\wx-2.9.4-msw']
```

This can be very useful for debugging why a module isn't getting imported. You can also modify the path. Because it's a list, we can add or delete paths from it. Here's how to add a path:

```
1  >>> sys.path.append("/path/to/my/module")
```

I'll leave deleting a path as an exercise for the reader.

sys.platform

The **sys.platform** value is a platform identifier. You can use this to append platform specific modules to **sys.path**, import different modules depending on platform or run different pieces of code. Let's take a look:

```
1  >>> import sys
2  >>> sys.platform
3  'win32'
```

This tells us that Python is running on a Windows machine. Here's an example of how we might use this information:

```
1  >>> os = sys.platform
2  >>> if os == "win32":
3          # use Window-related code here
4          import _winreg
5      elif os.startswith('linux'):
6          # do something Linux specific
7          import subprocess
8          subprocess.Popen(["ls, -l"])
```

The code above shows how we might check to see if we're using a particular operating system. If we're on Windows, we'll get some information from the Window's Registry using a Python module called **_winreg**. If we're on Linux, we might execute the **ls** command to get information about the directory we're in.

sys.stdin / stdout / stderr

The **stdin**, **stdout** and **stderr** map to file objects that correspond to the interpreter's standard input, output and error streams, respectively. **stdin** is used for all input given to the interpreter except for scripts whereas **stdout** is used for the output of **print** and **expression** statements. The primary reason I mention this is that you will sometimes need to redirect stdout or stderr or both to a file, such as a log or to some kind of display in a custom GUI you have created. You could also redirect stdin, but I have rarely seen this done.

Wrapping Up

There are many other values and methods in the **sys** module. Be sure to look it up in the Python documentation, section 27.1. You have learned a lot in this chapter. You now know how to exit a Python program, how to get platform information, working with arguments passed on the command line and much more. In the next chapter, we'll be learning about Python threads!

Chapter 21 - The threading module

Python has a number of different concurrency constructs such as threading, queues and multiprocessing. The threading module used to be the primary way of accomplishing concurrency. A few years ago, the multiprocessing module was added to the Python suite of standard libraries. This chapter will be focused on how to use threads and queues.

Using Threads

We will start with a simple example that just demonstrates how threads work. We will sub-class the **Thread** class and make it print out its name to stdout. Let's get coding!

```python
1   import random
2   import time
3
4   from threading import Thread
5
6   class MyThread(Thread):
7       """
8       A threading example
9       """
10
11      def __init__(self, name):
12          """Initialize the thread"""
13          Thread.__init__(self)
14          self.name = name
15
16      def run(self):
17          """Run the thread"""
18          amount = random.randint(3, 15)
19          time.sleep(amount)
20          msg = "%s is running" % self.name
21          print(msg)
22
23  def create_threads():
24      """
25      Create a group of threads
26      """
```

```
27        for i in range(5):
28            name = "Thread #%s" % (i+1)
29            my_thread = MyThread(name)
30            my_thread.start()
31
32    if __name__ == "__main__":
33        create_threads()
```

In the code above, we import Python's **random** module, the **time** module and we import the **Thread** class from the **threading** module. Next we sub-class Thread and make override its **__init__** method to accept an argument we label "name". To start a thread, you have to call its **start()** method. When you start a thread, it will automatically call the thread's **run** method. We have overridden the thread's run method to make it choose a random amount of time to sleep. The **random.randint** example here will cause Python to randomly choose a number from 3-15. Then we make the thread sleep the number of seconds that we just randomly chose to simulate it actually doing something. Finally we print out the name of the thread to let the user know that the thread has finished.

The create_threads function will create 5 threads, giving each of them a unique name. If you run this code, you should see something like this:

```
1  Thread #2 is running
2  Thread #3 is running
3  Thread #1 is running
4  Thread #4 is running
5  Thread #5 is running
```

The order of the output will be different each time. Try running the code a few times to see the order change. Now let's write something a little more practical!

Writing a Threaded Downloader

The previous example wasn't very useful other than as a tool to explain how threads work. So in this example, we will create a Thread class that can download files from the internet. The U.S. Internal Revenue Service has lots of PDF forms that it has its citizens use for taxes. We will use this free resource for our demo. Here's the code:

```python
1   # Python 2 version
2
3   import os
4   import urllib2
5
6   from threading import Thread
7
8   class DownloadThread(Thread):
9       """
10      A threading example that can download a file
11      """
12
13      def __init__(self, url, name):
14          """Initialize the thread"""
15          Thread.__init__(self)
16          self.name = name
17          self.url = url
18
19      def run(self):
20          """Run the thread"""
21          handle = urllib2.urlopen(self.url)
22          fname = os.path.basename(self.url)
23          with open(fname, "wb") as f_handler:
24              while True:
25                  chunk = handle.read(1024)
26                  if not chunk:
27                      break
28                  f_handler.write(chunk)
29          msg = "%s has finished downloading %s!" % (self.name,
30                                                     self.url)
31          print(msg)
32
33  def main(urls):
34      """
35      Run the program
36      """
37      for item, url in enumerate(urls):
38          name = "Thread %s" % (item+1)
39          thread = DownloadThread(url, name)
40          thread.start()
41
42  if __name__ == "__main__":
```

```
43      urls = ["http://www.irs.gov/pub/irs-pdf/f1040.pdf",
44              "http://www.irs.gov/pub/irs-pdf/f1040a.pdf",
45              "http://www.irs.gov/pub/irs-pdf/f1040ez.pdf",
46              "http://www.irs.gov/pub/irs-pdf/f1040es.pdf",
47              "http://www.irs.gov/pub/irs-pdf/f1040sb.pdf"]
48      main(urls)
```

This is basically a complete rewrite of the first script. In this one we import the os and urllib2 modules as well as the threading module. We will be using urllib2 to do the actual downloading inside the thread class. The os module is used to extract the name of the file we're downloading so we can use it to create a file with the same name on our machine. In the DownloadThread class, we set up the __init__ to accept a url and a name for the thread. In the run method, we open up the url, extract the filename and then use that filename for naming / creating the file on disk. Then we use a **while** loop to download the file a kilobyte at a time and write it to disk. Once the file is finished saving, we print out the name of the thread and which url has finished downloading.

The Python 3 version of the code is slightly different. You have to import **urllib** instead of **urllib2** and use **urllib.request.urlopen** instead of **urllib2.urlopen**. Here's the code so you can see the difference:

```python
1   # Python 3 version
2
3   import os
4   import urllib.request
5
6   from threading import Thread
7
8   class DownloadThread(Thread):
9       """
10      A threading example that can download a file
11      """
12
13      def __init__(self, url, name):
14          """Initialize the thread"""
15          Thread.__init__(self)
16          self.name = name
17          self.url = url
18
19      def run(self):
20          """Run the thread"""
21          handle = urllib.request.urlopen(self.url)
22          fname = os.path.basename(self.url)
23          with open(fname, "wb") as f_handler:
24              while True:
```

```
25              chunk = handle.read(1024)
26              if not chunk:
27                  break
28              f_handler.write(chunk)
29          msg = "%s has finished downloading %s!" % (self.name,
30                                                      self.url)
31          print(msg)
32
33  def main(urls):
34      """
35      Run the program
36      """
37      for item, url in enumerate(urls):
38          name = "Thread %s" % (item+1)
39          thread = DownloadThread(url, name)
40          thread.start()
41
42  if __name__ == "__main__":
43      urls = ["http://www.irs.gov/pub/irs-pdf/f1040.pdf",
44              "http://www.irs.gov/pub/irs-pdf/f1040a.pdf",
45              "http://www.irs.gov/pub/irs-pdf/f1040ez.pdf",
46              "http://www.irs.gov/pub/irs-pdf/f1040es.pdf",
47              "http://www.irs.gov/pub/irs-pdf/f1040sb.pdf"]
48      main(urls)
```

Using Queues

A Queue can be used for first-in-first-out (FIFO) or last-in-last-out (LILO) stack-like implementations if you just use them directly. In this section, we're going to mix threads in and create a simple file downloader script to demonstrate how Queues work for cases where we want concurrency.

To help explain how Queues work, we will rewrite the downloading script from the previous section to use Queues. Let's get started!

```python
import os
import threading
import urllib.request

from queue import Queue

class Downloader(threading.Thread):
    """Threaded File Downloader"""

    def __init__(self, queue):
        """Initialize the thread"""
        threading.Thread.__init__(self)
        self.queue = queue

    def run(self):
        """Run the thread"""
        while True:
            # gets the url from the queue
            url = self.queue.get()

            # download the file
            self.download_file(url)

            # send a signal to the queue that the job is done
            self.queue.task_done()

    def download_file(self, url):
        """Download the file"""
        handle = urllib.request.urlopen(url)
        fname = os.path.basename(url)
        with open(fname, "wb") as f:
            while True:
                chunk = handle.read(1024)
                if not chunk: break
                f.write(chunk)

def main(urls):
    """
    Run the program
    """
    queue = Queue()
```

```
43    # create a thread pool and give them a queue
44    for i in range(5):
45        t = Downloader(queue)
46        t.setDaemon(True)
47        t.start()
48
49    # give the queue some data
50    for url in urls:
51        queue.put(url)
52
53    # wait for the queue to finish
54    queue.join()
55
56 if __name__ == "__main__":
57    urls = ["http://www.irs.gov/pub/irs-pdf/f1040.pdf",
58            "http://www.irs.gov/pub/irs-pdf/f1040a.pdf",
59            "http://www.irs.gov/pub/irs-pdf/f1040ez.pdf",
60            "http://www.irs.gov/pub/irs-pdf/f1040es.pdf",
61            "http://www.irs.gov/pub/irs-pdf/f1040sb.pdf"]
62    main(urls)
```

Let's break this down a bit. First of all, we need to look at the main function definition to see how this all flows. Here we see that it accepts a list of urls. The main function then creates a queue instance that it passes to 5 daemonized threads. The main difference between daemonized and non-daemon threads is that you have to keep track of non-daemon threads and close them yourself whereas with a daemon thread you basically just set them and forget them and when your app closes, they close too. Next we load up the queue (using its put method) with the urls we passed in.

Finally we tell the queue to wait for the threads to do their processing via the join method. In the download class, we have the line **self.queue.get()** which blocks until the queue has something to return. That means the threads just sit idly waiting to pick something up. It also means that for a thread to **get** something from the queue, it must call the queue's **get** method. Thus as we add or put items in the queue, the thread pool will pick up or **get** items and process them. This is also known as **dequeing**. Once all the items in the queue are processed, the script ends and exits. On my machine, it downloads all 5 documents in under a second.

Wrapping Up

Now you know how to use threads and queues both in theory and in a practical way. Threads are especially useful when you are creating a user interface and you want to keep your interface usable. Without threads, the user interface would become unresponsive and would appear to hang while you did a large file download or a big query against a database. To keep that from happening, you do the long running processes in threads and then communicate back to your interface when you are done.

Chapter 22 - Working with Dates and Time

Python gives the developer several tools for working with dates and time. In this chapter, we will be looking at the **datetime** and **time** modules. We will study how they work and some common uses for them. Let's start with the **datetime** module!

The datetime Module

We will be learning about the following classes from the **datetime** module:

- datetime.date
- datetime.timedelta
- datetime.datetime

These will cover the majority of instances where you'll need to use date and datetime object in Python. There is also a **tzinfo** class for working with time zones that we won't be covering. Feel free to take a look at the Python documentation for more information on that class.

datetime.date

Python can represent dates several different ways. We're going to look at the **datetime.date** format first as it happens to be one of the simpler date objects.

```
1  >>> datetime.date(2012, 13, 14)
2  Traceback (most recent call last):
3    File "<string>", line 1, in <fragment>
4  builtins.ValueError: month must be in 1..12
5  >>> datetime.date(2012, 12, 14)
6  datetime.date(2012, 12, 14)
```

This code shows how to create a simple date object. The date class accepts three arguments: the year, the month and the day. If you pass it an invalid value, you will see a **ValueError**, like the one above. Otherwise you will see a **datetime.date** object returned. Let's take a look at another example:

```
1   >>> import datetime
2   >>> d = datetime.date(2012, 12, 14)
3   >>> d.year
4   2012
5   >>> d.day
6   14
7   >>> d.month
8   12
```

Here we assign the date object to the variable **d**. Now we can access the various date components by name, such as **d.year** or **d.month**. Now let's find out what day it is:

```
1   >>> datetime.date.today()
2   datetime.date(2014, 3, 5)
```

This can be helpful whenever you need to record what day it is. Or perhaps you need to do a date-based calculation based on today. It's a handy little convenience method though.

datetime.datetime

A **datetime.datetime** object contains all the information from a datetime.date plus a datetime.time object. Let's create a couple of examples so we can better understand the difference between this object and the datetime.date object.

```
1    >>> datetime.datetime(2014, 3, 5)
2    datetime.datetime(2014, 3, 5, 0, 0)
3    >>> datetime.datetime(2014, 3, 5, 12, 30, 10)
4    datetime.datetime(2014, 3, 5, 12, 30, 10)
5    >>> d = datetime.datetime(2014, 3, 5, 12, 30, 10)
6    >>> d.year
7    2014
8    >>> d.second
9    10
10   >>> d.hour
11   12
```

Here we can see that **datetime.datetime** accepts several additional arguments: year, month, day, hour, minute and second. It also allows you to specify microsecond and timezone information too. When you work with databases, you will find yourself using these types of objects a lot. Most of the time, you will need to convert from the Python date or datetime format to the SQL datetime or timestamp format. You can find out what today is with datetime.datetime using two different methods:

```
1  >>> datetime.datetime.today()
2  datetime.datetime(2014, 3, 5, 17, 56, 10, 737000)
3  >>> datetime.datetime.now()
4  datetime.datetime(2014, 3, 5, 17, 56, 15, 418000)
```

The datetime module has another method that you should be aware of called **strftime**. This method allows the developer to create a string that represents the time in a more human readable format. There's an entire table of formatting options that you should go read in the Python documentation, section 8.1.7. We're going to look at a couple of examples to show you the power of this method:

```
1  >>> datetime.datetime.today().strftime("%Y%m%d")
2  '20140305'
3  >>> today = datetime.datetime.today()
4  >>> today.strftime("%m/%d/%Y")
5  '03/05/2014'
6  >>> today.strftime("%Y-%m-%d-%H.%M.%S")
7  '2014-03-05-17.59.53'
```

The first example is kind of a hack. It shows how to convert today's datetime object into a string that follows the YYYYMMDD (year, month, day) format. The second example is better. Here we assign today's datetime object to a variable called **today** and then try out two different string formatting operations. The first one adds forward slashes between the datetime elements and also rearranges it so that it becomes month, day, year. The last example creates a timestamp of sorts that follows a fairly typical format: YYYY-MM-DD.HH.MM.SS. If you want to go to a two-digit year, you can swap out the %Y for %y.

datetime.timedelta

The **datetime.timedelta** object represents a time duration. In other words, it is the difference between two dates or times. Let's take a look at a simple example:

```
1  >>> now = datetime.datetime.now()
2  >>> now
3  datetime.datetime(2014, 3, 5, 18, 13, 51, 230000)
4  >>> then = datetime.datetime(2014, 2, 26)
5  >>> delta = now - then
6  >>> type(delta)
7  <type 'datetime.timedelta'>
8  >>> delta.days
9  7
10 >>> delta.seconds
11 65631
```

We create two datetime objects here. One for today and one for a week ago. Then we take the difference between them. This returns a timedelta object which we can then use to find out the number of days or seconds between the two dates. If you need to know the number of hours or minutes between the two, you'll have to use some math to figure it out. Here's one way to do it:

```
1  >>> seconds = delta.total_seconds()
2  >>> hours = seconds // 3600
3  >>> hours
4  186.0
5  >>> minutes = (seconds % 3600) // 60
6  >>> minutes
7  13.0
```

What this tells us is that there are 186 hours and 13 minutes in a week. Note that we are using a double-forward slash as our division operator. This is known as **floor division**.

Now we're ready to move on and learn a bit about the **time** module!

The time Module

The **time** module provides the Python developer access to various time-related functions. The time module is based around what it known as an **epoch**, the point when time starts. For Unix systems, the epoch was in 1970. To find out what the epoch is on your system, try running the following:

```
1  >>> import time
2  >>> time.gmtime(0)
3  time.struct_time(tm_year=1970, tm_mon=1, tm_mday=1, tm_hour=0, tm_min=0, tm_sec=\
4  0, tm_wday=3, tm_yday=1, tm_isdst=0)
```

I ran this on Windows 7 and it too seems to think that time began in 1970. Anyway, in this section, we will be studying the following time-related functions:

- time.ctime
- time.sleep
- time.strftime
- time.time

Let's get started!

time.ctime

The **time.ctime** function will convert a time in seconds since the epoch to a string representing local time. If you don't pass it anything, then the current time is returned. Let's try out a couple of examples:

```
1   >>> import time
2   >>> time.ctime()
3   'Thu Mar 06 07:28:48 2014'
4   >>> time.ctime(1384112639)
5   'Sun Nov 10 13:43:59 2013'
```

Here we show the results of calling **ctime** with nothing at all and with a fairly random number of seconds since the epoch. I have seen sort of thing used when someone saves the date as seconds since the epoch and then they want to convert it to something a human can understand. It's a bit simpler to save a big integer (or long) to a database then to mess with formatting it from a datetime object to whatever date object the database accepts. Of course, that also has the drawback that you do need to convert the integer or float value back into a string.

time.sleep

The **time.sleep** function gives the developer the ability to suspend execution of your script a given number of seconds. It's like adding a pause to your program. I have found this personally useful when I need to wait a second for a file to finish closing or a database commit to finish committing. Let's take a look at an example. Open a new window in IDLE and save the following code:

```
1   import time
2
3   for x in range(5):
4       time.sleep(2)
5       print("Slept for 2 seconds")
```

Now run the code in IDLE. You can do that by going to the **Run** menu and then choose the **Run module** menu item. When you do so, you will see it print out the phrase *Slept for 2 seconds* five times with a two second pause between each print. It's really that easy to use!

time.strftime

The **time** module has a **strftime** function that works in pretty much the same manner as the datetime version. The difference is mainly in what it accepts for input: a tuple or a **struct_time** object, like those that are returned when you call **time.gmtime()** or **time.localtime()**. Here's a little example:

```
1  >>> time.strftime("%Y-%m-%d-%H.%M.%S",
2                     time.localtime())
3  '2014-03-06-20.35.56'
```

This code is quite similar to the timestamp code we created in the datetime portion of this chapter. I think the datetime method is a little more intuitive in that you just create a **datetime.datetime** object and then call its **strftime** method with the format you want. With the time module, you have to pass the format plus a time tuple. It's really up to you to decide which one makes the most sense to you.

time.time

The **time.time** function will return the time in seconds since the epoch as a floating point number. Let's take a look:

```
1  >>> time.time()
2  1394199262.318
```

That was pretty simple. You could use this when you want to save the current time to a database but you didn't want to bother converting it to the database's datetime method. You might also recall that the **ctime** method accepts the time in seconds, so we could use **time.time** to get the number of seconds to pass to ctime, like this:

```
1  >>> time.ctime(time.time())
2  'Fri Mar 07 07:36:38 2014'
```

If you do some digging in the documentation for the time module or if you just experiment with it a bit, you will likely find a few other uses for this function.

Wrapping Up

At this point you should know how to work with dates and time using Python's standard modules. Python gives you a lot of power when it comes to working with dates. You will find these modules helpful if you ever need to create an application that keeps track of appointments or that needs to run on particular days. They are also useful when working with databases.

Chapter 23 - The xml module

Python has built-in XML parsing capabilities that you can access via its **xml** module. In this article, we will be focusing on two of the xml module's sub-modules:

- minidom
- ElementTree

We'll start with minidom simply because this used to be the de-facto method of XML parsing. Then we will look at how to use ElementTree instead.

Working with minidom

To start out, well need some actual XML to parse. Take a look at the following short example of XML:

```
1   <?xml version="1.0" ?>
2   <zAppointments reminder="15">
3       <appointment>
4           <begin>1181251680</begin>
5           <uid>040000008200E000</uid>
6           <alarmTime>1181572063</alarmTime>
7           <state></state>
8           <location></location>
9           <duration>1800</duration>
10          <subject>Bring pizza home</subject>
11      </appointment>
12  </zAppointments>
```

This is fairly typical XML and actually pretty intuitive to read. There is some really nasty XML out in the wild that you may have to work with. Anyway, save the XML code above with the following name: *appt.xml*

Let's spend some time getting acquainted with how to parse this file using Python's **minidom** module. This is a fairly long piece of code, so prepare yourself.

```
1    import xml.dom.minidom
2    import urllib.request
3
4    class ApptParser(object):
5
6        def __init__(self, url, flag='url'):
7            self.list = []
8            self.appt_list = []
9            self.flag = flag
10           self.rem_value = 0
11           xml = self.getXml(url)
12           self.handleXml(xml)
13
14       def getXml(self, url):
15           try:
16               print(url)
17               f = urllib.request.urlopen(url)
18           except:
19               f = url
20
21           doc = xml.dom.minidom.parse(f)
22           node = doc.documentElement
23           if node.nodeType == xml.dom.Node.ELEMENT_NODE:
24               print('Element name: %s' % node.nodeName)
25               for (name, value) in node.attributes.items():
26                   print('    Attr -- Name: %s  Value: %s' % (name, value))
27
28           return node
29
30       def handleXml(self, xml):
31           rem = xml.getElementsByTagName('zAppointments')
32           appointments = xml.getElementsByTagName("appointment")
33           self.handleAppts(appointments)
34
35       def getElement(self, element):
36           return self.getText(element.childNodes)
37
38       def handleAppts(self, appts):
39           for appt in appts:
40               self.handleAppt(appt)
41               self.list = []
42
```

```
43        def handleAppt(self, appt):
44            begin     = self.getElement(appt.getElementsByTagName("begin")[0])
45            duration  = self.getElement(appt.getElementsByTagName("duration")[0])
46            subject   = self.getElement(appt.getElementsByTagName("subject")[0])
47            location  = self.getElement(appt.getElementsByTagName("location")[0])
48            uid       = self.getElement(appt.getElementsByTagName("uid")[0])
49
50            self.list.append(begin)
51            self.list.append(duration)
52            self.list.append(subject)
53            self.list.append(location)
54            self.list.append(uid)
55            if self.flag == 'file':
56
57                try:
58                    state    = self.getElement(appt.getElementsByTagName("state")[0\
59    ])
60                    self.list.append(state)
61                    alarm      = self.getElement(appt.getElementsByTagName("alarmTime\
62    ")[0])
63                    self.list.append(alarm)
64                except Exception as e:
65                    print(e)
66
67            self.appt_list.append(self.list)
68
69        def getText(self, nodelist):
70            rc = ""
71            for node in nodelist:
72                if node.nodeType == node.TEXT_NODE:
73                    rc = rc + node.data
74            return rc
75
76    if __name__ == "__main__":
77        appt = ApptParser("appt.xml")
78        print(appt.appt_list)
```

This code is loosely based on an example from the Python documentation and I have to admit that I think my mutation of it is a bit ugly. Let's break this code down a bit. The url parameter you see in the **ApptParser** class can be either a url or a file. In the **getXml** method, we use an exception handler to try and open the url. If it happens to raise an error, than we assume that the url is actually a file path. Next we use minidom's **parse** method to parse the XML. Then we pull out a node from the XML. We'll ignore the conditional as it isn't important to this discussion. Finally, we return the **node** object.

Technically, the node is XML and we pass it on to the **handleXml** method. To grab all the appointment instances in the XML, we do this:

```
1  xml.getElementsByTagName("appointment").
```

Then we pass that information to the **handleAppts** method. That's a lot of passing information around. It might be a good idea to refactor this code a bit to make it so that instead of passing information around, it just set class variables and then called the next method without any arguments. I'll leave this as an exercise for the reader. Anyway, all the **handleAppts** method does is loop over each appointment and call the **handleAppt** method to pull some additional information out of it, add the data to a list and add that list to another list. The idea was to end up with a list of lists that held all the pertinent data regarding my appointments.

You will notice that the handleAppt method calls the **getElement** method which calls the **getText** method. Technically, you could skip the call to getElement and just call getText directly. On the other hand, you may need to add some additional processing to getElement to convert the text to some other type before returning it back. For example, you may want to convert numbers to integers, floats or decimal.Decimal objects.

Let's try one more example with minidom before we move on. We will use an XML example from Microsoft's MSDN website: http://msdn.microsoft.com/en-us/library/ms762271%28VS.85%29.aspx[13]. Save the following XML as *example.xml*

```
1   <?xml version="1.0"?>
2   <catalog>
3      <book id="bk101">
4         <author>Gambardella, Matthew</author>
5         <title>XML Developer's Guide</title>
6         <genre>Computer</genre>
7         <price>44.95</price>
8         <publish_date>2000-10-01</publish_date>
9         <description>An in-depth look at creating applications
10       with XML.</description>
11     </book>
12     <book id="bk102">
13        <author>Ralls, Kim</author>
14        <title>Midnight Rain</title>
15        <genre>Fantasy</genre>
16        <price>5.95</price>
```

---

[13]http://msdn.microsoft.com/en-us/library/ms762271%28VS.85%29.aspx

```
17        <publish_date>2000-12-16</publish_date>
18        <description>A former architect battles corporate zombies,
19        an evil sorceress, and her own childhood to become queen
20        of the world.</description>
21     </book>
22     <book id="bk103">
23        <author>Corets, Eva</author>
24        <title>Maeve Ascendant</title>
25        <genre>Fantasy</genre>
26        <price>5.95</price>
27        <publish_date>2000-11-17</publish_date>
28        <description>After the collapse of a nanotechnology
29        society in England, the young survivors lay the
30        foundation for a new society.</description>
31     </book>
32  </catalog>
```

For this example, we'll just parse the XML, extract the book titles and print them to stdout. Here's the code:

```
1   import xml.dom.minidom as minidom
2
3   def getTitles(xml):
4       """
5       Print out all titles found in xml
6       """
7       doc = minidom.parse(xml)
8       node = doc.documentElement
9       books = doc.getElementsByTagName("book")
10
11      titles = []
12      for book in books:
13          titleObj = book.getElementsByTagName("title")[0]
14          titles.append(titleObj)
15
16      for title in titles:
17          nodes = title.childNodes
18          for node in nodes:
19              if node.nodeType == node.TEXT_NODE:
20                  print(node.data)
21
22  if __name__ == "__main__":
```

```
23      document = 'example.xml'
24      getTitles(document)
```

This code is just one short function that accepts one argument, the XML file. We import the minidom module and give it the same name to make it easier to reference. Then we parse the XML. The first two lines in the function are pretty much the same as the previous example. We use the **getElementsByTagName** method to grab the parts of the XML that we want, then iterate over the result and extract the book titles from them. This actually extracts title objects, so we need to iterate over that as well and pull out the plain text, which is why we use a nested **for** loop.

Now let's spend a little time trying out a different sub-module of the xml module named **ElementTree**.

Parsing with ElementTree

In this section, you will learn how to create an XML file, edit XML and parse the XML with ElementTree. For comparison's sake, we'll use the same XML we used in the previous section to illustrate the differences between using minidom and ElementTree. Here is the original XML again:

```
1    <?xml version="1.0" ?>
2    <zAppointments reminder="15">
3        <appointment>
4            <begin>1181251680</begin>
5            <uid>040000008200E000</uid>
6            <alarmTime>1181572063</alarmTime>
7            <state></state>
8            <location></location>
9            <duration>1800</duration>
10           <subject>Bring pizza home</subject>
11       </appointment>
12   </zAppointments>
```

Let's begin by learning how to create this piece of XML programmatically using Python!

How to Create XML with ElementTree

Creating XML with ElementTree is very simple. In this section, we will attempt to create the XML above with Python. Here's the code:

```
1    import xml.etree.ElementTree as xml
2
3    def createXML(filename):
4        """
5        Create an example XML file
6        """
7        root = xml.Element("zAppointments")
8        appt = xml.Element("appointment")
9        root.append(appt)
10
11       # add appointment children
12       begin = xml.SubElement(appt, "begin")
13       begin.text = "1181251680"
14
15       uid = xml.SubElement(appt, "uid")
16       uid.text = "040000008200E000"
17
18       alarmTime = xml.SubElement(appt, "alarmTime")
19       alarmTime.text = "1181572063"
20
21       state = xml.SubElement(appt, "state")
22
23       location = xml.SubElement(appt, "location")
24
25       duration = xml.SubElement(appt, "duration")
26       duration.text = "1800"
27
28       subject = xml.SubElement(appt, "subject")
29
30       tree = xml.ElementTree(root)
31       with open(filename, "w") as fh:
32           tree.write(fh)
33
34   if __name__ == "__main__":
35       createXML("appt.xml")
```

If you run this code, you should get something like the following (probably all on one line):

```
 1  <zAppointments>
 2      <appointment>
 3          <begin>1181251680</begin>
 4          <uid>040000008200E000</uid>
 5          <alarmTime>1181572063</alarmTime>
 6          <state />
 7          <location />
 8          <duration>1800</duration>
 9          <subject />
10      </appointment>
11  </zAppointments>
```

This is pretty close to the original and is certainly valid XML. While it's not quite the same, it's close enough. Let's take a moment to review the code and make sure we understand it. First we create the root element by using ElementTree's Element function. Then we create an appointment element and append it to the root. Next we create SubElements by passing the appointment Element object (appt) to SubElement along with a name, like "begin". Then for each SubElement, we set its text property to give it a value. At the end of the script, we create an ElementTree and use it to write the XML out to a file.

Now we're ready to learn how to edit the file!

How to Edit XML with ElementTree

Editing XML with ElementTree is also easy. To make things a little more interesting though, we'll add another appointment block to the XML:

```
 1  <?xml version="1.0" ?>
 2  <zAppointments reminder="15">
 3      <appointment>
 4          <begin>1181251680</begin>
 5          <uid>040000008200E000</uid>
 6          <alarmTime>1181572063</alarmTime>
 7          <state></state>
 8          <location></location>
 9          <duration>1800</duration>
10          <subject>Bring pizza home</subject>
11      </appointment>
12          <appointment>
13          <begin>1181253977</begin>
14          <uid>sdlkjlkadhdakhdfd</uid>
15          <alarmTime>1181588888</alarmTime>
```

```
16              <state>TX</state>
17              <location>Dallas</location>
18              <duration>1800</duration>
19              <subject>Bring pizza home</subject>
20          </appointment>
21  </zAppointments>
```

Now let's write some code to change each of the begin tag's values from seconds since the epoch to something a little more readable. We'll use Python's **time** module to facilitate this:

```
1   import time
2   import xml.etree.cElementTree as ET
3
4   def editXML(filename):
5       """
6       Edit an example XML file
7       """
8       tree = ET.ElementTree(file=filename)
9       root = tree.getroot()
10
11      for begin_time in root.iter("begin"):
12          begin_time.text = time.ctime(int(begin_time.text))
13
14      tree = ET.ElementTree(root)
15      with open("updated.xml", "w") as f:
16          tree.write(f)
17
18  if __name__ == "__main__":
19      editXML("original_appt.xml")
```

Here we create an ElementTree object (tree) and we extract the **root** from it. Then we use ElementTree's **iter()** method to find all the tags that are labeled "begin". Note that the iter() method was added in Python 2.7. In our for loop, we set each item's text property to a more human readable time format via **time.ctime()**. You'll note that we had to convert the string to an integer when passing it to ctime. The output should look something like the following:

```
1   <zAppointments reminder="15">
2       <appointment>
3           <begin>Thu Jun 07 16:28:00 2007</begin>
4           <uid>040000008200E000</uid>
5           <alarmTime>1181572063</alarmTime>
6           <state />
7           <location />
8           <duration>1800</duration>
9           <subject>Bring pizza home</subject>
10      </appointment>
11      <appointment>
12          <begin>Thu Jun 07 17:06:17 2007</begin>
13          <uid>sdlkjlkadhdakhdfd</uid>
14          <alarmTime>1181588888</alarmTime>
15          <state>TX</state>
16          <location>Dallas</location>
17          <duration>1800</duration>
18          <subject>Bring pizza home</subject>
19      </appointment>
20  </zAppointments>
```

You can also use ElementTree's **find()** or **findall()** methods to search for specific tags in your XML. The find() method will just find the first instance whereas the findall() will find all the tags with the specified label. These are helpful for editing purposes or for parsing, which is our next topic!

How to Parse XML with ElementTree

Now we get to learn how to do some basic parsing with ElementTree. First we'll read through the code and then we'll go through bit by bit so we can understand it. Note that this code is based around the original example, but it should work on the second one as well.

```python
1   import xml.etree.cElementTree as ET
2
3   def parseXML(xml_file):
4       """
5       Parse XML with ElementTree
6       """
7       tree = ET.ElementTree(file=xml_file)
8       print(tree.getroot())
9       root = tree.getroot()
10      print("tag=%s, attrib=%s" % (root.tag, root.attrib))
```

```
11
12      for child in root:
13          print(child.tag, child.attrib)
14          if child.tag == "appointment":
15              for step_child in child:
16                  print(step_child.tag)
17
18      # iterate over the entire tree
19      print("-" * 40)
20      print("Iterating using a tree iterator")
21      print("-" * 40)
22      iter_ = tree.getiterator()
23      for elem in iter_:
24          print(elem.tag)
25
26      # get the information via the children!
27      print("-" * 40)
28      print("Iterating using getchildren()")
29      print("-" * 40)
30      appointments = root.getchildren()
31      for appointment in appointments:
32          appt_children = appointment.getchildren()
33          for appt_child in appt_children:
34              print("%s=%s" % (appt_child.tag, appt_child.text))
35
36  if __name__ == "__main__":
37      parseXML("appt.xml")
```

You may have already noticed this, but in this example and the last one, we've been importing cElementTree instead of the normal ElementTree. The main difference between the two is that cElementTree is C-based instead of Python-based, so it's much faster. Anyway, once again we create an ElementTree object and extract the root from it. You'll note that we print out the root and the root's tag and attributes. Next we show several ways of iterating over the tags. The first loop just iterates over the XML child by child. This would only print out the top level child (appointment) though, so we added an if statement to check for that child and iterate over its children too.

Next we grab an iterator from the tree object itself and iterate over it that way. You get the same information, but without the extra steps in the first example. The third method uses the root's **getchildren()** function. Here again we need an inner loop to grab all the children inside each appointment tag. The last example uses the root's **iter()** method to just loop over any tags that match the string "begin".

As mentioned in the last section, you could also use **find()** or **findall()** to help you find specific tags or sets of tags respectively. Also note that each Element object has a **tag** and a **text** property that you can use to acquire that exact information.

Wrapping Up

Now you know how to use minidom to parse XML. You have also learned how to use ElementTree to create, edit and parse XML. There are other libraries outside of Python that provide additional methods for working with XML too. Be sure you do some research to make sure you're using a tool that you understand as this topic can get pretty confusing if the tool you're using is obtuse.

Part III - Intermediate Odds and Ends

In Part III, you will learn about some Python internals that many would consider intermediate-level Python. You have graduated from the milk and you're ready for some meat! In this section, we will take a look at the following topics:

- Debugging
- Decorators
- The lambda statement
- Profiling your code
- Testing

The first chapter in this section will introduce you to Python's debugging module, **pdb** and how to use it to debug your code. The next chapter is all about decorators. You will learn about how to create them and about a few of the decorators that are built into Python. For the third chapter, we will be looking at the lambda statement, which basically creates a one-line anonymous function. It's a little weird, but fun! The fourth chapter will cover how you profile your code. This discipline gives you the ability to find possible bottlenecks in your code so that you know where to focus to optimize your code. The final chapter in this section is about testing your code. In it you will discover how to test your code using a couple of Python's own built-in modules.

I think you will find this section very helpful in continuing your Python education. Let's jump right in!

image

Chapter 24 - The Python Debugger

Python comes with its own debugger module that is named **pdb**. This module provides an interactive source code debugger for your Python programs. You can set breakpoints, step through your code, inspect stack frames and more. We will look at the following aspects of the module:

- How to start the debugger
- Stepping through your code
- Setting breakpoints

Let's start by creating a quick piece of code to attempt debugging with. Here's a silly example:

```
1   # debug_test.py
2
3   def doubler(a):
4       """"""
5       result = a*2
6       print(result)
7       return result
8
9   def main():
10      """"""
11      for i in range(1,10):
12          doubler(i)
13
14  if __name__ == "__main__":
15      main()
```

Now let's learn how to run the debugger against this piece of code.

How to Start the Debugger

You can start the debugger three different ways. The first is to just import it and insert **pdb.set_-trace()** into your code to start the debugger. You can import the debugger in IDLE and have it run your module. Or you can call the debugger on the command line. We'll focus on the last two methods in this section. We will start with using it in the interpreter (IDLE). Open up a terminal (command line window) and navigate to where you save the above code example. Then start Python. Now do the following:

```
1  >>> import debug_test
2  >>> import pdb
3  >>> pdb.run('debug_test.main()')
4  > <string>(1)<module>()
5  (Pdb) continue
6  2
7  4
8  6
9  8
10 10
11 12
12 14
13 16
14 18
15 >>>
```

Here we import our module and pdb. Then we execute pdb's **run** method and tell it to call our module's **main** method. This brings up the debugger's prompt. Here we typed **continue** to tell it to go ahead and run the script. You can also type the letter **c** as a shortcut for continue. When you **continue**, the debugger will continue execution until it reaches a breakpoint or the script ends.

The other way to start the debugger is to execute the following command via your terminal session:

```
1  python -m pdb debug_test.py
```

If you run it this way, you will see a slightly different result:

```
1  -> def doubler(a):
2  (Pdb) c
3  2
4  4
5  6
6  8
7  10
8  12
9  14
10 16
11 18
12 The program finished and will be restarted
```

You will note that in this example we used **c** instead of **continue**. You will also note that the debugger restarts at the end. This preserves the debugger's state (such as breakpoints) and can be more useful than having the debugger stop. Sometimes you'll need to go through the code several times to understand what's wrong with it.

Let's dig a little deeper and learn how to step through the code.

Stepping Through the Code

If you want to step through your code one line at a time, then you can use the **step** (or simply "s") command. Here's a session for your viewing pleasure:

```
 1  C:\Users\mike>cd c:\py101
 2
 3  c:\py101>python -m pdb debug_test.py
 4  > c:\py101\debug_test.py(4)<module>()
 5  -> def doubler(a):
 6  (Pdb) step
 7  > c:\py101\debug_test.py(11)<module>()
 8  -> def main():
 9  (Pdb) s
10  > c:\py101\debug_test.py(16)<module>()
11  -> if __name__ == "__main__":
12  (Pdb) s
13  > c:\py101\debug_test.py(17)<module>()
14  -> main()
15  (Pdb) s
16  --Call--
17  > c:\py101\debug_test.py(11)main()
18  -> def main():
19  (Pdb) next
20  > c:\py101\debug_test.py(13)main()
21  -> for i in range(1,10):
22  (Pdb) s
23  > c:\py101\debug_test.py(14)main()
24  -> doubler(i)
25  (Pdb)
```

Here we start up the debugger and tell it to step into the code. It starts at the top and goes through the first two function definitions. Then it reaches the conditional and finds that it's supposed to execute the **main** function. We step into the main function and then use the **next** command. The **next** command will execute a called function if it encounters it without stepping into it. If you want to step into the called function, then you'll only want to just use the **step** command.

When you see a line like > **c:py101debug_test.py(13)main()**, you will want to pay attention to the number that's in the parentheses. This number is the current line number in the code.

You can use the **args** (or **a**) to print the current argument list to the screen. Another handy command is **jump** (or **j**) followed by a space and the line number that you want to "jump" to. This gives you the ability to skip a bunch of monotonous stepping to get to the line that you want to get to. This leads us to learning about breakpoints!

Setting breakpoints

A breakpoint is a line in the code where you want to pause execution. You can set a breakpoint by calling the **break** (or **b**) command followed by a space and the line number that you want to break on. You can also prefix the line number with a filename and colon to specify a breakpoint in a different file. The break command also allows you to set a breakpoint with the **function** argument. There is also a **tbreak** command which will set a temporary breakpoint which is automatically removed when it gets hit.

Here's an example:

```
1   c:\py101>python -m pdb debug_test.py
2   > c:\py101\debug_test.py(4)<module>()
3   -> def doubler(a):
4   (Pdb) break 6
5   Breakpoint 1 at c:\py101\debug_test.py:6
6   (Pdb) c
7   > c:\py101\debug_test.py(6)doubler()
8   -> result = a*2
```

We start the debugger and then tell it to set a breakpoint on line 6. Then we continue and it stops on line 6 just like it's supposed to. Now would be a good time to check the argument list to see if it's what you expect. Give it a try by typing **args** now. Then do another **continue** and another **args** to see how it changed.

Wrapping Up

There are a lot of other commands that you can use in the debugger. I recommend reading the documentation to learn about the others. However, at this point you should be able to use the debugger effectively to debug your own code.

Chapter 25 - Decorators

Python decorators are really cool, but they can be a little hard to understand at first. A decorator in Python is a function that accepts another function as an argument. The decorator will usually modify or enhance the function it accepted and return the modified function. This means that when you call a decorated function, you will get a function that may be a little different that may have additional features compared with the base definition. But let's back up a bit. We should probably review the basic building block of a decorator, namely, the function.

A Simple Function

A function is a block of code that begins with the Python keyword **def** followed by the actual name of the function. A function can accept zero or more arguments, keyword arguments or a mixture of the two. A function always returns something. If you do not specify what a function should return, it will return **None**. Here is a very simple function that just returns a string:

```python
1  def a_function():
2      """A pretty useless function"""
3      return "1+1"
4
5  if __name__ == "__main__":
6      value = a_function()
7      print(value)
```

All we do in the code above is call the function and print the return value. Let's create another function:

```python
1   def another_function(func):
2       """
3       A function that accepts another function
4       """
5       def other_func():
6           val = "The result of %s is %s" % (func(),
7                                             eval(func())
8                                             )
9           return val
10      return other_func
```

159

This function accepts one argument and that argument has to be a function or callable. In fact, it really should only be called using the previously defined function. You will note that this function has a nested function inside of it that we are calling **other_func**. It will take the result of the function passed to it, evaluate it and create a string that tells us about what it did, which it then returns. Let's look at the full version of the code:

```
1   def another_function(func):
2       """
3       A function that accepts another function
4       """
5
6       def other_func():
7           val = "The result of %s is %s" % (func(),
8                                             eval(func())
9                                             )
10          return val
11      return other_func
12
13  def a_function():
14      """A pretty useless function"""
15      return "1+1"
16
17  if __name__ == "__main__":
18      value = a_function()
19      print(value)
20      decorator = another_function(a_function)
21      print(decorator())
```

This is how a decorator works. We create one function and then pass it into a second function. The second function is the **decorator** function. The decorator will modify or enhance the function that was passed to it and return the modification. If you run this code, you should see the following as output to stdout:

```
1   1+1
2   The result of 1+1 is 2
```

Let's change the code slightly to turn **another_function** into a decorator:

```
 1  def another_function(func):
 2      """
 3      A function that accepts another function
 4      """
 5
 6      def other_func():
 7          val = "The result of %s is %s" % (func(),
 8                                             eval(func())
 9                                             )
10          return val
11      return other_func
12
13  @another_function
14  def a_function():
15      """A pretty useless function"""
16      return "1+1"
17
18  if __name__ == "__main__":
19      value = a_function()
20      print(value)
```

You will note that in Python, a decorator starts with the <@*>* symbol followed by the name of the function that we will be using to "decorate" our regular with. To apply the decorator, you just put it on the line before the function definition. Now when we call **a_function, it will get decorated and we'll get the following result:

```
 1  The result of 1+1 is 2
```

Let's create a decorator that actually does something useful.

Creating a Logging Decorator

Sometimes you will want to create a log of what a function is doing. Most of the time, you will probably be doing your logging within the function itself. Occasionally you might want to do it at the function level to get an idea of the flow of the program or perhaps to fulfill some business rules, like auditing. Here's a little decorator that we can use to record any function's name and what it returns:

```
1   import logging
2
3   def log(func):
4       """
5       Log what function is called
6       """
7       def wrap_log(*args, **kwargs):
8           name = func.__name__
9           logger = logging.getLogger(name)
10          logger.setLevel(logging.INFO)
11
12          # add file handler
13          fh = logging.FileHandler("%s.log" % name)
14          fmt = '%(asctime)s - %(name)s - %(levelname)s - %(message)s'
15          formatter = logging.Formatter(fmt)
16          fh.setFormatter(formatter)
17          logger.addHandler(fh)
18
19          logger.info("Running function: %s" % name)
20          result = func(*args, **kwargs)
21          logger.info("Result: %s" % result)
22          return func
23      return wrap_log
24
25  @log
26  def double_function(a):
27      """
28      Double the input parameter
29      """
30      return a*2
31
32  if __name__ == "__main__":
33      value = double_function(2)
```

This little script has a **log** function that accepts a function as its sole argument. It will create a logger object and a log file name based on the name of the function. Then the log function will log what function was called and what the function returned, if anything.

Built-in Decorators

Python comes with several built-in decorators. The big three are:

- @classmethod
- @staticmethod
- @property

There are also decorators in various parts of Python's standard library. One example would be **functools.wraps**. We will be limiting our scope to the three above though.

@classmethod and @staticmethod

I have never actually used these myself, so I did a fair bit of research. The *<*@classmethod>** decorator can be called with with an instance of a class or directly by the class itself as its first argument. According to the Python documentation: *It can be called either on the class (such as C.f()) or on an instance (such as C().f()). The instance is ignored except for its class. If a class method is called for a derived class, the derived class object is passed as the implied first argument.* The primary use case of a @classmethod decorator that I have found in my research is as an alternate constructor or helper method for initialization.

The *<*@staticmethod>** decorator is just a function inside of a class. You can call it both with and without instantiating the class. A typical use case is when you have a function where you believe it has a connection with a class. It's a stylistic choice for the most part.

It might help to see a code example of how these two decorators work:

```
1  class DecoratorTest(object):
2      """
3      Test regular method vs @classmethod vs @staticmethod
4      """
5
6      def __init__(self):
7          """Constructor"""
8          pass
9
10     def doubler(self, x):
11         """"""
12         print("running doubler")
13         return x*2
14
15     @classmethod
16     def class_tripler(klass, x):
17         """"""
18         print("running tripler: %s" % klass)
19         return x*3
20
```

```
21        @staticmethod
22        def static_quad(x):
23            """"""
24            print("running quad")
25            return x*4
26
27 if __name__ == "__main__":
28        decor = DecoratorTest()
29        print(decor.doubler(5))
30        print(decor.class_tripler(3))
31        print(DecoratorTest.class_tripler(3))
32        print(DecoratorTest.static_quad(2))
33        print(decor.static_quad(3))
34
35        print(decor.doubler)
36        print(decor.class_tripler)
37        print(decor.static_quad)
```

This example demonstrates that you can call a regular method and both decorated methods in the same way. You will notice that you can call both the @classmethod and the @staticmethod decorated functions directly from the class or from an instance of the class. If you try to call a regular function with the class (i.e. DecoratorTest.doubler(2)) you will receive a **TypeError**. You will also note that the last print statement shows that decor.static_quad returns a regular function instead of a bound method.

Python Properties

Python has a neat little concept called a property that can do several useful things. We will be looking into how to do the following:

- Convert class methods into read-only attributes
- Reimplement setters and getters into an attribute

One of the simplest ways to use a property is to use it as a decorator of a method. This allows you to turn a class method into a class attribute. I find this useful when I need to do some kind of combination of values. Others have found it useful for writing conversion methods that they want to have access to as methods. Let's take a look at a simple example:

```
1  class Person(object):
2      """"""
3
4      def __init__(self, first_name, last_name):
5          """Constructor"""
6          self.first_name = first_name
7          self.last_name = last_name
8
9      @property
10     def full_name(self):
11         """
12         Return the full name
13         """
14         return "%s %s" % (self.first_name, self.last_name)
```

In the code above, we create two class attributes or properties: **self.first_name** and **self.last_name**. Next we create a **full_name** method that has a *<*@property>** decorator attached to it. This allows us to do the following in an interpreter session:

```
1  >>> person = Person("Mike", "Driscoll")
2  >>> person.full_name
3  'Mike Driscoll'
4  >>> person.first_name
5  'Mike'
6  >>> person.full_name = "Jackalope"
7  Traceback (most recent call last):
8    File "<string>", line 1, in <fragment>
9  AttributeError: can't set attribute
```

As you can see, because we turned the method into a property, we can access it using normal dot notation. However, if we try to set the property to something different, we will cause an **AttributeError** to be raised. The only way to change the **full_name** property is to do so indirectly:

```
1  >>> person.first_name = "Dan"
2  >>> person.full_name
3  'Dan Driscoll'
```

This is kind of limiting, so let's look at another example where we can make a property that does allow us to set it.

Replacing Setters and Getters with a Python property

Let's pretend that we have some legacy code that someone wrote who didn't understand Python very well. If you're like me, you've already seen this kind of code before:

```
1   from decimal import Decimal
2
3   class Fees(object):
4       """"""
5
6       def __init__(self):
7           """Constructor"""
8           self._fee = None
9
10      def get_fee(self):
11          """
12          Return the current fee
13          """
14          return self._fee
15
16      def set_fee(self, value):
17          """
18          Set the fee
19          """
20          if isinstance(value, str):
21              self._fee = Decimal(value)
22          elif isinstance(value, Decimal):
23              self._fee = value
```

To use this class, we have to use the setters and getters that are defined:

```
1   >>> f = Fees()
2   >>> f.set_fee("1")
3   >>> f.get_fee()
4   Decimal('1')
```

If you want to add the normal dot notation access of attributes to this code without breaking all the applications that depend on this piece of code, you can change it very simply by adding a property:

```
1   from decimal import Decimal
2
3   class Fees(object):
4       """"""
5
6       def __init__(self):
7           """Constructor"""
8           self._fee = None
9
10      def get_fee(self):
11          """
12          Return the current fee
13          """
14          return self._fee
15
16      def set_fee(self, value):
17          """
18          Set the fee
19          """
20          if isinstance(value, str):
21              self._fee = Decimal(value)
22          elif isinstance(value, Decimal):
23              self._fee = value
24
25      fee = property(get_fee, set_fee)
```

We added one line to the end of this code. Now we can do stuff like this:

```
1   >>> f = Fees()
2   >>> f.set_fee("1")
3   >>> f.fee
4   Decimal('1')
5   >>> f.fee = "2"
6   >>> f.get_fee()
7   Decimal('2')
```

As you can see, when we use **property** in this manner, it allows the fee property to set and get the value itself without breaking the legacy code. Let's rewrite this code using the property decorator and see if we can get it to allow setting.

```
1  from decimal import Decimal
2
3  class Fees(object):
4      """"""
5
6      def __init__(self):
7          """Constructor"""
8          self._fee = None
9
10     @property
11     def fee(self):
12         """
13         The fee property - the getter
14         """
15         return self._fee
16
17     @fee.setter
18     def fee(self, value):
19         """
20         The setter of the fee property
21         """
22         if isinstance(value, str):
23             self._fee = Decimal(value)
24         elif isinstance(value, Decimal):
25             self._fee = value
26
27 if __name__ == "__main__":
28     f = Fees()
```

The code above demonstrates how to create a "setter" for the **fee** property. You can do this by decorating a second method that is also called **fee** with a decorator called <**@fee.setter**>. The setter is invoked when you do something like this:

```
1  >>> f = Fees()
2  >>> f.fee = "1"
```

If you look at the signature for **property**, it has fget, fset, fdel and doc as "arguments". You can create another decorated method using the same name to correspond to a delete function using <**@fee.deleter*>*** if you want to catch the ****del** command against the attribute.

Wrapping Up

At this point you should know how to create your own decorators and how to use a few of Python's built-in decorators. We looked at @classmethod, @property and @staticmethod. I would be curious to know how my readers use the built-in decorators and how they use their own custom decorators.

Chapter 26 - The lambda

The Python lambda statement is an anonymous or unbound function and a pretty limited function at that. Let's take a look at a few typical examples and see if we can find a use case for it. The typical examples that one normally sees for teaching the lambda are some sort of boring doubling function. Just to be contrary, our simple example will show how to find the square root. First we'll show a normal function and then the lambda equivalent:

```python
import math

def sqroot(x):
    """
    Finds the square root of the number passed in
    """
    return math.sqrt(x)

square_rt = lambda x: math.sqrt(x)
```

If you try each of these functions, you'll end up with a float. Here are a couple examples:

```python
>>> sqroot(49)
7.0
>>> square_rt(64)
8.0
```

Pretty slick, right? But where would we actually use a lambda in real life? Maybe a calculator program? Well, that would work, but it's a pretty limited application for a builtin of Python! One of the major pieces of Python that lambda examples are applied to regularly are Tkinter callbacks. Tkinter is a toolkit for building GUIs that is included with Python.

Tkinter + lambda

We'll start with Tkinter since it's included with the standard Python package. Here's a really simple script with three buttons, two of which are bound to their event handler using a lambda:

```
1   import Tkinter as tk
2
3   class App:
4       """"""
5
6       def __init__(self, parent):
7           """Constructor"""
8           frame = tk.Frame(parent)
9           frame.pack()
10
11          btn22 = tk.Button(frame, text="22", command=lambda: self.printNum(22))
12          btn22.pack(side=tk.LEFT)
13          btn44 = tk.Button(frame, text="44", command=lambda: self.printNum(44))
14          btn44.pack(side=tk.LEFT)
15
16          quitBtn = tk.Button(frame, text="QUIT", fg="red", command=frame.quit)
17          quitBtn.pack(side=tk.LEFT)
18
19
20      def printNum(self, num):
21          """"""
22          print("You pressed the %s button" % num)
23
24  if __name__ == "__main__":
25      root = tk.Tk()
26      app = App(root)
27      root.mainloop()
```

Notice the btn22 and btn44 variables. This is where the action is. We create a tk.Button instance here and bind to our printNum method in one fell swoop. The lambda is assigned to the button's command parameter. What this means is that we're creating a one-off function for the command, much like in the quit button where we call the frame's quit method. The difference here is that this particular lambda is a method that calls another method and passes the latter an integer. In the printNum method, we print to stdout which button was pressed by using the information that was passed to it from the lambda function. Did you follow all that? If so, we can continue; if not, re-read this paragraph as many times as necessary until the information sinks in or you go crazy, whichever comes first.

Wrapping Up

The lambda statement is used in all kinds of other projects as well. If you Google a Python project name and lambda, you can find lots of live code out there. For example, if you search for "django lambda", you'll find out that django has a **modelformset** factory that utilizes lambdas. The Elixir plugin for SqlAlchemy also uses lambdas. Keep your eyes open and you'll be surprised how many times you'll stumble across this handy little function maker.

Chapter 27 - Code Profiling

Code profiling is an attempt to find bottlenecks in your code. Profiling is supposed to find what parts of your code take the longest. Once you know that, then you can look at those pieces of your code and try to find ways to optimize it. Python comes with three profilers built in: **cProfile**, **profile** and **hotshot**. According to the Python documentation, hotshot is "no longer maintained and may be dropped in a future version of Python". The **profile** module is a pure Python module, but adds a lot of overhead to profiled programs. Thus we will be focusing on **cProfile**, which has an interface that mimics the profile module.

Profiling Your Code with cProfile

Profiling code with cProfile is really quite easy. All you need to do is import the module and call its **run** function. Let's look at a simple example:

```
1  >>> import hashlib
2  >>> import cProfile
3  >>> cProfile.run("hashlib.md5(b'abcdefghijkl').digest()")
4          4 function calls in 0.000 CPU seconds
5
6     Ordered by: standard name
7
8     ncalls  tottime  percall  cumtime  percall filename:lineno(function)
9          1    0.000    0.000    0.000    0.000 <string>:1(<module>)
10         1    0.000    0.000    0.000    0.000 {_hashlib.openssl_md5}
11         1    0.000    0.000    0.000    0.000 {method 'digest' of '_hashlib.HASH\
12  ' objects}
13         1    0.000    0.000    0.000    0.000 {method 'disable' of '_lsprof.Prof\
14  iler' objects}
```

Here we import the **hashlib** module and use cProfile to profile the creation of an MD5 hash. The first line shows that there were 4 function calls. The next line tells us how the results are ordered. According to the documentation, standard name refers to the far right column. There are a number of columns here.

- **ncalls** is the number of calls made.
- **tottime** is a total of the time spent in the given function.

- **percall** refers to the quotient of tottime divided by ncalls
- **cumtime** is the cumulative time spent in this and all subfunctions. It's even accurate for recursive functions!
- The second **percall** column is the quotient of cumtime divided by primitive calls
- **filename:lineno(function)** provides the respective data of each function

A primitive call is one that was not induced via recursion.

This isn't a very interesting example as there are no obvious bottlenecks. Let's create a piece of code with some built in bottlenecks and see if the profiler detects them.

```python
1   import time
2
3   def fast():
4       """"""
5       print("I run fast!")
6
7   def slow():
8       """"""
9       time.sleep(3)
10      print("I run slow!")
11
12  def medium():
13      """"""
14      time.sleep(0.5)
15      print("I run a little slowly...")
16
17  def main():
18      """"""
19      fast()
20      slow()
21      medium()
22
23  if __name__ == '__main__':
24      main()
```

In this example, we create four functions. The first three run at different rates. The **fast** function will run at normal speed; the **medium** function will take approximately half a second to run and the **slow** function will take around 3 seconds to run. The **main** function calls the other three. Now let's run cProfile against this silly little program:

```
1  >>> import cProfile
2  >>> import ptest
3  >>> cProfile.run('ptest.main()')
4  I run fast!
5  I run slow!
6  I run a little slowly...
7          8 function calls in 3.500 seconds
8
9     Ordered by: standard name
10
11    ncalls  tottime  percall  cumtime  percall filename:lineno(function)
12         1    0.000    0.000    3.500    3.500 <string>:1(<module>)
13         1    0.000    0.000    0.500    0.500 ptest.py:15(medium)
14         1    0.000    0.000    3.500    3.500 ptest.py:21(main)
15         1    0.000    0.000    0.000    0.000 ptest.py:4(fast)
16         1    0.000    0.000    3.000    3.000 ptest.py:9(slow)
17         1    0.000    0.000    0.000    0.000 {method 'disable' of '_lsprof.Prof\
18 iler' objects}
19         2    3.499    1.750    3.499    1.750 {time.sleep}
```

This time around we see the program took 3.5 seconds to run. If you examine the results, you will see that cProfile has identified the **slow** function as taking 3 seconds to run. That's the biggest bottleneck after the **main** function. Normally when you find a bottleneck like this, you would try to find a faster way to execute your code or perhaps decide that the runtime was acceptable. In this example, we know that the best way to speed up the function is to remove the **time.sleep** call or at least reduce the sleep length.

You can also call cProfile on the command line rather than using it in the interpreter. Here's one way to do it:

```
1  python -m cProfile ptest.py
```

This will run cProfile against your script in much the same way as we did before. But what if you want to save the profiler's output? Well, that's easy with cProfile! All you need to do is pass it the **-o** command followed by the name (or path) of the output file. Here's an example:

```
1  python -m cProfile -o output.txt ptest.py
```

Unfortunately, the file it outputs isn't exactly human-readable. If you want to read the file, then you'll need to use Python's **pstats** module. You can use pstats to format the output in various ways. Here's some code that shows how to get some output that's similar to what we've seen so far:

```
1   >>> import pstats
2   >>> p = pstats.Stats("output.txt")
3   >>> p.strip_dirs().sort_stats(-1).print_stats()
4   Thu Mar 20 18:32:16 2014    output.txt
5
6            8 function calls in 3.501 seconds
7
8      Ordered by: standard name
9
10     ncalls  tottime  percall  cumtime  percall filename:lineno(function)
11          1    0.000    0.000    3.501    3.501 ptest.py:1(<module>)
12          1    0.001    0.001    0.500    0.500 ptest.py:15(medium)
13          1    0.000    0.000    3.501    3.501 ptest.py:21(main)
14          1    0.001    0.001    0.001    0.001 ptest.py:4(fast)
15          1    0.001    0.001    3.000    3.000 ptest.py:9(slow)
16          1    0.000    0.000    0.000    0.000 {method 'disable' of '_lsprof.Prof\
17  iler' objects}
18          2    3.499    1.750    3.499    1.750 {time.sleep}
19
20
21  <pstats.Stats instance at 0x017C9030>
```

The **strip_dirs** call will strip out all the paths to the modules from the output while the **sort_stats** call does the sorting that we're used to seeing. There are a bunch of really interesting examples in the cProfile documentation showing different ways to extract information using the pstats module.

Wrapping Up

At this point you should be able to use the **cProfile** module to help you diagnose why your code is so slow. You might also want to take a look at Python's **timeit** module. It allows you to time small pieces of your code if you don't want to deal with the complexities involved with profiling. There are also several other 3rd party modules that are good for profiling such as the line_profiler and the memory_profiler projects.

Chapter 28 - An Intro to Testing

Python includes a couple of built-in modules for testing your code. They two methods are called **doctest** and **unittest**. We will look at how to use **doctest** first and in the second section we will introduce unit tests using Test Driven Development techniques.

Testing with doctest

The doctest module will search for pieces of text in your code that resemble interactive Python sessions. It will then execute those sessions to verify that they work exactly as written. This means that if you wrote an example in a docstring that showed the output with a trailing space or tab, then the actual output of the function has to have that trailing whitespace too. Most of the time, the docstring is where you will want to put your tests. The following aspects of doctest will be covered:

- How to run doctest from the terminal
- How to use doctest inside a module
- How to run a doctest from a separate file

Let's get started!

Running doctest via the Terminal

We will start by creating a really simple function that will double whatever is given to it. We will include a couple of tests inside the function's **docstring**. Here's the code (be sure and save it as "dtest1.py"):

```
1   # dtest1.py
2
3   def double(a):
4       """
5       >>> double(4)
6       8
7       >>> double(9)
8       18
9       """
10      return a*2
```

177

Now we just need to run this code in **doctest**. Open up a terminal (or command line) and change directories to the folder that contains your script. Here's a screenshot of what I did:

image

You will notice that in the first example, I executed the following:

```
1   python -m doctest dtest1.py
```

That ran the test and nothing printed out to the screen. When you don't see anything printed, that means that all the tests passed successfully. The second example shows the following command:

```
1   python -m doctest -v dtest1.py
```

The "-v" means that we want verbose output, which is exactly what we received. Open up the code again and add a space after the "18" in the docstring. Then re-run the test. Here's the output I received:

image

The error message says it expected "18" and it got "18". What's going on here? Well we added a space after "18" to our docstring, so doctest actually expected the number "18" followed by a space. Also beware of putting dictionaries as output in your docstring examples. Dictionaries can be in any order, so the likelihood of it matching your actual output isn't very good.

Running doctest Inside a Module

Let's modify the example slightly so that we import the **doctest** module and use its **testmod** function.

```
1   def double(a):
2       """
3       >>> double(4)
4       8
5       >>> double(9)
6       18
7       """
8       return a*2
9
10  if __name__ == "__main__":
11      import doctest
12      doctest.testmod(verbose=True)
```

Here we import **doctest** and call **doctest.testmod**. We pass it the keyword argument of **verbose=True** so that we can see some output. Otherwise, this script will run with no output whatsoever, signifying that the tests ran successfully.

If you do not want to hard-code the verbose option, you can also do it on the command line:

```
1   python dtest2.py -v
```

Now we're ready to learn how to put the tests into a separate file.

Running doctest From a Separate File

The doctest module also supports putting the testing into a separate file. This allows us to separate the tests from the code. Let's strip the tests from the previous example and put them into a text file named **tests.txt**:

```
1   The following are tests for dtest2.py
2
3   >>> from dtest2 import double
4   >>> double(4)
5   8
6   >>> double(9)
7   18
```

Let's run this test file on the command line. Here's how:

```
C:\Windows\system32\cmd.exe

Microsoft Windows [Version 6.1.7601]
Copyright (c) 2009 Microsoft Corporation.  All rights reserved.

C:\Users\mdriscoll>cd c:\test

c:\test>python -m doctest tests.txt

c:\test>python -m doctest -v tests.txt
Trying:
    from dtest1 import double
Expecting nothing
ok
Trying:
    double(4)
Expecting:
    8
ok
Trying:
    double(9)
Expecting:
    18
ok
1 items passed all tests:
   3 tests in tests.txt
3 tests in 1 items.
3 passed and 0 failed.
Test passed.
```

image

You will notice that the syntax for calling doctest with a text file is the same as calling it with a Python file. The results are the same as well. In this case, there are three tests instead of two because we're also importing a module. You can also run the tests that are in a text file inside the Python interpreter. Here's one example:

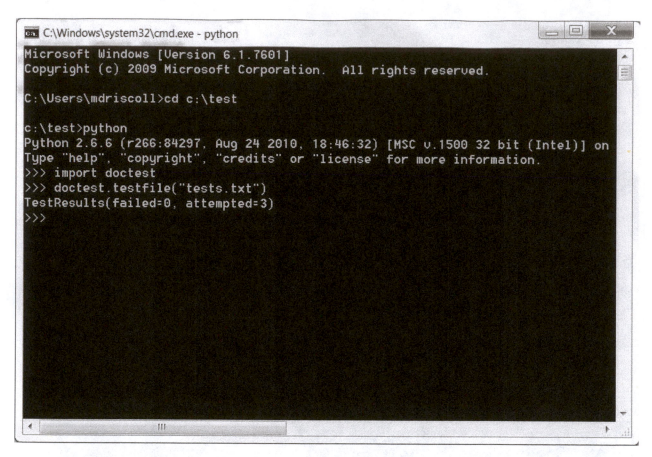

Microsoft Windows [Version 6.1.7601]
Copyright (c) 2009 Microsoft Corporation. All rights reserved.

C:\Users\mdriscoll>cd c:\test

c:\test>python
Python 2.6.6 (r266:84297, Aug 24 2010, 18:46:32) [MSC v.1500 32 bit (Intel)] on
Type "help", "copyright", "credits" or "license" for more information.
>>> import doctest
>>> doctest.testfile("tests.txt")
TestResults(failed=0, attempted=3)
>>>

image

Here we just import **doctest** and call its **testfile** method. Note that you need to also pass the filename or path to the **testfile** function. It will return a **TestResults** object that contains how many tests were attempted and how many failed.

Test Driven Development with unittest

In this section, you will learn about Test Driven Development (TDD) with Python using Python's built-in unittest module. I do want to thank Matt and Aaron for their assistance in showing me how TDD works in the real world. To demonstrate the concepts of TDD, we'll be covering how to score bowling in Python. You may want to use Google to look up the rules for bowling if you don't already know them. Once you know the rules, it's time to write some tests. In case you didn't know, the idea behind Test Driven Development is that you write the tests BEFORE you write the actual code. In this chapter, we will write a test, then some code to pass the test. We will iterate back and forth between writing tests and code until we're done. For this chapter, we'll write just three tests. Let's get started!

The First Test

Our first test will be to test our game object and see if it can calculate the correct total if we roll eleven times and only knock over one pin each time. This should give us a total of eleven.

```python
import unittest

class TestBowling(unittest.TestCase):
    """"""

    def test_all_ones(self):
        """Constructor"""
        game = Game()
        game.roll(11, 1)
        self.assertEqual(game.score, 11)
```

This is a pretty simple test. We create a game object and then call its **roll** method eleven times with a score of one each time. Then we use the **assertEqual** method from the **unittest** module to test if the game object's score is correct (i.e. eleven). The next step is to write the simplest code you can think of to make the test pass. Here's one example:

```python
class Game:
    """"""

    def __init__(self):
        """Constructor"""
        self.score = 0

    def roll(self, numOfRolls, pins):
        """"""
        for roll in numOfRolls:
            self.score += pins
```

For simplicity's sake, you can just copy and paste that into the same file with your test. We'll break them into two files for our next test. Anyway, as you can see, our **Game** class is super simple. All that was needed to pass the test was a score property and a **roll** method that can update it.

Let's run the test and see if it passes! The easiest way to run the tests is to add the following two lines of code to the bottom of the file:

```
1  if __name__ == '__main__':
2      unittest.main()
```

Then just run the Python file via the command line, If you do, you should get something like the following:

```
1  E
2  ----------------------------------------------------------------
3  ERROR: test_all_ones (__main__.TestBowling)
4  Constructor
5  ----------------------------------------------------------------
6  Traceback (most recent call last):
7    File "C:\Users\Mike\Documents\Scripts\Testing\bowling\test_one.py",
8    line 27, in test_all_ones
9      game.roll(11, 1)
10   File "C:\Users\Mike\Documents\Scripts\Testing\bowling\test_one.py",
11   line 15, in roll
12     for roll in numOfRolls:
13 TypeError: 'int' object is not iterable
14
15 ----------------------------------------------------------------
16 Ran 1 test in 0.001s
17
18 FAILED (errors=1)
```

Oops! We've got a mistake in there somewhere. It looks like we're passing an Integer and then trying to iterate over it. That doesn't work! We need to change our Game object's roll method to the following to make it work:

```
1  def roll(self, numOfRolls, pins):
2      """"""
3      for roll in range(numOfRolls):
4          self.score += pins
```

If you run the test now, you should get the following:

```
1    .
2    ----------------------------------------------------------------------
3    Ran 1 test in 0.000s
4
5    OK
```

Note the "." because it's important. That little dot means that one test has run and that it passed. The "OK" at the end clues you into that fact as well. If you study the original output, you'll notice it leads off with an "E" for error and there's no dot! Let's move on to test #2.

The Second Test

For the second test, we'll test what happens when we get a strike. We'll need to change the first test to use a list for the number of pins knocked down in each frame though, so we'll look at both tests here. You'll probably find this to be a fairly common process where you may need to edit a couple of tests due to fundamental changes in what you're testing for. Normally this will only happen at the beginning of your coding and you will get better later on such that you shouldn't need to do this. Since this is my first time doing this, I wasn't thinking far enough ahead. Anyway, let's take a look at the code:

```python
1    from game import Game
2    import unittest
3
4    class TestBowling(unittest.TestCase):
5        """"""
6
7        def test_all_ones(self):
8            """Constructor"""
9            game = Game()
10           pins = [1 for i in range(11)]
11           game.roll(11, pins)
12           self.assertEqual(game.score, 11)
13
14       def test_strike(self):
15           """
16           A strike is 10 + the value of the next two rolls. So in this case
17           the first frame will be 10+5+4 or 19 and the second will be
18           5+4. The total score would be 19+9 or 28.
19           """
20           game = Game()
21           game.roll(11, [10, 5, 4])
```

```
22            self.assertEqual(game.score, 28)
23
24    if __name__ == '__main__':
25        unittest.main()
```

Let's take a look at our first test and how it changed. Yes, we're breaking the rules here a bit when it comes to TDD. Feel free to NOT change the first test and see what breaks. In the **test_all_ones** method, we set the **pins** variable to equal a list comprehension which created a list of eleven ones. Then we passed that to our **game** object's **roll** method along with the number of rolls.

In the second test, we roll a strike in our first roll, a five in our second and a four in our third. Note that we went a head and told it that we were passing in eleven rolls and yet we only pass in three. This means that we need to set the other eight rolls to zeros. Next, we use our trusty **assertEqual** method to check if we get the right total. Finally, note that we're now importing the **Game** class rather than keeping it with the tests. Now we need to implement the code necessary to pass these two tests. Let's take a look at one possible solution:

```
1    class Game:
2        """"""
3
4        def __init__(self):
5            """Constructor"""
6            self.score = 0
7            self.pins = [0 for i in range(11)]
8
9        def roll(self, numOfRolls, pins):
10           """"""
11           x = 0
12           for pin in pins:
13               self.pins[x] = pin
14               x += 1
15           x = 0
16           for roll in range(numOfRolls):
17               if self.pins[x] == 10:
18                   self.score = self.pins[x] + self.pins[x+1] + self.pins[x+2]
19               else:
20                   self.score += self.pins[x]
21               x += 1
22           print(self.score)
```

Right off the bat, you will notice that we have a new class attribute called **self.pins** that holds the default pin list, which is eleven zeroes. Then in our **roll** method, we add the correct scores to the correct position in the self.pins list in the first loop. Then in the second loop, we check to see if the pins knocked down equals ten. If it does, we add it and the next two scores to score. Otherwise, we do what we did before. At the end of the method, we print out the score to check if it's what we expect. At this point, we're ready to code up our final test.

The Third (and Final) Test

Our last test will test for the correct score that would result should someone roll a spare. The test is easy, the solution is slightly more difficult. While we're at it, we're going to refactor the test code a bit. As usual, we will look at the test first.

```python
from game_v2 import Game
import unittest

class TestBowling(unittest.TestCase):
    """"""

    def setUp(self):
        """"""
        self.game = Game()

    def test_all_ones(self):
        """
        If you don't get a strike or a spare, then you just add up the
        face value of the frame. In this case, each frame is worth
        one point, so the total is eleven.
        """
        pins = [1 for i in range(11)]
        self.game.roll(11, pins)
        self.assertEqual(self.game.score, 11)

    def test_spare(self):
        """
        A spare is worth 10, plus the value of your next roll. So in this
        case, the first frame will be 5+5+5 or 15 and the second will be
        5+4 or 9. The total is 15+9, which equals 24,
        """
        self.game.roll(11, [5, 5, 5, 4])
        self.assertEqual(self.game.score, 24)

    def test_strike(self):
        """
```

```
32          A strike is 10 + the value of the next two rolls. So in this case
33          the first frame will be 10+5+4 or 19 and the second will be
34          5+4. The total score would be 19+9 or 28.
35          """
36          self.game.roll(11, [10, 5, 4])
37          self.assertEqual(self.game.score, 28)
38
39 if __name__ == '__main__':
40     unittest.main()
```

First off, we added a **setUp** method that will create a self.game object for us for each test. If we were accessing a database or something like that, we would probably have a tear down method too for closing connections or files or that sort of thing. These are run at the beginning and end of each test respectively should they exist. The **test_all_ones** and **test_strike** tests are basically the same except that they are using "self.game" now. The only the new test is **test_spare**. The docstring explains how spares work and the code is just two lines. Yes, you can figure this out. Let's look at the code we'll need to pass these tests:

```
1  # game_v2.py
2
3  class Game:
4      """"""
5
6      def __init__(self):
7          """Constructor"""
8          self.score = 0
9          self.pins = [0 for i in range(11)]
10
11     def roll(self, numOfRolls, pins):
12         """"""
13         x = 0
14         for pin in pins:
15             self.pins[x] = pin
16             x += 1
17         x = 0
18         spare_begin = 0
19         spare_end = 2
20         for roll in range(numOfRolls):
21             spare = sum(self.pins[spare_begin:spare_end])
22             if self.pins[x] == 10:
23                 self.score = self.pins[x] + self.pins[x+1] + self.pins[x+2]
24             elif spare == 10:
```

```
25              self.score = spare + self.pins[x+2]
26                  x += 1
27          else:
28              self.score += self.pins[x]
29          x += 1
30          if x == 11:
31              break
32          spare_begin += 2
33          spare_end += 2
34      print(self.score)
```

For this part of the puzzle, we add to our conditional statement in our loop. To calculate the spare's value, we use the **spare_begin** and **spare_end** list positions to get the right values from our list and then we sum them up. That's what the **spare** variable is for. That may be better placed in the elif, but I'll leave that for the reader to experiment with. Technically, that's just the first half of the spare score. The second half are the next two rolls, which is what you'll find in the calculation in the elif portion of the current code. The rest of the code is the same.

Other Notes

As you may have guessed, there is a whole lot more to the unittest module than what is covered here. There are lots of other asserts you can use to test results with. You can skip tests, run the tests from the command line, use a TestLoader to create a test suite and much, much more. Be sure to read the full documentation[14] when you get the chance as this tutorial barely scratches the surface of this library.

Wrapping Up

At this point, you should be able to understand how to use the doctest and unittest modules effectively in your own code. You should go and read the Python documentation about these two modules as there is additional information about other options and functionality that you might find useful. You also know a little about how to use the concepts of Test Driven Development when writing your own scripts.

---

[14]http://docs.python.org/2/library/unittest.html

Part IV - Tips, Tricks and Tutorials

In Part IV, you will learn how to install 3rd party packages from the Python Package Index (PyPI). You will learn a bit about **easy_install**, **pip** and **setup.py** and how to use these tools to install the packages. This is just the first chapter though. Here's a listing of the packages you will learn about:

- configobj - working with Config files in a more "Pythonic" way.
- lxml - a package for working with XML
- pylint / pyflakes - Python code analyzers
- requests - a Python-friendly version of urllib
- SQLAlchemy - an Object Relational Mapper for Python
- virtualenv - learn about virtual environments in Python

The reason we will be looking at **configobj** is because I think it works better than ConfigParser, the module that comes with Python. The configobj package has an interface that is just more intuitive and powerful than ConfigParser. In the next chapter, we'll look at the **lxml** module and learn a couple of new ways to read, parse and create XML. In the fourth chapter, we will look at **pylint** and **pyflakes**, which are great for code analysis. They can look at your module and check for errors. pylint can also be used to help you get your code to conform to PEP8, the Python style guide.

The **requests** package is great replacement for the **urllib** module. Its interface is simpler and the documentation is quite good. SQLAlchemy is the premier Object Relational Mapper for Python. It allows you to write SQL queries, tables, etc in Python code. One of its best features is that if you need to switch database backends, you won't have to change your code very much to continue working with said database. For the last chapter, we'll look at **virtualenv**, a neat module that allows you to create mini-virtual environments that you can write your code in. These virtual environments are especially handy for testing out new modules or just new releases of modules before you apply them to your Python core installation.

image

Chapter 29 - Installing Modules

When you're first starting out as a Python programmer, you don't think about how you might need to install an external package or module. But when that need appears, you'll want to know how to in a hurry! Python packages can be found all over the internet. Most of the popular ones can be found on the Python Package Index (PyPI). You will also find a lot of Python packages on github, bitbucket, and Google code. In this article, we will be covering the following methods of installing Python packages:

- Install from source
- easy_install
- pip
- Other ways to install packages

Installing from Source

Installing from source is a great skill to have. There are easier ways, which we'll be getting to later on in the article. However, there are some packages that you have to install from source. For example, to use **easy_install**, you will need to first install **setuptools**. To do that, you will want to download the tar or zip file from the Python Package Index and extract it somewhere on your system. Then look for the **setup.py** file. Open up a terminal session and change directories to the folder that contains the setup file. Then run the following command:

```
1   python setup.py install
```

If Python isn't on your system path, you will receive an error message stating that the *python* command wasn't found or is an unknown application. You can call this command by using the full path to Python instead. Here's how you might do it if you were on Windows:

```
1   c:\python34\python.exe setup.py install
```

This method is especially handy if you have multiple versions of Python installed and you need to install the package to different ones. All you need to do is type the full path to the right Python version and install the package against it.

Some packages contain C code, such as C header files that will need to be compiled for the package to install correctly. On Linux, you will normally already have a C/C++ compiler installed and you can get the package installed with minimal headaches. On Windows, you will need to have the correct version of Visual Studio installed to compile the package correctly. Some people say you can use MingW too, but I have yet to find a way to make that work. If the package has a Windows installer already pre-made, use it. Then you don't have to mess with compiling at all.

Using easy_install

Once you have **setuptools** installed, you can use **easy_install**. You can find it installed in your Python installation's **Scripts** folder. Be sure to add the Scripts folder to your system path so you can call easy_install on the command line without specifying its full path. Try running the following command to learn about all of easy_install's options:

```
1   easy_install -h
```

When you want to install a package with easy_install, all you have to do is this:

```
1   easy_install package_name
```

easy_install will attempt to download the package from PyPI, compile it (if necessary) and install it. If you go into your Python's **site-packages** directory, you will find a file named **easy-install.pth** that will contain an entry for all packages installed with easy_install. This file is used by Python to help in importing the module or package.

You can also tell easy_install to install from a URL or from a path on your computer. It can also install packages directly from a tar file. You can use easy_install to upgrade a package by using -**upgrade** (or **-U**). Finally, you can use easy_install to install Python eggs. You can find egg files on PyPI and other locations. An egg is basically a special zip file. In fact, if you change the extension to .zip, you can unzip the egg file.

Here are some examples:

```
1   easy_install -U SQLAlchemy
2   easy_install http://example.com/path/to/MyPackage-1.2.3.tgz
3   easy_install /path/to/downloaded/package
```

There are some issues with easy_install. It will try to install a package before it's finished downloading. There is no way to uninstall a package using easy_install. You will have to delete the package yourself and update the easy-install.pth file by removing the entry to the package. For these reasons and others, there was movement in the Python community to create something different, which caused **pip** to be born.

Using pip

The pip program actually comes with Python 3.4. If you have an older version of Python, then you will need to install pip manually. Installing pip is a little bit different than what we have previously discussed. You still go to PyPI, but instead of downloading the package and running its setup.py script, you will be asked to download a single script called **get-pip.py**. Then you will need to execute it by doing the following:

```
1  python get-pip.py
```

This will install **setuptools** or an alternative to setuptools called **distribute** if one of them is not already installed. It will also install pip. pip works with CPython versions 2.6, 2.7, 3.1, 3.2, 3.3, 3.4 and also pypy. You can use pip to install anything that easy_install can install, but the invocation is a bit different. To install a package, do the following:

```
1  pip install package_name
```

To upgrade a package, you would do this:

```
1  pip install -U PackageName
```

You may want to call **pip -h** to get a full listing of everything pip can do. One thing that pip can install that easy_install cannot is the Python **wheel** format. A wheel is a ZIP-format archive with a specially formatted filename and the **.whl** extension. You can also install wheels via its own command line utility. On the other hand, pip cannot install an egg. If you need to install an egg, you will want to use easy_install.

A Note on Dependencies

One of the many benefits of using **easy_install** and **pip** is that if the package has dependencies specified in their **setup.py** script, both **easy_install** and **pip** will attempt to download and install them too. This can alleviate a lot of frustration when you're trying new packages and you didn't realize that package A depended on Packages B, C and D. With **easy_install** or **pip**, you don't need to worry about that any more.

Wrapping Up

At this point, you should be able to install just about any package that you need, assuming the package supports your version of Python. There are a lot of tools available to the Python programmer. While packaging in Python is a bit confusing right now, once you know how to use the proper tools, you can usually get what you want installed or packaged up. We will be looking more at creating our own packages, eggs and wheels in Part V.

Chapter 30 - ConfigObj

Python comes with a handy module called **ConfigParser**. It's good for creating and reading configuration files (aka INI files). However, Michael Foord (author of IronPython in Action) and Nicola Larosa decided to write their own configuration module called **ConfigObj**. In many ways, it is an improvement over the standard library's module. For example, it will return a dictionary-like object when it reads a config file. ConfigObj can also understand some Python types. Another neat feature is that you can create a configuration spec that ConfigObj will use to validate the config file.

Getting Started

First of all, you need to go and get ConfigObj. This is a good time to use your knowledge from the last chapter on installing packages. Here is how you would get ConfigObj with pip:

```
1  pip install configobj
```

Once you have it installed, we can move on. To start off, open a text editor and create a file with some contents like this:

```
1  product = Sony PS3
2  accessories = controller, eye, memory stick
3  # This is a comment that will be ignored
4  retail_price = $400
```

Save it where ever you like. I'm going to call mine *config.ini*. Now let's see how ConfigObj can be used to extract that information:

```
1  >>> from configobj import ConfigObj
2  >>> config = ConfigObj(r"path to config.ini")
3  >>> config["product"]
4  'Sony PS3'
5  >>> config["accessories"]
6  ['controller', 'eye', 'memory stick']
7  >>> type(config["accessories"])
8  <type 'list'>
```

As you can see, ConfigObj uses Python's **dict** API to access the information it has extracted. All you had to do to get ConfigObj to parse the file was to pass the file's path to ConfigObj. Now, if the information had been under a section (i.e. [Sony]), then you would have had to do pre-pend everything with ["Sony"], like this: **config["Sony"]["product"]**. Also take note that the *accessories* section was returned as a list of strings. ConfigObj will take any valid line with a comma-separated list and return it as a Python list. You can also create multi-line strings in the config file as long as you enclose them with triple single or double quotes.

If you need to create a sub-section in the file, then use extra square brackets. For example, **[Sony]** is the top section, **[[Playstation]]** is the sub-section and **[[[PS3]]]** is the sub-section of the sub-section. You can create sub-sections up to any depth. For more information on the formatting of the file, I recommend reading ConfigObj's documentation.

Now we'll do the reverse and create the config file programmatically.

```
1   import configobj
2
3   def createConfig(path):
4       config = configobj.ConfigObj()
5       config.filename = path
6       config["Sony"] = {}
7       config["Sony"]["product"] = "Sony PS3"
8       config["Sony"]["accessories"] = ['controller', 'eye', 'memory stick']
9       config["Sony"]["retail price"] = "$400"
10      config.write()
11
12  if __name__ == "__main__":
13      createConfig("config.ini")
```

As you can see, all it took was 13 lines of code. In the code above, we create a function and pass it the path for our config file. Then we create a ConfigObj object and set its filename property. To create the section, we create an empty dict with the name "Sony". Then we pre-pend each line of the sections contents in the same way. Finally, we call our config object's write method to write the data to the file.

Using a configspec

ConfigObj also provides a way to validate your configuration files using a **configspec**. When I mentioned that I was going to write on this topic, Steven Sproat (creator of Whyteboard) volunteered his configspec code as an example. I took his specification and used it to create a default config file. In this example, we use Foord's validate module to do the validation. I don't think it's included in your ConfigObj download, so you may need to download it as well. Now, let's take a look at the code:

```
1   import configobj, validate
2
3   cfg = """
4   bmp_select_transparent = boolean(default=False)
5   canvas_border = integer(min=10, max=35, default=15)
6   colour1 = list(min=3, max=3, default=list('280', '0', '0'))
7   colour2 = list(min=3, max=3, default=list('255', '255', '0'))
8   colour3 = list(min=3, max=3, default=list('0', '255', '0'))
9   colour4 = list(min=3, max=3, default=list('255', '0', '0'))
10  colour5 = list(min=3, max=3, default=list('0', '0', '255'))
11  colour6 = list(min=3, max=3, default=list('160', '32', '240'))
12  colour7 = list(min=3, max=3, default=list('0', '255', '255'))
13  colour8 = list(min=3, max=3, default=list('255', '165', '0'))
14  colour9 = list(min=3, max=3, default=list('211', '211', '211'))
15  convert_quality = option('highest', 'high', 'normal', default='normal')
16  default_font = string
17  default_width = integer(min=1, max=12000, default=640)
18  default_height = integer(min=1, max=12000, default=480)
19  imagemagick_path = string
20  handle_size = integer(min=3, max=15, default=6)
21  language = option('English', 'English (United Kingdom)', 'Russian',
22                    'Hindi', default='English')
23  print_title = boolean(default=True)
24  statusbar = boolean(default=True)
25  toolbar = boolean(default=True)
26  toolbox = option('icon', 'text', default='icon')
27  undo_sheets = integer(min=5, max=50, default=10)
28  """
29
30  def createConfig(path):
31      """
32      Create a config file using a configspec
33      and validate it against a Validator object
34      """
35      spec = cfg.split("\n")
36      config = configobj.ConfigObj(path, configspec=spec)
37      validator = validate.Validator()
38      config.validate(validator, copy=True)
39      config.filename = path
40      config.write()
41
42  if __name__ == "__main__":
```

```
43      createConfig("config.ini")
```

The configspec allows the programmer the ability to specify what **types** are returned for each line in the configuration file. It also can be used to set a default value and a **min** and **max** values (among other things). If you run the code above, you will see a *config.ini* file generated in the current working directory that has just the default values. If the programmer didn't specify a default, then that line isn't even added to the configuration.

Let's take a closer look at what's going on just to make sure you understand. In the **createConfig** function, we create a ConfigObj instance by passing in the file path and setting the configspec. Note that the configspec can also be a normal text file or a python file rather than the string that is in this example. Next, we create a Validator object. Normal usage is to just call config.validate(validator), but in this code I set the copy argument to True so that I could create a file. Otherwise, all it would do is validate that the file I passed in fit the configspec's rules. Finally I set the config's filename and write the data out.

Wrapping Up

Now you know just enough to get you started on the ins and outs of ConfigObj. I hope you'll find it as helpful as I have. Be sure to go to the module's documentation and read more about what it and **validate** can do.

Chapter 31 - Parsing XML with lxml

In Part I, we looked at some of Python's built-in XML parsers. In this chapter, we will look at the fun third-party package, **lxml** from codespeak. It uses the ElementTree API, among other things. The lxml package has XPath and XSLT support, includes an API for SAX and a C-level API for compatibility with C/Pyrex modules. Here is what we will cover:

- How to Parse XML with lxml
- A Refactoring example
- How to Parse XML with lxml.objectify
- How to Create XML with lxml.objectify

For this chapter, we will use the examples from the **minidom** parsing example and see how to parse those with lxml. Here's an XML example from a program that was written for keeping track of appointments:

```xml
 1  <?xml version="1.0" ?>
 2  <zAppointments reminder="15">
 3      <appointment>
 4          <begin>1181251680</begin>
 5          <uid>040000008200E000</uid>
 6          <alarmTime>1181572063</alarmTime>
 7          <state></state>
 8          <location></location>
 9          <duration>1800</duration>
10          <subject>Bring pizza home</subject>
11      </appointment>
12      <appointment>
13          <begin>1234360800</begin>
14          <duration>1800</duration>
15          <subject>Check MS Office website for updates</subject>
16          <location></location>
17          <uid>604f4792-eb89-478b-a14f-dd34d3cc6c21-1234360800</uid>
18          <state>dismissed</state>
19      </appointment>
20  </zAppointments>
```

Let's learn how to parse this with lxml!

Parsing XML with lxml

The XML above shows two appointments. The beginning time is in seconds since the epoch; the uid is generated based on a hash of the beginning time and a key; the alarm time is the number of seconds since the epoch, but should be less than the beginning time; and the state is whether or not the appointment has been snoozed, dismissed or not. The rest of the XML is pretty self-explanatory. Now let's see how to parse it.

```
1   from lxml import etree
2
3   def parseXML(xmlFile):
4       """
5       Parse the xml
6       """
7       with open(xmlFile) as fobj:
8           xml = fobj.read()
9
10      root = etree.fromstring(xml)
11
12      for appt in root.getchildren():
13          for elem in appt.getchildren():
14              if not elem.text:
15                  text = "None"
16              else:
17                  text = elem.text
18              print(elem.tag + " => " + text)
19
20  if __name__ == "__main__":
21      parseXML("example.xml")
```

First off, we import the needed modules, namely the **etree** module from the lxml package and the **StringIO** function from the built-in **StringIO** module. Our **parseXML** function accepts one argument: the path to the XML file in question. We open the file, read it and close it. Now comes the fun part! We use etree's parse function to parse the XML code that is returned from the StringIO module. For reasons I don't completely understand, the parse function requires a file-like object.

Anyway, next we iterate over the context (i.e. the **lxml.etree.iterparse object**) and extract the tag elements. We add the conditional if statement to replace the empty fields with the word "None" to make the output a little clearer. And that's it.

Parsing the Book Example

Well, the result of that example was kind of boring. Most of the time, you want to save the data you extract and do something with it, not just print it out to stdout. So for our next example, we'll create a data structure to contain the results. Our data structure for this example will be a list of dicts. We'll use the MSDN book example here from the earlier chapter again. Save the following XML as *example.xml*

```
1  <?xml version="1.0"?>
2  <catalog>
3     <book id="bk101">
4        <author>Gambardella, Matthew</author>
5        <title>XML Developer's Guide</title>
6        <genre>Computer</genre>
7        <price>44.95</price>
8        <publish_date>2000-10-01</publish_date>
9        <description>An in-depth look at creating applications
10       with XML.</description>
11    </book>
12    <book id="bk102">
13       <author>Ralls, Kim</author>
14       <title>Midnight Rain</title>
15       <genre>Fantasy</genre>
16       <price>5.95</price>
17       <publish_date>2000-12-16</publish_date>
18       <description>A former architect battles corporate zombies,
19       an evil sorceress, and her own childhood to become queen
20       of the world.</description>
21    </book>
22    <book id="bk103">
23       <author>Corets, Eva</author>
24       <title>Maeve Ascendant</title>
25       <genre>Fantasy</genre>
26       <price>5.95</price>
27       <publish_date>2000-11-17</publish_date>
28       <description>After the collapse of a nanotechnology
29       society in England, the young survivors lay the
30       foundation for a new society.</description>
31    </book>
32  </catalog>
```

Now let's parse this XML and put it in our data structure!

```
1   from lxml import etree
2
3   def parseBookXML(xmlFile):
4
5       with open(xmlFile) as fobj:
6           xml = fobj.read()
7
8       root = etree.fromstring(xml)
9
10      book_dict = {}
11      books = []
12      for book in root.getchildren():
13          for elem in book.getchildren():
14              if not elem.text:
15                  text = "None"
16              else:
17                  text = elem.text
18              print(elem.tag + " => " + text)
19              book_dict[elem.tag] = text
20          if book.tag == "book":
21              books.append(book_dict)
22              book_dict = {}
23      return books
24
25  if __name__ == "__main__":
26      parseBookXML("books.xml")
```

This example is pretty similar to our last one, so we'll just focus on the differences present here. Right before we start iterating over the context, we create an empty dictionary object and an empty list. Then inside the loop, we create our dictionary like this:

```
1   book_dict[elem.tag] = text
```

The text is either **elem.text** or **None**. Finally, if the tag happens to be **book**, then we're at the end of a book section and need to add the dict to our list as well as reset the dict for the next book. As you can see, that is exactly what we have done. A more realistic example would be to put the extracted data into a **Book** class. I have done the latter with json feeds before.

Now we're ready to learn how to parse XML with **lxml.objectify**!

Parsing XML with lxml.objectify

The lxml module has a module called **objectify** that can turn XML documents into Python objects. I find "objectified" XML documents very easy to work with and I hope you will too. You may need to jump through a hoop or two to install it as **pip** doesn't work with lxml on Windows. Be sure to go to the Python Package index and look for a version that's been made for your version of Python. Also note that the latest pre-built installer for lxml only supports Python 3.2 (at the time of writing), so if you have a newer version of Python, you may have some difficulty getting lxml installed for your version.

Anyway, once you have it installed, we can start going over this wonderful piece of XML again:

```
1   <?xml version="1.0" ?>
2   <zAppointments reminder="15">
3       <appointment>
4           <begin>1181251680</begin>
5           <uid>040000008200E000</uid>
6           <alarmTime>1181572063</alarmTime>
7           <state></state>
8           <location></location>
9           <duration>1800</duration>
10          <subject>Bring pizza home</subject>
11      </appointment>
12      <appointment>
13          <begin>1234360800</begin>
14          <duration>1800</duration>
15          <subject>Check MS Office website for updates</subject>
16          <location></location>
17          <uid>604f4792-eb89-478b-a14f-dd34d3cc6c21-1234360800</uid>
18          <state>dismissed</state>
19      </appointment>
20  </zAppointments>
```

Now we need to write some code that can parse and modify the XML. Let's take a look at this little demo that shows a bunch of the neat abilities that objectify provides.

```
1   from lxml import etree, objectify
2
3   def parseXML(xmlFile):
4       """Parse the XML file"""
5       with open(xmlFile) as f:
6           xml = f.read()
7
8       root = objectify.fromstring(xml)
9
10      # returns attributes in element node as dict
11      attrib = root.attrib
```

```
12
13      # how to extract element data
14      begin = root.appointment.begin
15      uid = root.appointment.uid
16
17      # loop over elements and print their tags and text
18      for appt in root.getchildren():
19          for e in appt.getchildren():
20              print("%s => %s" % (e.tag, e.text))
21          print()
22
23      # how to change an element's text
24      root.appointment.begin = "something else"
25      print(root.appointment.begin)
26
27      # how to add a new element
28      root.appointment.new_element = "new data"
29
30      # remove the py:pytype stuff
31      objectify.deannotate(root)
32      etree.cleanup_namespaces(root)
33      obj_xml = etree.tostring(root, pretty_print=True)
34      print(obj_xml)
35
36      # save your xml
37      with open("new.xml", "w") as f:
38          f.write(obj_xml)
39
40  if __name__ == "__main__":
41      f = r'path\to\sample.xml'
42      parseXML(f)
```

The code is pretty well commented, but we'll spend a little time going over it anyway. First we pass it our sample XML file and **objectify** it. If you want to get access to a tag's attributes, use the **attrib** property. It will return a dictionary of the attributes of the tag. To get to sub-tag elements, you just use dot notation. As you can see, to get to the **begin** tag's value, we can just do something like this:

```
1   begin = root.appointment.begin
```

One thing to be aware of is if the value happens to have leading zeroes, the returned value may have them truncated. If that is important to you, then you should use the following syntax instead:

```
1  begin = root.appointment.begin.text
```

If you need to iterate over the children elements, you can use the **iterchildren** method. You may have to use a nested for loop structure to get everything. Changing an element's value is as simple as just assigning it a new value.

```
1  root.appointment.new_element = "new data"
```

Now we're ready to learn how to create XML using **lxml.objectify**.

Creating XML with lxml.objectify

The lxml.objectify sub-package is extremely handy for parsing and creating XML. In this section, we will show how to create XML using the lxml.objectify module. We'll start with some simple XML and then try to replicate it. Let's get started!

We will continue using the following XML for our example:

```
1  <?xml version="1.0" ?>
2  <zAppointments reminder="15">
3      <appointment>
4          <begin>1181251680</begin>
5          <uid>040000008200E000</uid>
6          <alarmTime>1181572063</alarmTime>
7          <state></state>
8          <location></location>
9          <duration>1800</duration>
10         <subject>Bring pizza home</subject>
11     </appointment>
12     <appointment>
13         <begin>1234360800</begin>
14         <duration>1800</duration>
15         <subject>Check MS Office website for updates</subject>
16         <location></location>
17         <uid>604f4792-eb89-478b-a14f-dd34d3cc6c21-1234360800</uid>
18         <state>dismissed</state>
19     </appointment>
20  </zAppointments>
```

Let's see how we can use lxml.objectify to recreate this XML:

```python
 1  from lxml import etree, objectify
 2
 3  def create_appt(data):
 4      """
 5      Create an appointment XML element
 6      """
 7      appt = objectify.Element("appointment")
 8      appt.begin = data["begin"]
 9      appt.uid = data["uid"]
10      appt.alarmTime = data["alarmTime"]
11      appt.state = data["state"]
12      appt.location = data["location"]
13      appt.duration = data["duration"]
14      appt.subject = data["subject"]
15      return appt
16
17  def create_xml():
18      """
19      Create an XML file
20      """
21
22      xml = '''<?xml version="1.0" encoding="UTF-8"?>
23      <zAppointments>
24      </zAppointments>
25      '''
26
27      root = objectify.fromstring(xml)
28      root.set("reminder", "15")
29
30      appt = create_appt({"begin":1181251680,
31                          "uid":"040000008200E000",
32                          "alarmTime":1181572063,
33                          "state":"",
34                          "location":"",
35                          "duration":1800,
36                          "subject":"Bring pizza home"}
37                         )
38      root.append(appt)
39
40      uid = "604f4792-eb89-478b-a14f-dd34d3cc6c21-1234360800"
41      appt = create_appt({"begin":1234360800,
42                          "uid":uid,
```

```
43                              "alarmTime":1181572063,
44                              "state":"dismissed",
45                              "location":"",
46                              "duration":1800,
47                              "subject":"Check MS Office website for updates"}
48                          )
49      root.append(appt)
50
51      # remove lxml annotation
52      objectify.deannotate(root)
53      etree.cleanup_namespaces(root)
54
55      # create the xml string
56      obj_xml = etree.tostring(root,
57                              pretty_print=True,
58                              xml_declaration=True)
59
60      try:
61          with open("example.xml", "wb") as xml_writer:
62              xml_writer.write(obj_xml)
63      except IOError:
64          pass
65
66  if __name__ == "__main__":
67      create_xml()
```

Let's break this down a bit. We will start with the **create_xml** function. In it we create an XML root object using the objectify module's **fromstring** function. The root object will contain **zAppointment** as its tag. We set the root's **reminder** attribute and then we call our **create_appt** function using a dictionary for its argument. In the **create_appt** function, we create an instance of an Element (technically, it's an **ObjectifiedElement**) that we assign to our **appt** variable. Here we use **dotnotation** to create the tags for this element. Finally we return the **appt** element back and append it to our **root** object. We repeat the process for the second appointment instance.

The next section of the **create_xml** function will remove the lxml annotation. If you do not do this, your XML will end up looking like the following:

```
1   <?xml version="1.0" ?>
2   <zAppointments py:pytype="TREE" reminder="15">
3       <appointment py:pytype="TREE">
4           <begin py:pytype="int">1181251680</begin>
5           <uid py:pytype="str">040000008200E000</uid>
6           <alarmTime py:pytype="int">1181572063</alarmTime>
7           <state py:pytype="str"/>
8           <location py:pytype="str"/>
9           <duration py:pytype="int">1800</duration>
10          <subject py:pytype="str">Bring pizza home</subject>
11      </appointment><appointment py:pytype="TREE">
12          <begin py:pytype="int">1234360800</begin>
13          <uid py:pytype="str">604f4792-eb89-478b-a14f-dd34d3cc6c21-1234360800</ui\
14  d>
15          <alarmTime py:pytype="int">1181572063</alarmTime>
16          <state py:pytype="str">dismissed</state>
17          <location py:pytype="str"/>
18          <duration py:pytype="int">1800</duration>
19          <subject py:pytype="str">Check MS Office website for updates</subject>
20      </appointment>
21  </zAppointments>
```

To remove all that unwanted annotation, we call the following two functions:

```
1   objectify.deannotate(root)
2   etree.cleanup_namespaces(root)
```

The last piece of the puzzle is to get lxml to generate the XML itself. Here we use lxml's **etree** module to do the hard work:

```
1   obj_xml = etree.tostring(root,
2                           pretty_print=True,
3                           xml_declaration=True)
```

The tostring function will return a nice string of the XML and if you set **pretty_print** to True, it will usually return the XML in a nice format too. The **xml_declaration** keyword argument tells the etree module whether or not to include the first declaration line (i.e. **<?xml version="1.0" ?>**.

Wrapping Up

Now you know how to use lxml's etree and objectify modules to parse XML. You also know how to use objectify to create XML. Knowing how to use more than one module to accomplish the same task can be valuable in seeing how to approach the same problem from different angles. It will also help you choose the tool that you're most comfortable with.

Chapter 32 - Python Code Analysis

Python code analysis can be a heavy subject, but it can be very helpful in making your programs better. There are several Python code analyzers that you can use to check your code and see if they conform to standards. pylint is probably the most popular. It's very configurable, customizable and pluggable too. It also checks your code to see if it conforms to PEP8, the official style guide of Python Core and it looks for programming errors too.

Note that pylint checks your code against most, but not all of PEP8's standards. We will spend a little time learning about another code analysis package that is called **pyflakes**.

Getting Started with pylint

The pylint package isn't included with Python, so you will need to go to the Python Package Index (PyPI) or the package's website to download it. You can use the following command to do all the work for you:

```
1   pip install pylint
```

If everything goes as planned, you should now have **pylint** installed and we'll be ready to continue.

Analyzing Your Code

Once pylint is installed, you can run it on the command line without any arguments to see what options it accepts. If that doesn't work, you can type out the full path like this:

```
1   c:\Python34\Scripts\pylint
```

Now we need some code to analyze. Here's a piece of code that has four errors in it. Save this to a file named *crummy_code.py*:

```
1   import sys
2
3   class CarClass:
4       """"""
5
6       def __init__(self, color, make, model, year):
7           """Constructor"""
8           self.color = color
9           self.make = make
10          self.model = model
11          self.year = year
12
13          if "Windows" in platform.platform():
14              print("You're using Windows!")
15
16          self.weight = self.getWeight(1, 2, 3)
17
18      def getWeight(this):
19          """"""
20          return "2000 lbs"
```

Can you spot the errors without running the code? Let's see if pylint can find the issues!

```
1   pylint crummy_code.py
```

When you run this command, you will see a lot of output sent to your screen. Here's a partial example:

```
1   c:\py101>c:\Python34\Scripts\pylint crummy_code.py
2   No config file found, using default configuration
3   ************ Module crummy_code
4   C:  2, 0: Trailing whitespace (trailing-whitespace)
5   C:  5, 0: Trailing whitespace (trailing-whitespace)
6   C: 12, 0: Trailing whitespace (trailing-whitespace)
7   C: 15, 0: Trailing whitespace (trailing-whitespace)
8   C: 17, 0: Trailing whitespace (trailing-whitespace)
9   C:  1, 0: Missing module docstring (missing-docstring)
10  C:  3, 0: Empty class docstring (empty-docstring)
11  C:  3, 0: Old-style class defined. (old-style-class)
12  E: 13,24: Undefined variable 'platform' (undefined-variable)
13  E: 16,36: Too many positional arguments for function call (too-many-function-arg\
14  s)
```

```
15  C: 18, 4: Invalid method name "getWeight" (invalid-name)
16  C: 18, 4: Empty method docstring (empty-docstring)
17  E: 18, 4: Method should have "self" as first argument (no-self-argument)
18  R: 18, 4: Method could be a function (no-self-use)
19  R:  3, 0: Too few public methods (1/2) (too-few-public-methods)
20  W:  1, 0: Unused import sys (unused-import)
```

Let's take a moment to break this down a bit. First we need to figure out what the letters designate: C is for convention, R is refactor, W is warning and E is error. pylint found 3 errors, 4 convention issues, 2 lines that might be worth refactoring and 1 warning. The 3 errors plus the warning were what I was looking for. We should try to make this crummy code better and reduce the number of issues. We'll fix the imports and change the getWeight function to get_weight since camelCase isn't allowed for method names. We also need to fix the call to get_weight so it passes the right number of arguments and fix it so it has "self" as the first argument. Here's the new code:

```python
1   # crummy_code_fixed.py
2   import platform
3
4   class CarClass:
5       """ """
6
7       def __init__(self, color, make, model, year):
8           """Constructor"""
9           self.color = color
10          self.make = make
11          self.model = model
12          self.year = year
13
14          if "Windows" in platform.platform():
15              print("You're using Windows!")
16
17          self.weight = self.get_weight(3)
18
19      def get_weight(self, this):
20          """ """
21          return "2000 lbs"
```

Let's run this new code against pylint and see how much we've improved the results. For brevity, we'll just show the first section again:

```
1  c:\py101>c:\Python34\Scripts\pylint crummy_code_fixed.py
2  No config file found, using default configuration
3  ************* Module crummy_code_fixed
4  C: 1,0: Missing docstring
5  C: 4,0:CarClass: Empty docstring
6  C: 21,4:CarClass.get_weight: Empty docstring
7  W: 21,25:CarClass.get_weight: Unused argument 'this'
8  R: 21,4:CarClass.get_weight: Method could be a function
9  R: 4,0:CarClass: Too few public methods (1/2)
```

That helped a lot! If we added docstrings, we could halve the number of issues. Now we're ready to take a look at pyflakes!

Getting Started with pyflakes

The **pyflakes** project is a part of something known as the Divmod Project. Pyflakes doesn't actually execute the code it checks much like pylint doesn't execute the code it analyzes. You can install pyflakes using pip, easy_install or from source.

We will start by running pyflakes against the original version of the same piece of code that we used with pylint. Here it is again:

```python
1  import sys
2
3  class CarClass:
4      """"""
5
6      def __init__(self, color, make, model, year):
7          """Constructor"""
8          self.color = color
9          self.make = make
10         self.model = model
11         self.year = year
12
13         if "Windows" in platform.platform():
14             print("You're using Windows!")
15
16         self.weight = self.getWeight(1, 2, 3)
17
18     def getWeight(this):
19         """"""
20         return "2000 lbs"
```

As was noted in the previous section, this silly piece of code has 4 issues, 3 of which would stop the program from running. Let's see what pyflakes can find! Try running the following command and you'll see the following output:

```
1   c:\py101>c:\Python34\Scripts\pyflakes.exe crummy_code.py
2   crummy_code.py:1: 'sys' imported but unused
3   crummy_code.py:13: undefined name 'platform'
```

While pyflakes was super fast at returning this output, it didn't find all the errors. The **getWeight** method call is passing too many arguments and the **getWeight** method itself is defined incorrectly as it doesn't have a **self** argument. Well, you can actually call the first argument anything you want, but by convention it's usually called **self**. If you fixed your code according to what pyflakes told you, your code still wouldn't work.

Wrapping Up

The next step would be to try running pylint and pyflakes against some of your own code or against a Python package like SQLAlchemy and seeing what you get for output. You can learn a lot about your own code using these tools. pylint is integrated with many popular Python IDEs, such as Wingware, Editra, and PyDev. You may find some of the warnings from pylint to be annoying or not even really applicable. There are ways to suppress such things as deprecation warnings through command line options. Or you can use the **-generate-rcfile** to create an example config file that will help you control pylint. Note that pylint and pyflakes does not import your code, so you don't have to worry about undesirable side effects.

Chapter 33 - The requests package

The **requests** package is a more Pythonic replacement for Python's own **urllib**. You will find that requests package's API is quite a bit simpler to work with. You can install the requests library by using pip or easy_install or from source.

Using requests

Let's take a look at a few examples of how to use the requests package. We will use a series of small code snippets to help explain how to use this library.

```
1  >>> r = requests.get("http://www.google.com")
```

This example returns a **Response** object. You can use the Response object's methods to learn a lot about how you can use requests. Let's use Python's **dir** function to find out what methods we have available:

```
1  >>> dir(r)
2  ['__attrs__', '__bool__', '__class__', '__delattr__', '__dict__',
3  '__dir__', '__doc__', '__eq__', '__format__', '__ge__', '__getattribute__',
4  '__getstate__', '__gt__', '__hash__', '__init__', '__iter__', '__le__', '__lt__',
5  '__module__', '__ne__', '__new__', '__nonzero__', '__reduce__', '__reduce_ex__',
6  '__repr__', '__setattr__', '__setstate__', '__sizeof__', '__str__', '__subclassh\
7  ook__',
8  '__weakref__', '_content', '_content_consumed', 'apparent_encoding', 'close',
9  'connection', 'content', 'cookies', 'elapsed', 'encoding', 'headers', 'history',
10 'iter_content', 'iter_lines', 'json', 'links', 'ok', 'raise_for_status', 'raw',
11 'reason', 'request', 'status_code', 'text', 'url']
```

If you run the following method, you can see the web page's source code:

```
1  >>> r.content()
```

The output from this command is way too long to include in the book, so be sure to try it out yourself. If you'd like to take a look at the web pages headers, you can run the following:

214

```
1  >>> r.headers
```

Note that the **headers** attribute returns a dict-like object and isn't a function call. We're not showing the output as web page headers tend to be too wide to show correctly in a book. There are a bunch of other great functions and attributes in the Response object. For example, you can get the cookies, the links in the page, and the status_code that the page returned.

The requests package supports the following HTTP request types: POST, GET, PUT, DELETE, HEAD and OPTIONS. If the page returns json, you can access it by calling the Response object's **json** method. Let's take a look at a practical example.

How to Submit a Web Form

In this section, we will compare how to submit a web form with requests versus urllib. Let's start by learning how to submit a web form. We will be doing a web search with **duckduckgo.com** searching on the term *python* and saving the result as an HTML file. We'll start with an example that uses urllib:

```
1  import urllib.request
2  import urllib.parse
3  import webbrowser
4
5  data = urllib.parse.urlencode({'q': 'Python'})
6  url = 'http://duckduckgo.com/html/'
7  full_url = url + '?' + data
8  response = urllib.request.urlopen(full_url)
9  with open("results.html", "wb") as f:
10     f.write(response.read())
11
12 webbrowser.open("results.html")
```

The first thing you have to do when you want to submit a web form is figure out what the form is called and what the url is that you will be posting to. If you go to duckduckgo's website and view the source, you'll notice that its action is pointing to a relative link, "/html". So our url is "http://duckduckgo.com/html". The input field is named "q", so to pass duckduckgo a search term, we have to concatenate the url to the "q" field. The results are read and written to disk. Now let's find out how this process differs when using the requests package.

The requests package does form submissions a little bit more elegantly. Let's take a look:

```
1  import requests
2
3  url = 'https://duckduckgo.com/html/'
4  payload = {'q':'python'}
5  r = requests.get(url, params=payload)
6  with open("requests_results.html", "wb") as f:
7      f.write(r.content)
```

With requests, you just need to create a dictionary with the field name as the key and the search term as the value. Then you use **requests.get** to do the search. Finally you use the resulting requests object, "r", and access its content property which you save to disk.

Wrapping Up

Now you know the basics of the **requests** package. I would recommend reading the package's online documentation as it has many additional examples that you may find useful. I personally think this module is more intuitive to use than the standard library's equivalent.

Chapter 34 - SQLAlchemy

SQLAlchemy is usually referred to as an **Object Relational Mapper (ORM)**, although it is much more full featured than any of the other Python ORMs that I've used, such as SqlObject or the one that's built into Django. SQLAlchemy was created by a fellow named Michael Bayer. Since I'm a music nut, we'll be creating a simple database to store album information. A database isn't a database without some relationships, so we'll create two tables and connect them. Here are a few other things we'll be learning:

- Adding data to each table
- Modifying data
- Deleting data
- Basic queries

But first we need to actually make the database, so that's where we'll begin our journey. You will need to install SQLAlchemy to follow along in this tutorial. We'll use pip to get this job done:

```
1  pip install sqlalchemy
```

Now we're ready to get started!

How to Create a Database

Creating a database with SQLAlchemy is really easy. SQLAlchemy uses a **Declarative** method for creating databases. We will write some code to generate the database and then explain how the code works. If you want a way to view your SQLite database, I would recommend the SQLite Manager plugin for Firefox. Here's some code to create our database tables:

```
1   # table_def.py
2   from sqlalchemy import create_engine, ForeignKey
3   from sqlalchemy import Column, Date, Integer, String
4   from sqlalchemy.ext.declarative import declarative_base
5   from sqlalchemy.orm import relationship, backref
6
7   engine = create_engine('sqlite:///mymusic.db', echo=True)
8   Base = declarative_base()
9
10  class Artist(Base):
11      """"""
12      __tablename__ = "artists"
13
14      id = Column(Integer, primary_key=True)
15      name = Column(String)
16
17  class Album(Base):
18      """"""
19      __tablename__ = "albums"
20
21      id = Column(Integer, primary_key=True)
22      title = Column(String)
23      release_date = Column(Date)
24      publisher = Column(String)
25      media_type = Column(String)
26
27      artist_id = Column(Integer, ForeignKey("artists.id"))
28      artist = relationship("Artist", backref=backref("albums", order_by=id))
29
30  # create tables
31  Base.metadata.create_all(engine)
```

If you run this code, then you should see something similar to the following output:

```
1   2014-04-03 09:43:57,541 INFO sqlalchemy.engine.base.Engine SELECT CAST('test pla\
2   in returns' AS VARCHAR(60)) AS anon_1
3   2014-04-03 09:43:57,551 INFO sqlalchemy.engine.base.Engine ()
4   2014-04-03 09:43:57,551 INFO sqlalchemy.engine.base.Engine SELECT CAST('test uni\
5   code returns' AS VARCHAR(60)) AS anon_1
6   2014-04-03 09:43:57,551 INFO sqlalchemy.engine.base.Engine ()
7   2014-04-03 09:43:57,551 INFO sqlalchemy.engine.base.Engine PRAGMA table_info("ar\
8   tists")
9   2014-04-03 09:43:57,551 INFO sqlalchemy.engine.base.Engine ()
10  2014-04-03 09:43:57,551 INFO sqlalchemy.engine.base.Engine PRAGMA table_info("al\
11  bums")
12  2014-04-03 09:43:57,551 INFO sqlalchemy.engine.base.Engine ()
13  2014-04-03 09:43:57,551 INFO sqlalchemy.engine.base.Engine
14  CREATE TABLE artists (
15      id INTEGER NOT NULL,
16      name VARCHAR,
17      PRIMARY KEY (id)
18  )
19
20
21  2014-04-03 09:43:57,551 INFO sqlalchemy.engine.base.Engine ()
22  2014-04-03 09:43:57,661 INFO sqlalchemy.engine.base.Engine COMMIT
23  2014-04-03 09:43:57,661 INFO sqlalchemy.engine.base.Engine
24  CREATE TABLE albums (
25      id INTEGER NOT NULL,
26      title VARCHAR,
27      release_date DATE,
28      publisher VARCHAR,
29      media_type VARCHAR,
30      artist_id INTEGER,
31      PRIMARY KEY (id),
32      FOREIGN KEY(artist_id) REFERENCES artists (id)
33  )
34
35
36  2014-04-03 09:43:57,661 INFO sqlalchemy.engine.base.Engine ()
37  2014-04-03 09:43:57,741 INFO sqlalchemy.engine.base.Engine COMMIT
```

Why did this happen? Because when we created the engine object, we set its **echo** parameter to **True**. The engine is where the database connection information is and it has all the DBAPI stuff in it that makes communication with your database possible. You'll note that we're creating a SQLite database. Ever since Python 2.5, SQLite has been supported by the language. If you want to connect to some other database, then you'll need to edit the connection string. Just in case you're confused about what we're talking about, here is the code in question:

```
1   engine = create_engine('sqlite:///mymusic.db', echo=True)
```

The string, **sqlite:///mymusic.db**, is our connection string. Next we create an instance of the declarative base, which is what we'll be basing our table classes on. Next we have two classes, **Artist** and **Album** that define what our database tables will look like. You'll notice that we have **Columns**, but no column names. SQLAlchemy actually used the variable names as the column names unless you specifically specify one in the **Column** definition. You'll note that we are using an **id** Integer field as our primary key in both classes. This field will auto-increment. The other columns are pretty self-explanatory until you get to the **ForeignKey**. Here you'll see that we're tying the **artist_id** to the **id** in the **Artist** table. The relationship directive tells SQLAlchemy to tie the Album class/table to the Artist table. Due to the way we set up the ForeignKey, the relationship directive tells SQLAlchemy that this is a **many-to-one relationship**, which is what we want. Many albums to one artist. You can read more about table relationships here[15].

The last line of the script will create the tables in the database. If you run this script multiple times, it won't do anything new after the first time as the tables are already created. You could add another table though and then it would create the new one.

How to Insert / Add Data to Your Tables

A database isn't very useful unless it has some data in it. In this section we'll show you how to connect to your database and add some data to the two tables. It's much easier to take a look at some code and then explain it, so let's do that!

```
1   # add_data.py
2   import datetime
3   from sqlalchemy import create_engine
4   from sqlalchemy.orm import sessionmaker
5   from table_def import Album, Artist
6
7   engine = create_engine('sqlite:///mymusic.db', echo=True)
8
9   # create a Session
10  Session = sessionmaker(bind=engine)
11  session = Session()
12
13  # Create an artist
```

---

[15]http://docs.sqlalchemy.org/en/rel_0_7/orm/relationships.html#relationship-patterns

```
14  new_artist = Artist(name="Newsboys")
15
16  new_artist.albums = [Album(title="Read All About It",
17                             release_date=datetime.date(1988,12,1),
18                             publisher="Refuge", media_type="CD")]
19
20  # add more albums
21  more_albums = [Album(title="Hell Is for Wimps",
22                       release_date=datetime.date(1990,7,31),
23                       publisher="Star Song", media_type="CD"),
24                 Album(title="Love Liberty Disco",
25                       release_date=datetime.date(1999,11,16),
26                       publisher="Sparrow", media_type="CD"),
27                 Album(title="Thrive",
28                       release_date=datetime.date(2002,3,26),
29                       publisher="Sparrow", media_type="CD")]
30  new_artist.albums.extend(more_albums)
31
32  # Add the record to the session object
33  session.add(new_artist)
34  # commit the record the database
35  session.commit()
36
37  # Add several artists
38  session.add_all([
39      Artist(name="MXPX"),
40      Artist(name="Kutless"),
41      Artist(name="Thousand Foot Krutch")
42      ])
43  session.commit()
```

First we need to import our table definitions from the previous script. Then we connect to the database with our engine and create something new, the **Session** object. The **session** is our handle to the database and lets us interact with it. We use it to create, modify, and delete records and we also use sessions to query the database. Next we create an **Artist** object and add an album. You'll note that to add an album, you just create a list of **Album** objects and set the artist object's "albums" property to that list or you can extend it, as you see in the second part of the example. At the end of the script, we add three additional Artists using the **add_all**. As you have probably noticed by now, you need to use the session object's **commit** method to write the data to the database. Now it's time to turn our attention to modifying the data.

How to Modify Records with SQLAlchemy

What happens if you saved some bad data. For example, you typed your favorite album's title incorrectly or you got the release date wrong for that fan edition you own? Well you need to learn how to modify that record! This will actually be our jumping off point into learning SQLAlchemy queries as you need to find the record that you need to change and that means you need to write a query for it. Here's some code that shows us the way:

```python
# modify_data.py
from sqlalchemy import create_engine
from sqlalchemy.orm import sessionmaker
from table_def import Album, Artist

engine = create_engine('sqlite:///mymusic.db', echo=True)

# create a Session
Session = sessionmaker(bind=engine)
session = Session()

# querying for a record in the Artist table
res = session.query(Artist).filter(Artist.name=="Kutless").first()
print(res.name)

# changing the name
res.name = "Beach Boys"
session.commit()

# editing Album data
artist, album = session.query(Artist, Album).filter(
    Artist.id==Album.artist_id).filter(Album.title=="Thrive").first()
album.title = "Step Up to the Microphone"
session.commit()
```

Our first query goes out and looks up an Artist by name using the **filter** method. The **.first()** tells SQLAlchemy that we only want the first result. We could have used **.all()** if we thought there would be multiple results and we wanted all of them. Anyway, this query returns an Artist object that we can manipulate. As you can see, we changed the **name** from **Kutless** to **Beach Boys** and then committed out changes.

Querying a joined table is a little bit more complicated. This time we wrote a query that queries both our tables. It filters using the Artist id AND the Album title. It returns two objects: an artist and an album. Once we have those, we can easily change the title for the album. Wasn't that easy? At this point, we should probably note that if we add stuff to the session erroneously, we can **rollback** our changes/adds/deletes by using **session.rollback()**. Speaking of deleting, let's tackle that subject!

How to Delete Records in SQLAlchemy

Sometimes you just have to delete a record. Whether it's because you're involved in a cover-up or because you don't want people to know about your love of Britney Spears music, you just have to get rid of the evidence. In this section, we'll show you how to do just that! Fortunately for us, SQLAlchemy makes deleting records really easy. Just take a look at the following code!

```
1  # deleting_data.py
2  from sqlalchemy import create_engine
3  from sqlalchemy.orm import sessionmaker
4  from table_def import Album, Artist
5
6  engine = create_engine('sqlite:///mymusic.db', echo=True)
7
8  # create a Session
9  Session = sessionmaker(bind=engine)
10 session = Session()
11
12 res = session.query(Artist).filter(Artist.name=="MXPX").first()
13
14 session.delete(res)
15 session.commit()
```

As you can see, all you had to do was create another SQL query to find the record you want to delete and then call **session.delete(res)**. In this case, we deleted our MXPX record. Some people think punk will never die, but they must not know any DBAs! We've already seen queries in action, but let's take a closer look and see if we can learn anything new.

The Basic SQL Queries of SQLAlchemy

SQLAlchemy provides all the queries you'll probably ever need. We'll be spending a little time just looking at a few of the basic ones though, such as a couple simple SELECTs, a JOINed SELECT and using the LIKE query. You'll also learn where to go for information on other types of queries. For now, let's look at some code:

```python
1    # queries.py
2    from sqlalchemy import create_engine
3    from sqlalchemy.orm import sessionmaker
4    from table_def import Album, Artist
5
6    engine = create_engine('sqlite:///mymusic.db', echo=True)
7
8    # create a Session
9    Session = sessionmaker(bind=engine)
10   session = Session()
11
12   # how to do a SELECT * (i.e. all)
13   res = session.query(Artist).all()
14   for artist in res:
15       print(artist.name)
16
17   # how to SELECT the first result
18   res = session.query(Artist).filter(Artist.name=="Newsboys").first()
19
20   # how to sort the results (ORDER_BY)
21   res = session.query(Album).order_by(Album.title).all()
22   for album in res:
23       print(album.title)
24
25   # how to do a JOINed query
26   qry = session.query(Artist, Album)
27   qry = qry.filter(Artist.id==Album.artist_id)
28   artist, album = qry.filter(Album.title=="Step Up to the Microphone").first()
29
30   # how to use LIKE in a query
31   res = session.query(Album).filter(Album.publisher.like("S%a%")).all()
32   for item in res:
33       print(item.publisher)
```

The first query we run will grab all the artists in the database (a SELECT) *and print out each of their name fields. Next you'll see how to just do a query for a specific artist and return just the first result. The third query shows how do a SELECT* on the Album table and order the results by album title. The fourth query is the same query (a query on a JOIN) we used in our editing section except that we've broken it down to better fit PEP8 standards regarding line length. Another reason to break down long queries is that they become more readable and easier to fix later on if you messed something up. The last query uses LIKE, which allows us to pattern match or look for something that's "like" a specified string. In this case, we wanted to find any records that had a Publisher that started with a capital "S", some character, an "a" and then anything else. So this will match the publishers Sparrow and Star, for example.

SQLAlchemy also supports IN, IS NULL, NOT, AND, OR and all the other filtering keywords that most DBAs use. SQLAlchemy also supports literal SQL, scalars, etc, etc.

Wrapping Up

At this point you should know SQLAlchemy well enough to get started using it confidently. The project also has excellent documentation that you should be able to use to answer just about anything you need to know. If you get stuck, the SQLAlchemy users group / mailing list is very responsive to new users and even the main developers are there to help you figure things out.

Chapter 35 - virtualenv

Virtual environments can be really handy for testing software. That's true in programming circles too. Ian Bicking created the virtualenv project, which is a tool for creating isolated Python environments. You can use these environments to test out new versions of your software, new versions of packages you depend on or just as a sandbox for trying out some new package in general. You can also use virtualenv as a workspace when you can't copy files into site-packages because it's on a shared host. When you create a virtual environment with virtualenv, it creates a folder and copies Python into it along with a site-packages folder and a couple others. It also installs pip. Once your virtual environment is active, it's just like using your normal Python. And when you're done, you can just delete the folder to cleanup. No muss, no fuss. Alternatively, you can keep on using it for development.

In this chapter, we'll spend some time getting to know virtualenv and how to use it to make our own magic.

Installation

First of all, you probably need to install virtualenv. You can use pip or easy_install to install it or you can download the virtualenv.py file from their website and install it from source using its **setup.py** script.

If you have Python 3.4, you will find that you actually have the **venv** module, which follows an API that is very similar to the **virtualenv** package. This chapter will focus on just the virtualenv package, however.

Creating a Virtual Environment

Creating a virtual sandbox with the virtualenv package is quite easy. All you need to do is the following:

```
1   python virtualenv.py FOLDER_NAME
```

Where **FOLDER_NAME** is the name of the folder that you want your sandbox to go. On my Windows 7 machine, I have **C:\Python34\Scripts** added to my path so I can just call **virtualenv.py** FOLDER_NAME without the python part. If you don't pass it anything, then you'll get a list of options printed out on your screen. Let's say we create a project called **sandbox**. How do we use it? Well, we need to **activate**. it. Here's how:

226

On Posix you would do source bin/activate while on Windows, you would do .**\path\to\env\Scripts\activate**. on the command line. Let's actually go through these steps. We'll create the sandbox folder on our desktop so you can see an example. Here's what it looks like on my machine:

```
1  C:\Users\mdriscoll\Desktop>virtualenv sandbox
2  New python executable in sandbox\Scripts\python.exe
3  Installing setuptools...............done.
4  Installing pip..................done.
5
6  C:\Users\mdriscoll\Desktop>sandbox\Scripts\activate
7  (sandbox) C:\Users\mdriscoll\Desktop>
```

You'll note that once your virtual environment is activated, you'll see your prompt change to include a prefix of the folder name that you created, which is **sandbox** in this case. This lets you know that you're using your sandbox. Now you can use pip to install other packages to your virtual environment. When you're done, you just call the deactivate script to exit the environment.

There are a couple of flags you can pass to virtualenv when creating your virtual playground that you should be aware of. For example, you can use -**system-site-packages** to inherit the packages from your default Python's site packages. If you want to use distribute rather than setuptools, you can pass virtualenv the -**distribute** flag.

virtualenv also provides a way for you to just install libraries but use the system Python itself to run them. According to the documentation, you just create a special script to do it.

There's also a neat (and experimental) flag called -**relocatable** that can be used to make the folder relocatable. However, this does NOT work on Windows at the time of this writing, so I wasn't able to test it out.

Finally, there's an -**extra-search-dir** flag that you can use to keep your virtual environment offline. Basically it allows you to add a directory to the search path for distributions that pip or easy_install can install from. In this way, you don't need to have access to the internet to install packages.

Wrapping Up

At this point, you should be able to use virtualenv yourself. There are a couple of other projects worth mentioning at this point. There's Doug Hellman's **virtualenvwrapper** library that makes it even easier to create, delete and manage virtual environments and then there's **zc.buildout** which is probably the closest thing to virtualenv that could be called a competitor. I recommend checking them both out as they might help you in your programming adventures.

Part V - Packaging and Distribution

In Part V you will learn about Python packaging and the various methods to distribute your code. You will learn about the following:

- How to create a module and package
- Publishing your Packages to the Python Packaging Index (PyPI)
- Python eggs
- Python wheels
- py2exe
- bb_freeze
- cx_Freeze
- PyInstaller
- GUI2Exe
- How to Create an Installer with InnoSetup

The first chapter of this section describes how to create a module or package. Then in the following chapter, we will go over publishing our package to PyPI. Next up, we will learn how to create and install a Python egg and the Python wheel.

The next four chapters will cover how to create binaries using the following 3rd party packages: py2exe, bb_freeze, cx_Freeze and PyInstaller. The only package in this list that is actually compatible with Python 3 is cx_Freeze. Because of this fact, we will be showing Python 2 examples in these four chapters so that we can easily compare all 4 packages and their capabilities.

The next to last chapter will show you how to use GUI2Exe, a neat little user interface that was created to go on top of py2exe, bb_freeze, etc. GUI2Exe makes creating binaries even easier!

The last chapter of this section will show how to create an installer using InnoSetup. Let's get started!

image

Chapter 36 - Creating Modules and Packages

Creating Python modules is something that most Python programmers do every day without even thinking about it. Any time you save a new Python script, you have created a new module. You can import your module into other modules. A package is a collection of related modules. The things you import into your scripts from the standard library are modules or packages. In this chapter, we will learn how to create modules and packages. We'll spend more time on packages since they're more complicated than modules.

How to Create a Python Module

We will begin by creating a super simple module. This module will provide us with basic arithmetic and no error handling. Here's our first example:

```python
def add(x, y):
    return x + y

def division(x, y):
    return x / y

def multiply(x, y):
    return x * y

def subtract(x, y):
    return x - y
```

This code has issues, of course. If you pass in two Integers to the **division** method, then you'll end up getting an Integer back if you are using Python 2.x. This may not be what you're expecting. There's also no error checking for division by zero or mixing of strings and numbers. But that's not the point. The point is that if you save this code, you have a fully qualified module. Let's call it **arithmetic.py**. Now what can you do with a module anyway? You can import it and use any of the defined functions or classes that are inside it. And we could make it **executable** with a little spit and polish. Let's do both!

First we'll write a little script that imports our module and runs the functions in it. Save the following as **math_test.py**:

```
1  import arithmetic
2
3  print(arithmetic.add(5, 8))
4  print(arithmetic.subtract(10, 5))
5  print(arithmetic.division(2, 7))
6  print(arithmetic.multiply(12, 6))
```

Now let's modify the original script so that we can run it from the command line. Here's one of the simplest ways to do it:

```
1  def add(x, y):
2      return x + y
3
4  def division(x, y):
5      return x / y
6
7  def multiply(x, y):
8      return x * y
9
10 def subtract(x, y):
11     return x - y
12
13 if __name__ == "__main__":
14     import sys
15     print(sys.argv)
16     v = sys.argv[1].lower()
17     valOne = int(sys.argv[2])
18     valTwo = int(sys.argv[3])
19     if v == "a":
20         print(add(valOne, valTwo))
21     elif v == "d":
22         print(division(valOne, valTwo))
23     elif v == "m":
24         print(multiply(valOne, valTwo))
25     elif v == "s":
26         print(subtract(valOne, valTwo))
27     else:
28         pass
```

The proper way to do this script would be to use Python's **optparse (pre-2.7)** or **argparse (2.7+)** module. You should spend some time to figure out one of these modules as a learning exercise. In the meantime, we will move on to packages!

How to Create a Python Package

The main difference between a module and a package is that a package is a collection of modules AND it has an **__init__.py** file. Depending on the complexity of the package, it may have more than one **__init__.py**. Let's take a look at a simple folder structure to make this more obvious, then we'll create some simple code to follow the structure we define.

```
1  mymath/
2      __init__.py
3      adv/
4          __init__.py
5          sqrt.py
6      add.py
7      subtract.py
8      multiply.py
9      divide.py
```

Now we just need to replicate this structure in our own package. Let's give that a whirl! Create each of these files in a folder tree like the above example. For the add, subtract, multiply and divide files, you can use the functions we created in the earlier example. For the **sqrt.py** module, we'll use the following code.

```
1  # sqrt.py
2  import math
3
4  def squareroot(n):
5      return math.sqrt(n)
```

You can leave both **__init__.py** files blank, but then you'll have to write code like **mymath.add.add(x,y)** which is pretty ugly, so we'll add the following code to the outer **__init__.py** to make using our package easier to understand and use.

```
1  # outer __init__.py
2  from . add import add
3  from . divide import division
4  from . multiply import multiply
5  from . subtract import subtract
6  from .adv.sqrt import squareroot
```

Now we should be able to use our module once we have it on our Python path. You can copy the folder into your Python's **site-packages** folder to do this. On Windows it's in the following general location: **C:\Python34\Lib\site-packages**. Alternatively, you can edit the path on the fly in your test code. Let's see how that's done:

```
1  import sys
2
3  # modify this path to match your environment
4  sys.path.append('C:\Users\mdriscoll\Documents')
5
6  import mymath
7
8  print(mymath.add(4,5))
9  print(mymath.division(4, 2))
10 print(mymath.multiply(10, 5))
11 print(mymath.squareroot(48))
```

Note that my path does NOT include the **mymath** folder. You want to append the parent folder that holds your new module, NOT the module folder itself. If you do this, then the code above should work.

You can also create a **setup.py** script and install your package in **develop** mode. Here's an example setup.py script:

```
1  #!/usr/bin/env python
2
3  from setuptools import setup
4
5
6  # This setup is suitable for "python setup.py develop".
7
8  setup(name='mymath',
9        version='0.1',
10       description='A silly math package',
11       author='Mike Driscoll',
12       author_email='mike@mymath.org',
13       url='http://www.mymath.org/',
14       packages=['mymath', 'mymath.adv'],
15       )
```

You would save this script one level above the **mymath** folder. To install the package in develop mode, you would do the following:

```
1  python setup.py develop
```

This will install a link file in the site-packages folder that points to where ever your package resides. This is great for testing without actually installing your package.

Congratulations! You've just created a Python package!

Wrapping Up

You've just learned how to create your very own, custom-made modules and packages. You will find that the more you code, the more often you'll create programs that have parts that you want to re-use. You can put those reusable pieces of code into modules. Eventually you will have enough related modules that you may want to turn them into a package. Now you have the tools to actually do that!

Chapter 37 - How to Add Your Code to PyPI

We created a package called **mymath** in the previous chapter. In this chapter, we will learn how to share it on the Python Packaging Index (PyPI). To do that, we will first need to learn how to create a **setup.py** file. Just to review, here is our current folder hierarchy:

```
1  mymath/
2      __init__.py
3      adv/
4          __init__.py
5          sqrt.py
6      add.py
7      subtract.py
8      multiply.py
9      divide.py
```

This means that you have a **mymath** folder with the following files in it: **__init__.py, add.py, subtract.py, multiply.py** and **divide.py**. You will also have an **adv** folder inside the **mymath** folder. In the **adv** folder, you will have two files: **__init__.py** and **sqrt.py**.

Creating a setup.py File

We will start out by creating a super simple **setup.py** script. Here's a bare-bones one:

```
1  from distutils.core import setup
2
3  setup(name='mymath',
4        version='0.1',
5        packages=['mymath', 'mymath.adv'],
6        )
```

This is something you might write for a package internally. To upload to PyPI, you will need to include a little more information:

```
1   from distutils.core import setup
2
3   setup(name='mymath',
4         version='0.1',
5         description='A silly math package',
6         author='Mike Driscoll',
7         author_email='mike@mymath.org',
8         url='http://www.mymath.org/',
9         packages=['mymath', 'mymath.adv'],
10        )
```

Now that we're done with that, we should test our script. You can create a virtual environment using the directions from chapter 35 or you can just install your code to your Python installation by calling the following command:

```
1   python setup.py install
```

Alternatively, you can use the method at the end of the last chapter in which you created a special **setup.py** that you installed in **develop** mode. You will note that in the last chapter, we used **setuptools** whereas in this chapter we used **distutils**. The only reason we did this is that setuptools has the **develop** command and distutils does not.

Now we need to register our package with PyPI!

Registering Packages

Registering you package is very easy. Since this is your first package, you will want to register with the Test PyPI server instead of the real one. You may need to create a **.pypirc** file and enter the Test PyPI server address. See the next section for more information. Once you have done that, you just need to run the following command:

```
1   python setup.py register
```

You will receive a list of options that ask you to login, register, have the server send you a password or quit. If you have your username and password saved on your machine, you won't see that message. If you're already registered, you can login and your package's metadata will be uploaded.

Uploading Packages to PyPI

You will probably want to start out by testing with PyPI's test server, which is at https://testpypi. python.org/pypi. You will have to register with that site too as it uses a different database than the main site. Once you've done that, you may want to create a **.pypirc** file somewhere on your operating system's path. On Linux, you can use **$HOME** to find it and on Windows, you can use the **HOME** environ variable. This path is where you would save that file. Following is a sample of what could go in your pypirc file from https://wiki.python.org/moin/TestPyPI:

```
1  [distutils]
2  index-servers=
3      pypi
4      test
5
6  [test]
7  repository = https://testpypi.python.org/pypi
8  username = richard
9  password = <your password goes here>
10
11  [pypi]
12  repository = http://pypi.python.org/pypi
13  username = richard
14  password = <your password goes here>
```

I would highly recommend that you read the documentation in depth to understand all the options you can add to this configuration file.

To upload some files to PyPI, you will need to create some distributions.

```
1  python setup.py sdist bdist_wininst upload
```

When you run the command above, it will create a **dist** folder. The **sdist** command will create an archive file (a zip on Windows, a tarball on Linux). The **bdist_wininst** will create a simple Windows installer executable. The **upload** command will then upload these two files to PyPI.

In your **setup.py** file, you can add a **long_description** field that will be used by PyPI to generate a home page for your package on PyPI. You can use reStructuredText to format your description. Or you can skip adding the description and accept PyPI's default formatting.

If you would like a full listing of the commands you can use with **setup.py**, try running the following command:

```
1   python setup.py --help-commands
```

You should also add a **README.txt** file that explains how to install and use your package. It can also contain a "Thank You" section if you have a lot of contributors.

Wrapping Up

Now you know the basics for adding your package to the Python Packaging Index. If you want to add a Python egg to PyPI, you will need to use easy_install instead of distutils. When you release your next version, you may want to add a **CHANGES.txt** file that lists the changes to your code. There is a great website called **The Hitchhiker's Guide to Packaging** which would be a great place for you to check out for additional information on this exciting topic. Alternatively, you may also want to check out this tutorial[16] by Scott Torborg to get a different take on the process.

---

[16]http://www.scotttorborg.com/python-packaging/index.html

Chapter 38 - The Python egg

Python **eggs** are an older distribution format for Python. The new format is called a Python **wheel**, which we will look at in the next chapter. An egg file is basically a zip file with a different extension. Python can import directly from an egg. You will need the **SetupTools** package to work with eggs. SetupTools is the original mainstream method of downloading and installing Python packages from PyPI and other sources via the command line, kind of like apt-get for Python. There was a fork of SetupTools called **distribute** that was eventually merged back into SetupTools. I only mention it because you may see references to that fork if you do much reading about Python eggs outside of this book.

While the egg format is being migrated away from, you do still need to know about it as there are many packages that are distributed using this technology. It will probably be years before everyone has stopped using eggs. Let's learn how to make our own!

Creating an egg

You can think of an egg as just an alternative to a source distribution or Windows executable, but it should be noted that for pure Python eggs, the egg file is completely cross-platform. We will take a look at how to create our own egg using the package we created in a previous modules and packages chapter. To get started creating an egg, you will need to create a new folder and put the **mymath** folder inside it. Then create a **setup.py** file in the parent directory to mymath with the following contents:

```
1  from setuptools import setup, find_packages
2
3  setup(
4      name = "mymath",
5      version = "0.1",
6      packages = find_packages()
7      )
```

Python has its own package for creating distributions that is called **distutils**. However instead of using Python's **distutils' setup** function, we're using **setuptools' setup**. We're also using setuptools' **find_packages** function which will automatically look for any packages in the current directory and add them to the egg. To create said egg, you'll need to run the following from the command line:

```
1   c:\Python34\python.exe setup.py bdist_egg
```

This will generate a lot of output, but when it's done you'll see that you have three new folders: **build**, **dist**, and **mymath.egg-info**. The only one we care about is the **dist** folder in which you will find your egg file, **mymath-0.1-py3.4.egg**. Note that on my machine, I forced it to run against Python 3.4 so that it would create the egg against that version of Python. The egg file itself is basically a zip file. If you change the extension to "zip", you can look inside it and see that it has two folders: **mymath** and **EGG-INFO**. At this point, you should be able to point **easy_install** at your egg on your file system and have it install your package.

Wrapping Up

Now it's your turn. Go onto the Python Package Index and find some pure Python modules to download. Then try creating eggs using the techniques you learned in this chapter. If you want to install an egg, you can use **easy_install**. Uninstalling an egg is a bit tougher. You will have to go to its install location and delete the folder and / or egg file it installed as well as remove the entry for the package from the **easy-install.pth** file. All of these items can be found in your Python's **site-packages** folder.

Chapter 39 - Python wheels

Python's first mainstream packaging format was the .egg file. Now there's a new format in town called the **wheel** (*.whl*). *According to the Python Packaging Index's description, a wheel is designed to contain all the files for a PEP 376 compatible install in a way that is very close to the on-disk format**. In this chapter, we will learn how to create a wheel and then install our wheel in a **virtualenv**.

Getting Started

Using pip is the recommended way to work with wheels. Make sure you have installed the latest copy of pip as older versions did not support the wheel format. If you're not sure if you have the latest pip, you can run the following command:

```
1  pip install --upgrade pip
```

If you didn't have the latest, then this command will upgrade pip. Now we're ready to create a wheel!

Creating a wheel

First of all, you will need to install the wheel package:

```
1  pip install wheel
```

That was easy! Next, we'll be using the **unidecode** package for creating our first wheel as it doesn't already have one made at the time of writing and I've used this package myself in several projects. The unidecode package will take a string of text and attempt to replace any unicode with its ASCII equivalent. This is extremely handy for when you have to scrub user provided data of weird anomalies. Here's the command you should run to create a wheel for this package:

```
1  pip wheel --wheel-dir=my_wheels Unidecode
```

Here's a screenshot of the output I received when I ran this:

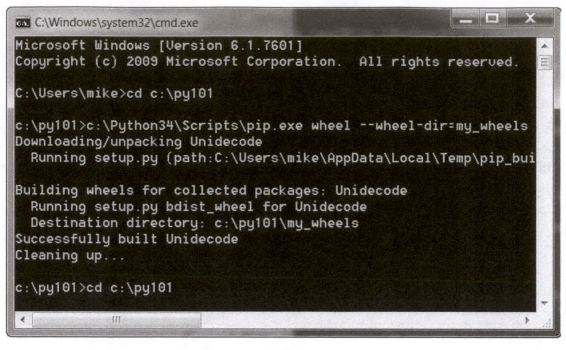

image

Now you should have a wheel named **Unidecode-0.04.14-py26-none-any.whl** in a folder named my_wheels. Let's learn how to install our new wheel!

Installing a Python wheel

Let's create a virtualenv to test with. We will use the following command to create our virtual testing environment:

```
1  virtualenv test
```

This assumes that **virtualenv** is on your system path. If you get an **unrecognized command** error, then you'll probably have to specify the full path (i.e. **c:\Python34\Scripts\virtualenv**). Running this command will create a virtual sandbox for us to play in that includes pip. Be sure to run the **activate** script from the **test** folder's Scripts folder to enable the virtuanenv before continuing. Your virtualenv does not include wheel, so you'll have to install wheel again:

```
1  pip install wheel
```

Once that is installed, we can install our wheel with the following command:

```
1   pip install --use-wheel --no-index --find-links=path/to/my_wheels Unidecode
```

To test that this worked, run Python from the Scripts folder in your virtualenv and try importing unidecode. If it imports, then you successfully installed your wheel!

The *.whl file is similar to an.*egg in that it's basically a *.zip file in disguise. If you rename the extension from.*whl to *.zip, you can open it up with your zip application of choice and examine the files and folders inside at your leisure.

Wrapping Up

Now you should be ready to create your own wheels. They are a nice way to create a local repository of dependencies for your project(s) that you can install quickly. You could create several different wheel repositories to easily switch between different version sets for testing purposes. When combined with virtualenv, you have a really easy way to see how newer versions of dependencies could affect your project without needing to download them multiple times.

Chapter 40 - py2exe

The py2exe project used to be the primary way to create Windows executables from your Python applications. The regular version of py2exe just supports Python 2.3-2.7. There is a new version listed on PyPI[17] that will work with Python 3.4 as well. We will focus on the Python 2.x version, although this chapter should work with the Python 3 version too.

You have several choices for your application. You can create a program that only runs in a terminal, you can create a desktop graphical user interface (GUI) or you can create a web application. We will create a very simple desktop interface that doesn't do anything except display a form that the user can fill out. We will use the wxPython GUI toolkit to help demonstrate how py2exe can pick up packages without us telling it to.

Creating a Simple GUI

You will want to go to wxPython's website (www.wxpython.org) and download a copy that matches your Python version. If you have a 32-bit Python, make sure you download a 32-bit wxPython. You cannot use easy_install or pip to install wxPython unless you get the bleeding edge Phoenix version of wxPython, so you'll have to grab a copy that is pre-built for your system either from the wxPython website or from your system's package manager. I recommend using at least wxPython 2.9 or higher.

Let's write some code!

```
1   import wx
2
3   class DemoPanel(wx.Panel):
4       """"""
5
6       def __init__(self, parent):
7           """Constructor"""
8           wx.Panel.__init__(self, parent)
9
10          labels = ["Name", "Address", "City", "State", "Zip",
11                    "Phone", "Email", "Notes"]
12
13          mainSizer = wx.BoxSizer(wx.VERTICAL)
14          lbl = wx.StaticText(self, label="Please enter your information here:")
```

---

[17]https://pypi.python.org/pypi/py2exe/0.9.2.0/

```
15              lbl.SetFont(wx.Font(12, wx.SWISS, wx.NORMAL, wx.BOLD))
16          mainSizer.Add(lbl, 0, wx.ALL, 5)
17          for lbl in labels:
18              sizer = self.buildControls(lbl)
19              mainSizer.Add(sizer, 1, wx.EXPAND)
20          self.SetSizer(mainSizer)
21          mainSizer.Layout()
22
23      def buildControls(self, label):
24          """
25          Put the widgets together
26          """
27          sizer = wx.BoxSizer(wx.HORIZONTAL)
28          size = (80,40)
29          font = wx.Font(12, wx.SWISS, wx.NORMAL, wx.BOLD)
30
31          lbl = wx.StaticText(self, label=label, size=size)
32          lbl.SetFont(font)
33          sizer.Add(lbl, 0, wx.ALL|wx.CENTER, 5)
34          if label != "Notes":
35              txt = wx.TextCtrl(self, name=label)
36          else:
37              txt = wx.TextCtrl(self, style=wx.TE_MULTILINE, name=label)
38          sizer.Add(txt, 1, wx.ALL, 5)
39          return sizer
40
41  class DemoFrame(wx.Frame):
42      """
43      Frame that holds all other widgets
44      """
45
46      def __init__(self):
47          """Constructor"""
48          wx.Frame.__init__(self, None, wx.ID_ANY,
49                            "Py2Exe Tutorial",
50                            size=(600,400)
51                            )
52          panel = DemoPanel(self)
53          self.Show()
54
55  if __name__ == "__main__":
56      app = wx.App(False)
```

```
57      frame = DemoFrame()
58      app.MainLoop()
```

If you run the code above, you should see something like the following:

image

Let's break this down a bit. We create two classes, **DemoPanel** and **DemoFrame**. In wxPython, the **wx.Frame** object is what you use to create the actual "window" that you see in most cases. You add a **wx.Panel** to give your application the proper look and feel and to add tabbing between fields. The panel object's parent is the frame. The frame, being the top level widget, has no parent. The panel contains all the other widgets in this example. We use sizers to help layout the widgets. Sizers allow the developer to create widgets that will resize appropriately when the window itself is resized. You can also place the widgets on the panel using absolute positioning, which is not recommended. We call the **MainLoop** method of the **wx.App** object at the end to start the event loop, which allows wxPython to respond to mouse and keyboard events (like clicking, typing, etc).

Now we're ready to learn how to package this application up into an executable!

Note: I tested on Windows 7 using Python 2.7.3, wxPython 2.9.4.0 (classic) and py2exe 0.6.9.

The py2exe setup.py file

The key to any py2exe script is the **setup.py** file. This file controls what gets included or excluded, how much we compress and bundle, and much more! Here is the simplest setup that we can use with the wx script above:

```
1   from distutils.core import setup
2   import py2exe
3
4   setup(windows=['sampleApp.py'])
```

As you can see, we import the **setup** method from **distutils.core** and then we import **py2exe**. Next we call setup with a **windows** keyword parameter and pass it the name of the main file inside a python list object. If you were creating a non-GUI project, than you would use the **console** key instead of **windows**. To run this snippet, save it into the same folder as your wxPython script, open up a command prompt and navigate to the location that you saved the two files. Then type **python setup.py py2exe** to run it. If all goes well, you will see a lot of output ending with something like this:

image

If you happen to use Python 2.6, you might get an error about **MSVCP90.dll** not being found. Should you see that error, you will probably need to go find the **Microsoft Visual C++ 2008 Redistributable Package** and install it to make the DLL available on your system. Occasionally you will create the executable and then when you run it, it just won't load correctly. A log file is normally created when this happens that you can use to try to figure out what happened. I have also found a tool called **Dependency Walker** that you can run against your executable and it can tell you about non-Python items that are missing (like DLLs, etc).

I would like to point out that the **setup.py** file doesn't explicitly include wxPython. That means that py2exe was smart enough to include the wxPython package automatically. Let's spend some time learning a bit more about including and excluding packages.

Creating an Advanced setup.py File

Let's see what other options py2exe gives us for creating binaries by creating a more complex **setup.py** file.

```
1   from distutils.core import setup
2   import py2exe
3
4   includes = []
5   excludes = ['_gtkagg', '_tkagg', 'bsddb', 'curses', 'email', 'pywin.debugger',
6               'pywin.debugger.dbgcon', 'pywin.dialogs', 'tcl',
7               'Tkconstants', 'Tkinter']
8   packages = []
9   dll_excludes = ['libgdk-win32-2.0-0.dll', 'libgobject-2.0-0.dll', 'tcl84.dll',
10                  'tk84.dll']
11
12  setup(
13      options = {"py2exe": {"compressed": 2,
14                            "optimize": 2,
15                            "includes": includes,
16                            "excludes": excludes,
17                            "packages": packages,
18                            "dll_excludes": dll_excludes,
19                            "bundle_files": 3,
20                            "dist_dir": "dist",
21                            "xref": False,
22                            "skip_archive": False,
23                            "ascii": False,
24                            "custom_boot_script": '',
25                            }
26                 },
27      windows=['sampleApp.py']
28      )
```

This is pretty self-explanatory, but let's unpack it anyway. First we set up a few lists that we pass to the options parameter of the setup function.

- The **includes** list is for special modules that you need to specifically include. Sometimes py2exe can't find certain modules, so you get to manually specify them here.
- The **excludes** list is a list of which modules to exclude from your program. In this case, we don't need Tkinter since we're using wxPython. This list of excludes is what GUI2Exe will exclude by default.
- The **packages** list is a list of specific packages to include. Again, sometimes py2exe just can't find something. I've had to include email, PyCrypto, or lxml here before. Note that if the excludes list contains something you're trying to include in the packages or includes lists, py2exe may continue to exclude them.
- **dll_excludes** - excludes dlls that we don't need in our project.

In the **options** dictionary, we have a few other options to look at. The **compressed** key tells py2exe whether or not to compress the zipfile, if it's set. The **optimize** key sets the optimization level. Zero is no optimization and 2 is the highest. By setting **optimize** to 2, we can reduce the size of folder by about one megabyte. The **bundle_files** key bundles dlls in the zipfile or the exe. Valid values for bundle_files are:

- 1 = bundle everything, including the Python interpreter.
- 2 = bundle everything but the Python interpreter
- 3 = don't bundle (default)

A few years ago, when I was first learning py2exe, I asked on their mailing list what the best option was because I was having issues with bundle option 1. I was told that 3 was probably the most stable. I went with that and stopped having random problems, so that's what I currently recommend. If you don't like distributing more than one file, zip them up or create an installer. The only other option I use in this list is the **dist_dir** one. I use it to experiment with different build options or to create custom builds when I don't want to overwrite my main good build. You can read about all the other options on the py2exe website.

The py2exe package does not support including Python eggs in its binaries, so if you have installed a package that your application depends on as an egg, when you go to create the executable, it won't work. You will have to make sure your dependencies are installed normally.

Wrapping Up

At this point, you should know enough to get started using py2exe yourself. You can get busy and start distributing your latest creation now. It should be noted that there are several alternatives to py2exe, such as **bbfreeze**, **cx_freeze** and **PyInstaller**. You should try at least a couple of the others to see how they compare. Creating executables can be frustrating, but have patience and persevere through it. The Python packaging community is quite willing to help. All you need to do is ask.

Chapter 41 - bbfreeze

The **bbfreeze** package also allows us to create binaries, but only on Linux and Windows. When you create a binary on Linux, the result will only run on machines that have the same hardware architecture and version of libc, which limits its usefulness on Linux. It should also be noted that bbfreeze only works with Python versions 2.4 - 2.7. You can use easy_install or pip to install the bbfreeze package onto your system. The bbfreeze package includes egg support, so it can include egg dependencies in your binary, unlike py2exe. You can also freeze multiple scripts at once, include the Python interpreter and more.

Getting Started with bbfreeze

You can use easy_install to download and install bbfreeze or you can just download its source or the egg file directly from the Python Package Index (PyPI). In this article, we'll try using it on a simple configuration file generator script and we'll also try it against the wxPython program from the py2exe chapter.

Note: I tested on Windows 7 using Python 2.7.3, wxPython 2.9.4.0 (classic) and bbfreeze 1.1.3

```
1   # config_1.py
2   import configobj
3
4   def createConfig(configFile):
5       """
6       Create the configuration file
7       """
8       config = configobj.ConfigObj()
9       inifile = configFile
10      config.filename = inifile
11      config['server'] = "http://www.google.com"
12      config['username'] = "mike"
13      config['password'] = "dingbat"
14      config['update interval'] = 2
15      config.write()
16
17  def getConfig(configFile):
18      """
19      Open the config file and return a configobj
```

```
20          """
21          return configobj.ConfigObj(configFile)
22
23   def createConfig2(path):
24          """
25          Create a config file
26          """
27          config = configobj.ConfigObj()
28          config.filename = path
29          config["Sony"] = {}
30          config["Sony"]["product"] = "Sony PS3"
31          config["Sony"]["accessories"] = ['controller', 'eye', 'memory stick']
32          config["Sony"]["retail price"] = "$400"
33          config.write()
34
35   if __name__ == "__main__":
36          createConfig2("sampleConfig2.ini")
```

This script has a couple of functions that are pretty pointless, but we'll leave them in for illustrative purposes. According to the bbfreeze documentation, we should be able to create a binary with the following string typed into the command line:

```
1   bb-freeze config_1.py
```

This assumes that you have **C:\Python27\Scripts** on your path. If you don't, you'll need to type the complete path out (i.e. **C:\Python27\Scripts\bb-freeze config_1.py**). If you run this, you should see a folder named **dist** get created. Here's what mine looked like after I ran **config_1.exe**:

image

You will note that when you run the executable, it creates a config file named **sampleconfig2.ini**. You may see a warning about the **pywin32** package not being installed. You can ignore the warning or download and install pywin32.

Now we're ready to move on and try to create an executable from code that use wxPython!

Using bbfreeze's Advanced Configuration

The PyPI page for bbfreeze (which is also its home page) has very little documentation. However, the page does say that the preferred way to use bbfreeze is with little scripts. We're going to try creating a binary with the wxPython example, mentioned earlier. Here's the wx code:

```
1   import wx
2
3   class DemoPanel(wx.Panel):
4       """"""
5
6       def __init__(self, parent):
7           """Constructor"""
8           wx.Panel.__init__(self, parent)
9
10          labels = ["Name", "Address", "City", "State", "Zip",
11                    "Phone", "Email", "Notes"]
12
```

```
13              mainSizer = wx.BoxSizer(wx.VERTICAL)
14              lbl = wx.StaticText(self, label="Please enter your information here:")
15              lbl.SetFont(wx.Font(12, wx.SWISS, wx.NORMAL, wx.BOLD))
16              mainSizer.Add(lbl, 0, wx.ALL, 5)
17              for lbl in labels:
18                  sizer = self.buildControls(lbl)
19                  mainSizer.Add(sizer, 1, wx.EXPAND)
20              self.SetSizer(mainSizer)
21              mainSizer.Layout()
22
23          def buildControls(self, label):
24              """
25              Put the widgets together
26              """
27              sizer = wx.BoxSizer(wx.HORIZONTAL)
28              size = (80,40)
29              font = wx.Font(12, wx.SWISS, wx.NORMAL, wx.BOLD)
30
31              lbl = wx.StaticText(self, label=label, size=size)
32              lbl.SetFont(font)
33              sizer.Add(lbl, 0, wx.ALL|wx.CENTER, 5)
34              if label != "Notes":
35                  txt = wx.TextCtrl(self, name=label)
36              else:
37                  txt = wx.TextCtrl(self, style=wx.TE_MULTILINE, name=label)
38              sizer.Add(txt, 1, wx.ALL, 5)
39              return sizer
40
41  class DemoFrame(wx.Frame):
42      """
43      Frame that holds all other widgets
44      """
45
46          def __init__(self):
47              """Constructor"""
48              wx.Frame.__init__(self, None, wx.ID_ANY,
49                                "Py2Exe Tutorial",
50                                size=(600,400)
51                                )
52              panel = DemoPanel(self)
53              self.Show()
54
```

```
55  if __name__ == "__main__":
56      app = wx.App(False)
57      frame = DemoFrame()
58      app.MainLoop()
```

Now let's create a simple freezing script!

```
1  # bb_setup.py
2  from bbfreeze import Freezer
3
4  f = Freezer(distdir="bb-binary")
5  f.addScript("sampleApp.py")
6  f()
```

First off, we import the **Freezer** class from the **bbfreeze** package. Freezer accepts three arguments: a destination folder, an **includes** iterable and an **excludes** iterable (i.e. a tuple or list). Just to see how well bbfreeze works with only its defaults, we leave out the includes and excludes tuples/lists. Once you have a Freezer object, you can add your script(s) by calling the Freezer object name's addScript method. Then you just need to call the object (i.e. **f()**).

Note: You may see a warning about bb_freeze not being able to find "MSVCP90.dll" or similar. If you see that message, you may need to include it explicitly or add it as a dependency when you create an installer. We will be learning about how to create an installer in a later chapter.

To run this script, you just have to do something like this:

```
1  python bb_setup.py
```

When I ran this script, it created a folder named **bb-binary** that contained 19 files that weighed in at 17.2 MB. When I ran the **sampleApp.exe** file, it ran just fine and was properly themed, however it also had a console screen. We'll have to edit our script a bit to fix that:

```
1   # bb_setup2.py
2   from bbfreeze import Freezer
3
4   includes = []
5   excludes = ['_gtkagg', '_tkagg', 'bsddb', 'curses', 'email', 'pywin.debugger',
6               'pywin.debugger.dbgcon', 'pywin.dialogs', 'tcl',
7               'Tkconstants', 'Tkinter']
8
9   bbFreeze_Class = Freezer('dist', includes=includes, excludes=excludes)
10
```

```
11   bbFreeze_Class.addScript("sampleApp.py", gui_only=True)
12
13   bbFreeze_Class.use_compression = 0
14   bbFreeze_Class.include_py = True
15   bbFreeze_Class()
```

If you run this, you should end up with a **dist** folder with about 19 files, but a slightly different size of 19.6 MB. Notice that we added a second argument to the addScript method: gui_only=True. This makes that annoying console go away. We also set compression to zero (no compression) and include the Python interpreter. Turning on compression only reduced the result back down to 17.2 MB though.

The bbfreeze package also handles "recipes" and includes several examples, however they are not documented well either. Feel free to study them yourself as an exercise.

Wrapping Up

Now you should know the basics of using bbfreeze to create binaries from your programs. I noticed that when I ran bbfreeze on my machine, it was considerably slower in producing the wxPython executable compared with py2exe. This is one of those things that you will have to experiment with when you are determining which tool to use to create your binaries.

Chapter 42 - cx_Freeze

In this chapter, we will be learning about **cx_Freeze**, a cross-platform set of scripts designed to **freeze** Python scripts into executables in a manner similar to py2exe, PyInstaller, etc. We will freeze one console script and one window (i.e GUI) script, using the examples from the previous chapter. The cx_Freeze tool is the **only** binary creation tool that can work with both Python 2.x and 3.x on multiple operating systems at this time. We will be using it with Python 2.7 in this chapter only because we want to compare it directly to the other binary creation tools.

You can install cx_Freeze using one of their Windows installers, via their provided Linux RPMs, via a source RPM or directly from source. You can also use **pip** to install cx_Freeze.

Note: I tested on Windows 7 using Python 2.7.3, wxPython 2.9.4.0 (classic) and cx_Freeze 4.3.2.

Getting Started with cx_Freeze

As mentioned on the cx_Freeze website, there are three ways to use this script. The first is to just use the included cxfreeze script; the second is to create a distutils setup script (think py2exe) which you can save for future use; and the third is to work with the internals of cxfreeze. We will focus on the first two ways of using cx_Freeze. We'll begin with the console script:

```
1   # config_1.py
2   import configobj
3
4   def createConfig(configFile):
5       """
6       Create the configuration file
7       """
8       config = configobj.ConfigObj()
9       inifile = configFile
10      config.filename = inifile
11      config['server'] = "http://www.google.com"
12      config['username'] = "mike"
13      config['password'] = "dingbat"
14      config['update interval'] = 2
15      config.write()
16
17  def getConfig(configFile):
18      """
```

256

```
19        Open the config file and return a configobj
20        """
21        return configobj.ConfigObj(configFile)
22
23  def createConfig2(path):
24        """
25        Create a config file
26        """
27        config = configobj.ConfigObj()
28        config.filename = path
29        config["Sony"] = {}
30        config["Sony"]["product"] = "Sony PS3"
31        config["Sony"]["accessories"] = ['controller', 'eye', 'memory stick']
32        config["Sony"]["retail price"] = "$400"
33        config.write()
34
35  if __name__ == "__main__":
36        createConfig2("sampleConfig2.ini")
```

All this script does is create a really simple configuration file using Michael Foord's **configobj** module. You can set it up to read the config too, but for this example, we'll skip that. Let's find out how to build a binary with cx_Freeze! According to the documentation, all it should take is the following string on the command line (assuming you are in the correct directory):

```
1  cxfreeze config_1.py --target-dir dirName
```

This assumes that you have **C:\PythonXX\Scripts** on your path. If not, you'll either have to fix that or type out the fully qualified path. Anyway, if the cxfreeze script runs correctly, you should have a folder with the following contents:

Name	Date modified	Type	Size
_hashlib.pyd	4/10/2012 11:31 PM	PYD File	279 KB
_socket.pyd	4/10/2012 11:31 PM	PYD File	40 KB
_ssl.pyd	4/10/2012 11:31 PM	PYD File	705 KB
bz2.pyd	4/10/2012 11:31 PM	PYD File	59 KB
config_1.exe	4/18/2014 2:32 PM	Application	1,155 KB
python27.dll	4/10/2012 11:31 PM	Application extens...	2,250 KB
sampleConfig2.ini	4/18/2014 2:32 PM	Configuration setti...	1 KB
unicodedata.pyd	4/10/2012 11:31 PM	PYD File	671 KB

image

As you can see, the total file size should around 5 megabytes. That was pretty easy. It even picked up the configobj module without our having to tell it to. There are 18 command line arguments you can pass to cx_Freeze to control how it does things. These range from what modules to include or exclude, optimization, compression, include a zip file, path manipulation and more.

Now let's try something a little more advanced.

Advanced cx_Freeze - Using a setup.py File

First off we need a script to use. We will use the wxPython form example from the previous chapters.

```python
import wx

class DemoPanel(wx.Panel):
    """"""

    def __init__(self, parent):
        """Constructor"""
        wx.Panel.__init__(self, parent)

        labels = ["Name", "Address", "City", "State", "Zip",
                  "Phone", "Email", "Notes"]

        mainSizer = wx.BoxSizer(wx.VERTICAL)
        lbl = wx.StaticText(self, label="Please enter your information here:")
        lbl.SetFont(wx.Font(12, wx.SWISS, wx.NORMAL, wx.BOLD))
        mainSizer.Add(lbl, 0, wx.ALL, 5)
        for lbl in labels:
            sizer = self.buildControls(lbl)
            mainSizer.Add(sizer, 1, wx.EXPAND)
        self.SetSizer(mainSizer)
        mainSizer.Layout()

    def buildControls(self, label):
        """
        Put the widgets together
        """
        sizer = wx.BoxSizer(wx.HORIZONTAL)
        size = (80,40)
        font = wx.Font(12, wx.SWISS, wx.NORMAL, wx.BOLD)

        lbl = wx.StaticText(self, label=label, size=size)
```

```
32            lbl.SetFont(font)
33            sizer.Add(lbl, 0, wx.ALL|wx.CENTER, 5)
34            if label != "Notes":
35                txt = wx.TextCtrl(self, name=label)
36            else:
37                txt = wx.TextCtrl(self, style=wx.TE_MULTILINE, name=label)
38            sizer.Add(txt, 1, wx.ALL, 5)
39            return sizer
40
41  class DemoFrame(wx.Frame):
42        """
43        Frame that holds all other widgets
44        """
45
46      def __init__(self):
47          """Constructor"""
48          wx.Frame.__init__(self, None, wx.ID_ANY,
49                            "Py2Exe Tutorial",
50                            size=(600,400)
51                            )
52          panel = DemoPanel(self)
53          self.Show()
54
55  if __name__ == "__main__":
56      app = wx.App(False)
57      frame = DemoFrame()
58      app.MainLoop()
```

Now let's create a **setup.py** file in the cx_Freeze style:

```
1  # setup.py
2  from cx_Freeze import setup, Executable
3
4  setup(
5      name = "wxSampleApp",
6      version = "0.1",
7      description = "An example wxPython script",
8      executables = [Executable("sampleApp.py")]
9      )
```

As you can see, this is a pretty simple one. We import a couple classes from cx_Freeze and pass some parameters into them. In this case, we give the setup class a name, version, description and

Executable class. The Executable class also gets one parameter, the script name that it will use to create the binary from.

Alternatively, you can create a simple setup.py using cx_Freeze's quickstart command (assuming it's on your system's path) in the same folder as your code:

cxfreeze-quickstart

To get the setup.py to build the binary, you need to do the following on the command line:

```
1   python setup.py build
```

After running this, you should end up with the following folders: **build** **exe.win32-2.7**. Inside that last folder I ended up with 15 files that total 16.6 MB. When you run the sampleApp.exe file, you will notice that we've screwed something up. There's a console window loading in addition to our GUI! To rectify this, we'll need to change our setup file slightly. Take a look at our new one:

```
1   from cx_Freeze import setup, Executable
2
3   exe = Executable(
4       script="sampleApp.py",
5       base="Win32GUI",
6       )
7
8   setup(
9       name = "wxSampleApp",
10      version = "0.1",
11      description = "An example wxPython script",
12      executables = [exe]
13      )
```

First off, we separated the Executable class from the setup class and assigned the Executable class to a variable. We also added a second parameter to the Executable class that is key. That parameter is called **base**. By setting **base="Win32GUI"**, we are able to suppress the console window. The documentation on the cx_Freeze website shows the many other options that the Executable class takes.

Wrapping Up

Now you should know how to create binaries with cx_Freeze. It's pretty easy to do and it ran a lot faster than bbfreeze did in my testing. If you have the need to create binaries for both Python 2.x and 3.x on all major platforms, then this is the tool for you!

Chapter 43 - PyInstaller

PyInstaller is the last tool we will be looking at for creating binaries. It supports Python 2.4 - 2.7. We will continue to use our simple console and wxPython GUI scripts for our testing. PyInstaller is supposed to work on Windows, Linux, Mac, Solaris and AIX. The support for Solaris and AIX is experimental. PyInstaller supports code-signing (Windows), eggs, hidden imports, single executable, single directory, and lots more!

Note: I tested on Windows 7 using Python 2.7.3, wxPython 2.9.4.0 (classic) and PyInstaller 2.1.

Getting Started with PyInstaller

To install PyInstaller, you can download the source code in a tarball or zip archive, decompress it and run its **setup.py** file:

```
1  python setup.py install
```

You can also install PyInstaller using pip. We will start with our little piece of config creation code:

```
1  # config_1.py
2  import configobj
3
4  def createConfig(configFile):
5      """
6      Create the configuration file
7      """
8      config = configobj.ConfigObj()
9      inifile = configFile
10     config.filename = inifile
11     config['server'] = "http://www.google.com"
12     config['username'] = "mike"
13     config['password'] = "dingbat"
14     config['update interval'] = 2
15     config.write()
16
17  def getConfig(configFile):
18      """
19      Open the config file and return a configobj
```

```
20         """
21         return configobj.ConfigObj(configFile)
22
23   def createConfig2(path):
24         """
25         Create a config file
26         """
27         config = configobj.ConfigObj()
28         config.filename = path
29         config["Sony"] = {}
30         config["Sony"]["product"] = "Sony PS3"
31         config["Sony"]["accessories"] = ['controller', 'eye', 'memory stick']
32         config["Sony"]["retail price"] = "$400"
33         config.write()
34
35   if __name__ == "__main__":
36         createConfig2("sampleConfig2.ini")
```

Now let's try to create an executable! You should be able to just do this to get PyInstaller to work:

```
1   pyinstaller config_1.py
```

When I ran this, I got the following error:

```
1   Error: PyInstaller for Python 2.6+ on Windows needs pywin32.
2   Please install from http://sourceforge.net/projects/pywin32/
```

To use PyInstaller on Windows, you will need to install **PyWin32** first! Once you have PyWin32 installed, try re-running that command. You should see a lot of output sent to the screen and you should also see these two folders appear next to your script: **build** and **dist**. If you go into the **dist** folder, and then into its **config_1** folder, you should see something like this:

Name	Date modified	Type	Size
_hashlib.pyd	4/10/2012 11:31 PM	PYD File	279 KB
_socket.pyd	4/10/2012 11:31 PM	PYD File	40 KB
_ssl.pyd	4/10/2012 11:31 PM	PYD File	705 KB
bz2.pyd	4/10/2012 11:31 PM	PYD File	59 KB
config_1.exe	4/18/2014 3:26 PM	Application	1,287 KB
config_1.exe.manifest	4/18/2014 3:26 PM	MANIFEST File	1 KB
Microsoft.VC90.CRT.manifest	10/15/2012 9:20 PM	MANIFEST File	2 KB
msvcm90.dll	10/15/2012 9:20 PM	Application exte...	220 KB
msvcp90.dll	10/15/2012 9:20 PM	Application exte...	556 KB
msvcr90.dll	10/15/2012 9:20 PM	Application exte...	641 KB
python27.dll	4/10/2012 11:31 PM	Application exte...	2,250 KB
sampleConfig2.ini	4/18/2014 3:26 PM	Configuration se...	1 KB
select.pyd	4/10/2012 11:31 PM	PYD File	10 KB
unicodedata.pyd	4/10/2012 11:31 PM	PYD File	671 KB

image

When I ran the executable, it created the config file just as it should. You will notice that PyInstaller was able to grab **configobj** without you needing to tell it to.

PyInstaller and wxPython

Now let's try creating a binary from a simple wxPython script. Here's the wxPython code that we've been using in previous chapters:

```
1    import wx
2
3    class DemoPanel(wx.Panel):
4        """"""
5
6        def __init__(self, parent):
7            """Constructor"""
8            wx.Panel.__init__(self, parent)
9
10           labels = ["Name", "Address", "City", "State", "Zip",
11                     "Phone", "Email", "Notes"]
12
13           mainSizer = wx.BoxSizer(wx.VERTICAL)
14           lbl = wx.StaticText(self, label="Please enter your information here:")
```

```
15          lbl.SetFont(wx.Font(12, wx.SWISS, wx.NORMAL, wx.BOLD))
16          mainSizer.Add(lbl, 0, wx.ALL, 5)
17          for lbl in labels:
18              sizer = self.buildControls(lbl)
19              mainSizer.Add(sizer, 1, wx.EXPAND)
20          self.SetSizer(mainSizer)
21          mainSizer.Layout()
22
23      def buildControls(self, label):
24          """
25          Put the widgets together
26          """
27          sizer = wx.BoxSizer(wx.HORIZONTAL)
28          size = (80,40)
29          font = wx.Font(12, wx.SWISS, wx.NORMAL, wx.BOLD)
30
31          lbl = wx.StaticText(self, label=label, size=size)
32          lbl.SetFont(font)
33          sizer.Add(lbl, 0, wx.ALL|wx.CENTER, 5)
34          if label != "Notes":
35              txt = wx.TextCtrl(self, name=label)
36          else:
37              txt = wx.TextCtrl(self, style=wx.TE_MULTILINE, name=label)
38          sizer.Add(txt, 1, wx.ALL, 5)
39          return sizer
40
41  class DemoFrame(wx.Frame):
42      """
43      Frame that holds all other widgets
44      """
45
46      def __init__(self):
47          """Constructor"""
48          wx.Frame.__init__(self, None, wx.ID_ANY,
49                            "Py2Exe Tutorial",
50                            size=(600,400)
51                            )
52          panel = DemoPanel(self)
53          self.Show()
54
55  if __name__ == "__main__":
56      app = wx.App(False)
```

```
57        frame = DemoFrame()
58        app.MainLoop()
```

If you execute the **pyinstaller** command against this script, you will see ever more output sent to the screen. It will create 23 files that total 19.4 MB. You will also notice that when you run the **sampleApp.exe**, it shows a console window in addition to your GUI, which is not what we want. The simplest way to fix that is to call PyInstaller with the **-w** command which tells PyInstaller to suppress the console window:

```
1  pyinstaller -w sampleApp.py
```

The PyInstaller package has many command line options that you can use to change the way PyInstaller processes your program. Whenever you run PyInstaller, it will create a **spec** file that it uses to process your program. If you'd like to save a copy of the spec file to help you better understand what PyInstaller is doing, you can do so using the following command:

```
1  pyi-makespec sampleApp.py
```

You can pass the same commands to **pyi-makespec** as you do to PyInstaller, which will change the spec appropriately. Here's the contents of the spec that was created with the previous command:

```
1  # -*- mode: python -*-
2  a = Analysis(['sampleApp.py'],
3               pathex=['c:\\py101\\wxpy'],
4               hiddenimports=[],
5               hookspath=None,
6               runtime_hooks=None)
7  pyz = PYZ(a.pure)
8  exe = EXE(pyz,
9            a.scripts,
10           exclude_binaries=True,
11           name='sampleApp.exe',
12           debug=False,
13           strip=None,
14           upx=True,
15           console=False )
16 coll = COLLECT(exe,
17               a.binaries,
18               a.zipfiles,
19               a.datas,
20               strip=None,
21               upx=True,
22               name='sampleApp')
```

In earlier versions of PyInstaller, you would actually create the spec file and edit it directly. Now unless you need something really special, you can generate the right spec by just using flags. Be sure to read the documentation for full details as there are many flags and describing them all is outside the scope of this chapter.

Wrapping Up

This ends our quick tour of PyInstaller. I hope you found this helpful in your Python binary-making endeavors. The PyInstaller project is pretty well documented and worth your time to check out.

Chapter 44 - Creating an Installer

In this chapter, we will walk you through the process of creating an executable and then packaging it up into an installer. We will be using a really neat little user interface called GUI2Exe that was written by Andrea Gavana to create the executable. It is based on wxPython, so you will need to have that installed to use it. GUI2Exe supports py2exe, bbfreeze, cx_Freeze, PyInstaller and py2app. Then once we have the **dist** folder created, we will use **Inno Setup** to create our installer.

We will be using the following code once more:

```python
# sampleApp.py

import wx

class DemoPanel(wx.Panel):
    """"""

    def __init__(self, parent):
        """Constructor"""
        wx.Panel.__init__(self, parent)

        labels = ["Name", "Address", "City", "State", "Zip",
                  "Phone", "Email", "Notes"]

        mainSizer = wx.BoxSizer(wx.VERTICAL)
        lbl = wx.StaticText(self, label="Please enter your information here:")
        lbl.SetFont(wx.Font(12, wx.SWISS, wx.NORMAL, wx.BOLD))
        mainSizer.Add(lbl, 0, wx.ALL, 5)
        for lbl in labels:
            sizer = self.buildControls(lbl)
            mainSizer.Add(sizer, 1, wx.EXPAND)
        self.SetSizer(mainSizer)
        mainSizer.Layout()

    def buildControls(self, label):
        """
        Put the widgets together
        """
        sizer = wx.BoxSizer(wx.HORIZONTAL)
```

```
30              size = (80,40)
31              font = wx.Font(12, wx.SWISS, wx.NORMAL, wx.BOLD)
32
33              lbl = wx.StaticText(self, label=label, size=size)
34              lbl.SetFont(font)
35              sizer.Add(lbl, 0, wx.ALL|wx.CENTER, 5)
36              if label != "Notes":
37                  txt = wx.TextCtrl(self, name=label)
38              else:
39                  txt = wx.TextCtrl(self, style=wx.TE_MULTILINE, name=label)
40              sizer.Add(txt, 1, wx.ALL, 5)
41              return sizer
42
43  class DemoFrame(wx.Frame):
44      """
45      Frame that holds all other widgets
46      """
47
48      def __init__(self):
49          """Constructor"""
50          wx.Frame.__init__(self, None, wx.ID_ANY,
51                            "Py2Exe Tutorial",
52                            size=(600,400)
53                            )
54          panel = DemoPanel(self)
55          self.Show()
56
57  if __name__ == "__main__":
58      app = wx.App(False)
59      frame = DemoFrame()
60      app.MainLoop()
```

Let's get started!

Getting Started with GUI2Exe

To use GUI2Exe, you just have to go to its website (http://code.google.com/p/gui2exe/) and download a release. Then you unzip it and run the script that's called **GUI2Exe.py**. The GUI2Exe project is based on wxPython, so make sure you have that installed as well. I ran mine successfully with wxPython 2.9. Here's how you would call it:

```
1    python GUI2Exe.py
```

If that executed successfully, you should see a screen similar to this one:

image

Now go to File -> New Project and give your project a name. In this case, I called the project **wxForm**. If you want to, you can add a fake Company Name, Copyright and give it a Program Name. Be sure to also browse for your main Python script (i.e. **sampleApp.py**). According to Andrea's website, you should set **Optimize** to **2**, **Compressed** to **2** and **Bundled Files** to **1**. This seems to work most of the time, but I've had some screwy errors that seem to stem from setting the last one to **1**. In fact, according to one of my contacts on the py2exe mailing list, the **bundle** option should be set to **3** to minimize errors. The nice thing about setting bundle to "1" is that you end up with just one file, but since I'm going to roll it up with Inno I'm going to go with option 3 to make sure my program works well.

Once you have everything the way you want it, click the **Compile** button in the lower right-hand corner. This will create all the files you want to distribute in the **dist** folder unless you have changed the name by checking the **dist checkbox** and editing the subsequent textbox. When it's done compiling, GUI2Exe will ask you if you want to test your executable. Go ahead and hit **Yes**. If you receive any errors about missing modules, you can add them in the **Python Modules** or **Python Packages** section as appropriate. For this example, you shouldn't have that issue though.

Now we're ready to learn about creating the installer!

Let's Make an Installer!

Now that we have an executable and a bunch of dependencies, how do we make an installer? For this chapter we'll be using Inno Setup, but you could also use NSIS or a Microsoft branded installer. You will need to go to their website (http://www.jrsoftware.org/isdl.php), download the program and install it. Then run the program. You should see the main program along with the following dialog on top of it:

image

Choose the **Create a new script using the Script Wizard** option and then press the OK button. Click **Next** and you should see something like this:

image

Fill this out however you like and click **Next** (I called mine **wxForm**). This next screen allows you to choose where you want the application to be installed by default. It defaults to **Program Files** which is fine. Click **Next**. Now you should see the following screen:

image

Browse to the executable you created to add it. Then click the **Add file(s)**... button to add the rest. You can actually select all of the files except for the exe and hit OK. This is how mine turned out:

image

Now you're ready to click **Next**. Make sure the Start Menu folder has the right name (in this case, **wxForm**) and continue. You can ignore the next two screens or experiment with them if you like. I'm not using a license or putting information files in to display to the user though. The last screen before finishing allows you to choose a directory to put the output into. I just left that empty since it defaults to where the executable is located, which is fine with this example. Click **Next**, **Next** and **Finish**. This will generate a full-fledged **.iss** file, which is what Inno Setup uses to turn your application into an installer. It will ask you if you'd like to go ahead and compile the script now. Go ahead and do that. Then it will ask if you'd like to save your **.iss** script. That's a good idea, so go ahead and do that too. Hopefully you didn't receive any errors and you can try out your new installer.

If you're interested in learning about Inno's scripting language, feel free to read Inno's Documentation. You can do quite a bit with it. If you happen to make changes to your build script, you can rebuild your installer by going to the **build** menu and choosing the **compile** menu item.

Wrapping Up

At this point, you now know how to create a real, live installer that you can use to install your application and any files it needs to run. This is especially handy when you have a lot of custom icons for your toolbars or a default database, config file, etc that you need to distribute with your application. Go back and try creating the installer again, but choose different options to see what else you can do. Experimenting is a great way to learn. Just make sure you always have a backup in case something goes wrong!

Appendix A: Putting It All Together

Now that you've finished reading the book, what do you do? Most beginner programming books I've read would leave you hanging at this point, but not this one. In this chapter, we will take what we've learned and apply it to create a real program! First we need some background and a set of requirements. In the business world, we might call this a **specification**. The more specific the specification is, the more likely your code will match the customer's expectations. Unfortunately, you will find that in the real world, good specifications are hard to come by and you have to spend a lot of time nailing down exactly what the customer wants. But I digress. Let's get started on our program!

The Background

This book was written using a markup language called **RestructuredText**. Each chapter of the book was saved in its own file (Ex. chapter1.rst) as I have found that my proofers would rather proof individual chapters than get overwhelmed by large chunks of the book. Here is a really short example that demonstrates how to create a chapter heading:

```
chapter_1.rst
1   ****************
2   Chapter 1 - IDLE
3   ****************
4
5   This chapter will be about the IDLE editor included with Python!
```

image

You may want to take a look at this Quick Reference[18] to learn more about RestructuredText.

The Specification

What I need to be able to do is find a way to produce a PDF out of these individual chapters, add the customer's name and email address to each page and email the PDF to each customer. This was

---

[18]http://docutils.sourceforge.net/docs/user/rst/quickref.html

my original idea for distributing the book to my Kickstarter backers. Note that Kickstarter provides the customer information in a CSV file.

Breaking the Specification Down

Most programs that you will write can be broken down into smaller programs. In fact, you will want to do this to make your code more **modular**. This means that if you break the code down into small enough pieces that the pieces can be reused by other programs. We won't go that far in this example, but you should have an idea of how to do that by the end of this chapter.

Let's break the specification down a bit. Here are the tasks that occurred to me:

- Write a program to put all the chapters into one book file
- Figure out how to add a footer
- Find some way to turn the book file into a PDF
- Write a program that can email PDFs

Let's start with the first two items since they're related.

Turning Chapters Into a Book

I went the easy route and just created a Python list of the chapters in the order that I wanted them to appear in the book. I could have used Python's **glob** module to grab all the files in a folder that had the **.rst** extension, but then they might not have been in the right order.

Let's take a look at a simple example of what I did:

```python
import os
import subprocess

chapters = ['chapter_1.rst',
            'chapter_2.rst',
            'chapter_3.rst']

def read_chapter(chapter):
    """
    Reads a chapter and returns the stream
    """
    path = os.path.join("data", chapter)
    try:
        with open(path) as chp_handler:
```

```
15              data = chp_handler.read()
16       except (IOError, OSError):
17           raise Exception("Unable to open chapter: %s" % chapter)
18
19       return data
20
21   def make_book(name="Mike", email_address="test@py.com"):
22       """
23       Creates Python 101 book
24       """
25       book_path = "output/python101.rst"
26       pdf_path = "output/python101.pdf"
27       page_break = """
28   .. raw:: pdf
29
30       PageBreak
31       """
32       footer = """
33   .. footer::
34
35       Copyright |copy| 2014 by Michael Driscoll, all rights reserved.
36
37       Licensed to %s <%s>
38
39   .. |copy| unicode:: 0xA9 .. copyright sign
40       """ % (name, email_address)
41       try:
42           with open(book_path, "w") as book:
43               book.write(footer + "\n")
44               for chapter in chapters:
45                   data = read_chapter(chapter)
46                   book.write(data)
47                   book.write("\n")
48                   book.write(page_break + "\n")
49       except:
50           print("Error writing book!")
51           raise
52
53       cmd = [r"C:\Python27\Scripts\rst2pdf.exe",
54               book_path, "-o", pdf_path]
55       subprocess.call(cmd)
56
```

```
57  if __name__ == "__main__":
58      make_book()
```

Let's break this down a bit. At the beginning of the script, we import two modules: **os** and **subprocess**. Then we create a really simple function that will open a chapter file that's located in the **data** folder, read the chapter and return the file's contents. The meat of the program is in the **make_book** function. Here we set up the names of the RestructuredText file and the PDF. Then we create a **page_break** variable and a **footer** variable. These two variables contain RestructuredText that we insert into the document. Right now, the program does not insert a customer's name or email, but will just use a couple of defaults instead.

Next we open the RestructuredText book document in **write** mode and write the footer text to it. Then we loop over the chapters, writing them to disk with a page break between each of them. Then at the very end of the script, we call a program called **rst2pdf** that will turn our new book file into a PDF. At this point, we have about a third of the program written. Now we just need to figure out how to read CSV file and email the PDF.

Reading the Customer CSV File

You may recall that we already covered a module that can help us in this quest back in Chapter 13. It's the **csv** module, of course! I won't reveal exactly what information Kickstarter has in their files, but we can create our own pretend version. Let's say it's something like this:

```
1  Mike Driscoll,test@py.com
2  Andy Hunter,andwa@hunter.org
3  Toby Mac,macdaddy@gotee.com
```

Let's create a quick function that can extract the name and email address from this file.

```
1   import csv
2
3   def read_csv(path):
4       """"""
5       try:
6           with open(path) as csv_file:
7               reader = csv.reader(csv_file)
8               for line in reader:
9                   name, email = line
10                  print(name)
11                  print(email)
12      except IOError:
```

```
13          print("Error reading file: %s" % path)
14          raise
15
16 if __name__ == "__main__":
17      path = "backers.csv"
18      read_csv(path)
```

All this script does is read the CSV file and print out the name and email address. Let's rename the function to **main** and have it call our **make_book** function:

```
1 def main(path):
2      """"""
3      try:
4          with open(path) as csv_file:
5              reader = csv.reader(csv_file)
6              for line in reader:
7                  name, email = line
8                  make_book(name, email)
9      except IOError:
10          print("Error reading file: %s" % path)
11          raise
12
13 if __name__ == "__main__":
14      main("backers.csv")
```

This will call the **make_book** function 3 times, so we will create the PDF 3 times and overwrite each time. You can check the file at the end of the run to see which name and email address is in the footer. This gets us two-thirds of the way there. All that's left is to figure out how to send the PDF out in an email. Fortunately, we covered that back in Chapter 17 when you learned about the **email** and **smtplib** modules!

Emailing the PDF

Let's spend a few minutes putting together a simple program that can email PDFs. Here's a fairly simple example:

```python
1    import os
2    import smtplib
3
4    from email import encoders
5    from email.mime.text import MIMEText
6    from email.mime.base import MIMEBase
7    from email.mime.multipart import MIMEMultipart
8    from email.utils import formatdate
9
10   def send_email(email, pdf):
11       """
12       Send an email out
13       """
14       header0 = 'Content-Disposition'
15       header1 ='attachment; filename="%s"' % os.path.basename(pdf)
16       header = header0, header1
17
18       host  = "mail.server.com"
19       server = smtplib.SMTP(host)
20       subject = "Test email from Python"
21       to = email
22       from_addr = "test@pylib.com"
23       body_text = "Here is the Alpha copy of Python 101, Part I"
24
25       # create the message
26       msg = MIMEMultipart()
27       msg["From"] = from_addr
28       msg["Subject"] = subject
29       msg["Date"] = formatdate(localtime=True)
30       msg["To"] = email
31
32       msg.attach( MIMEText(body_text) )
33
34       attachment = MIMEBase('application', "octet-stream")
35       try:
36           with open(pdf, "rb") as fh:
37               data = fh.read()
38           attachment.set_payload( data )
39           encoders.encode_base64(attachment)
40           attachment.add_header(*header)
41           msg.attach(attachment)
42       except IOError:
```

```
43          msg = "Error opening attachment file %s" % file_to_attach
44        print(msg)
45
46      server.sendmail(from_addr, to, msg.as_string())
47
48  if __name__ == "__main__":
49      send_email("mike@example.org", "output/python101.pdf")
```

This is basically a modified example of the email attachment code from earlier in the book. This function is made to accept two arguments: an email address and a path to a PDF file. Technically, you could pass it any type of file and it would work. You will need to modify the **host** variable to point to your own SMTP server. I tested this on my machine with the proper host name and it worked great. Now we just need to integrate this code into the main code.

Putting it all Together

Now we get to put all the code together and see it as a whole. Here it is:

```
1  import csv
2  import os
3  import smtplib
4  import subprocess
5
6  from email import encoders
7  from email.mime.text import MIMEText
8  from email.mime.base import MIMEBase
9  from email.mime.multipart import MIMEMultipart
10 from email.utils import formatdate
11
12 chapters = ['chapter_1.rst',
13             'chapter_2.rst',
14             'chapter_3.rst']
15
16 def make_book(name="Mike", email_address="test@py.com"):
17     """
18     Creates Python 101 book
19     """
20     book_path = "output/python101.rst"
21     pdf_path = "output/python101.pdf"
22     page_break = """
23  .. raw:: pdf
```

```
24
25          PageBreak
26          """
27          footer = """
28   .. footer::
29
30      Copyright |copy| 2014 by Michael Driscoll, all rights reserved.
31
32      Licensed to %s <%s>
33
34   .. |copy| unicode:: 0xA9 .. copyright sign
35          """ % (name, email_address)
36          try:
37              with open(book_path, "w") as book:
38                  book.write(footer + "\n")
39                  for chapter in chapters:
40                      data = read_chapter(chapter)
41                      book.write(data)
42                      book.write("\n")
43                      book.write(page_break + "\n")
44          except:
45              print("Error writing book!")
46              raise
47
48          cmd = [r"C:\Python27\Scripts\rst2pdf.exe",
49                 book_path, "-o", pdf_path]
50          subprocess.call(cmd)
51          return pdf_path
52
53   def read_chapter(chapter):
54          """
55          Reads a chapter and returns the stream
56          """
57          path = os.path.join("data", chapter)
58          try:
59              with open(path) as chp_handler:
60                  data = chp_handler.read()
61          except (IOError, OSError):
62              raise Exception("Unable to open chapter: %s" % chapter)
63
64          return data
65
```

```python
66  def send_email(email, pdf):
67      """
68      Send an email out
69      """
70      header0 = 'Content-Disposition'
71      header1 ='attachment; filename="%s"' % os.path.basename(pdf)
72      header = header0, header1
73
74      host  = "mail.server.com"
75      server = smtplib.SMTP(host)
76      subject = "Test email from Python"
77      to = email
78      from_addr = "test@pylib.com"
79      body_text = "Here is the Alpha copy of Python 101, Part I"
80
81      # create the message
82      msg = MIMEMultipart()
83      msg["From"] = from_addr
84      msg["Subject"] = subject
85      msg["Date"] = formatdate(localtime=True)
86      msg["To"] = email
87
88      msg.attach( MIMEText(body_text) )
89
90      attachment = MIMEBase('application', "octet-stream")
91      try:
92          with open(pdf, "rb") as fh:
93              data = fh.read()
94          attachment.set_payload( data )
95          encoders.encode_base64(attachment)
96          attachment.add_header(*header)
97          msg.attach(attachment)
98      except IOError:
99          msg = "Error opening attachment file %s" % file_to_attach
100         print(msg)
101
102     server.sendmail(from_addr, to, msg.as_string())
103
104 def main(path):
105     """"""""
106     try:
107         with open(path) as csv_file:
```

```
108                 reader = csv.reader(csv_file)
109                 for line in reader:
110                     name, email = line
111                     pdf = make_book(name, email)
112                     send_email(email, pdf)
113         except IOError:
114             print("Error reading file: %s" % path)
115             raise
116
117  if __name__ == "__main__":
118      main("backers.csv")
```

Let's go over the minor changes. First off, we had to change the **make_book** function so that it returned the PDF path. Then we changed the **main** function so that it took that path and passed it to the **send_email** function along with the email address. Two changes and we're done!

Wrapping Up

Now you have the knowledge to take apart a new program and turn it into a set of smaller tasks. Then you can join the smaller programs into one large program. There are lots of different ways we could have done this. For example, we could have left each piece in its own file or module. Then we could import each piece into a different script and run them that way. That would be a good exercise for to try on your own.

When I did this, I ran into issues with my email host. Most email hosts will not let you send out lots of emails per hour or even make many connections at once. You can find a few services on the internet that you can use instead of your own internet provider that may work better for you.

I hope you found this chapter helpful in your own endeavours. Thanks for reading!